Studies of Organized Crime

Volume 12

Series Editor

Dina Siegel

For further volumes:
http://www.springer.com/series/6564

Nicoletta Serenata
Editor

The 'Ndrangheta and Sacra Corona Unita

The History, Organization and Operations
of Two Unknown Mafia Groups

 Springer

Editor
Nicoletta Serenata
Auburn University
Auburn
Alabama
USA

ISSN 1571-5493
ISBN 978-3-319-04929-8   ISBN 978-3-319-04930-4 (eBook)
DOI 10.1007/978-3-319-04930-4
Springer Cham Heidelberg New York Dordrecht London

Library of Congress Control Number: 2014938107

Springer is part of Springer Science+Business Media (www.springer.com)

Preface

The Italian Mafia is a general term indicating those criminal organizations originally routed in the South of Italy whose influences have been extending in the northern regions of Italy and in other foreign countries as well. Italian Mafia has attracted the attention of both media and scholars, who focused mainly on the well-known Sicilian Mafia, called Cosa Nostra and more recently, on Camorra, a criminal organization primarily operating in Campania. In the last few years, many scholars deemed that the field of studies concerning the Italian Mafia had little to add to the understanding of the phenomenon. I disagree. In fact, I strongly believe that there are many areas that are yet to be explored, and the present volume represents an attempt in that direction. Unlike other published works, this volume focuses on two relatively unknown Italian criminal organizations—the *'Ndrangheta*, based in Calabria, and the *Sacra Corona Unita*, based in Apulia. Neither of these organizations has received much attention in English-language literature.

The idea of editing this volume came to my mind while I was attending Graduate School at The Ohio State University. Researching the Italian Mafia, I realized that almost nothing about the 'Ndrangheta and Sacra Corona Unita (SCU) was available in the English language. The scarcity of material was a sign of how little these two organizations have been examined outside Italy, and how little the general public knows about them. Nowadays, news about these two organizations appear more frequently in Italian newspapers, especially the 'Ndrangheta after the *Operazione Crimine* in 2010—a crucial judicial operation that shed more light on the Calabrian organization.

The realization of this volume derives from the desire to redeem my land and open people's eyes on what is happening over there. As a child growing up in a neighborhood controlled by one of the most dangerous Mafia families in Bari, I felt their presence. Although, I am perfectly aware that this published volume will neither change nor defeat a criminal organization, I believe that spreading the knowledge of Sacra Corona Unita can foster awareness and inspire hope in future generations to avoid mistakes similar to the ones made by the past generations.

I would like to express my gratitude to the many people who helped me through this work. Special thanks go to all the Italian authors who believed in this project and felt the obligation to describe these two groups outside Italy. I am honored to have worked with them.

I am especially grateful to the two clerks of the Tribunale di Bari, Dr. Francesco Susca and Nicola Pansini, who in several warm summer days, helped me in the search of important documents regarding the Sacra Corona Unita. Francesco Forleo, clerk of the Tribunale di Brindisi, merits a sincere and thoughtful appreciation for his professionalism that led me to a copy of the Statute of the Sacra Corona Unita, a document difficult to find in Italian judiciary archives. Francesco Flora, Maresciallo Aiutante of the Guardia di Finanza (Financial Police), who in his spare time searched for documents and reports of the 'Ndrangheta, difficult to find as well; the journalist of La Repubblica di Bari, Mara Chiarelli, provided updated information that lead to the realization of the map of the Apulian Mafia.

I would like to thank Springer for enabling me to publish this volume and Katherine Chabalko for her effort in making this book possible.

Above all, I want to thank Giacomo who encouraged and believed in me despite all the time it took me away from us.

I am grateful to Matthew Amburgy and Christina Angelilli for correcting and editing the drafts of the manuscript.

Contents

Abbreviations

The following acronyms are used in the volume:

DIA—Direzione Investigativa Antimafia (Anti-Mafia Investigation Unit)
DDA—Direzione Distrettuale Antimafia (District Anti-Mafia Office)
DNA—Direzione Nazionale Antimafia (National Anti-Mafia Office)
DA—District Attorney
SCU—Sacra Conora Unita (United Sacred Crown)

Some Italian words have not been translated since their significance is known in English:

Carabinieri (Italian police)
cosca or cosche (clan or clans)
Mafioso (person belonging to a Mafia organization)
omertà (silence)
pizzo (blackmail money)
pentito (collaborator of justice)
vendetta (revenge)
maxiprocesso (large trial with the involment of Mafia people)

The word "State" is the Italian Republic which is often referred to as Stato in Italian.

Contributors

A. Apollonio Dipartimento di Giurisprudenza—Diritto e procedura penale, Università di Pavia, Pavia, Italy

E. Ciconte Rome, Italy

O. Ingrascì Altre. Atelier di ricerca sociale, Milano, Italy

M. Longo Department of History, Society and Human Studies, Università del Salento, Lecce, Italy

M. Massari Department of Political Sciences, University of Naples "Federico II", Naples, Italy

E. G. Parini Dipartimento di Scienze politiche e sociali, Università della Calabria, Arcavacata di Rende, CS, Italy

R. Sciarrone Culture, Politics and Society Department, University of Turin, Turin, Italy

N. Serenata Foreign Languages and Literatures Department, Auburn University, Auburn, AL, USA

R. Siebert Dipartimento di Sociologia, Università della Calabria, Rende (CS), Italy

About the Authors

Renate Siebert is an Emeritus Full Professor of Sociology at the University of Calabria. She has been a part of several national and international research projects funded by public institutions and Ministries. Her various research focuses on development and underdevelopment and social representations of inequality, ethnic prejudice and racism; women in the postcolonial context; family structures and social-health services; illegality, Mafia violence, totalitarian organizations and their impact over civil society and women life; memory and oblivion, mourning elaboration which becomes civil commitment; women and politics, local administration and gender issues; the role of women within Mafia-type organizations. In her publications, there are *Le donne, la mafia* (Milan, il Saggiatore 1994) that has been translated in English *Secrets of Life and Death. Women and the Mafia* (London-New York, Verso 1996); *Mafia e quotidianità* (Milan, Il Saggiatore-Flammarion 1996); and with Felia Allum she wrote *Organized Crime and the Challenge to Democracy* (London, Routledge 2003).

Ercole Giap Parini is a researcher in the Department of Political Science at the University of Calabria. He is a member of *Standing Group on Organized Crime* of the European Consortium for Political Research (ECPR) focusing on the effects on social-political and institutional contests. His publications are *Mafia, politica e società civile. Due casi in Calabria* (Soveria Mannelli, Rubettino 1999), *Mafia e antimafia, quali prospettive?* in *Relazioni pericolose: criminalità e sviluppo nel Mezzogiorno* edited by Renate Siebert (Soveria Mannelli, Rubettino 2000), and the words *cosca, 'ndrangheta, racket,* and *territorio* in *Dizionario di Mafia e Antimafia* (Turin, Narcomafie-Gruppo Abele 2008).

Enzo Ciconte has been from 1987 to 2008, a Member of the Parliament and of the Justice Committee; from 1997 until 2008 a Counselor for the Parliament Committee of Italian Mafia Investigations Department. He wrote the first book on the Calabrian Mafia. Among his publications are *'Ndrangheta dall'unità ad oggi* (Bari-Rome, Laterza 1992), *Processo alla 'Ndrangheta* (Bari-Rome, Laterza 1996), *Mafia, Camorra e 'Ndrangheta in Emilia-Romagna* (Rimini, Panozzo 1998), *'Ndrangheta* (Soveria Mannelli, Rubbettino 2008), *Storia criminale. La resistibile ascesa* *di mafia, 'ndrangheta e camorra dall'Ottocento ai giorni nostri* (Soveria Mannelli, Rubbettino 2008), and *'Ndrangheta padana* (Soveria Mannelli, Rubbettino 2010).

Rocco Sciarrone is an Associate Professor in Sociology at the University of Turin. In 2012, he was nominated as delegate, for the University of Turin, in the Special Commission for the Promotion of Legality and the Contrast of Mafia Phenomenon in the city of Turin. His research focuses on the analysis of the Mafia phenomenon, analyzing in particular, the process of territorial development and expansion, territorial control, and collusion and complicity relations; processes of regulation and criminal networks, and foreign immigration. He is an author of *Mafie vecchie, mafie nuove. Radicamento ed espansione* (Rome, Donzelli 2009), and editor of *Alleanze nell'ombra. Mafie ed economie locali in Sicilia e nelMezzogiorno* (Rome, Donzelli 2011).

Ombretta Ingrascì has a Ph.D. in History at University of London with a thesis titled "*Mafia Women in the Contemporary Italy. The Changing Role of Women in the Italian Mafia since 1945.*" She is currently a member of the Anti-Mafia Committee of the city of Milan and President of the Italian Ngo *Altre. Atelier di ricerca sociale* (www.altrericerche.it). She is the Deputy Director of the Summer School on Organized Crime at the State University of Milan. Among her publications are: *Donne d'onore. Storie di mafia al femminile* (Milan, Mondadori 2007) which has been translated in Spanish and Polish; *Confessioni di un padre. Il pentito Emilio di Giovine racconta la 'ndrangheta alla figlia.* (Milan, Melampo 2013).

Monica Massari works at the Department of Political Sciences of the University of Naples "Federico II" where she teaches Sociology. Since the mid-1990s, her research activities have addressed issues related to social change and social control, in particular, the historic and social evolution and the dynamics of expansion of organized crime both at national, international, and transnational levels and the relationships between globalization, organized crime and illegal markets (specifically drugs, trafficking in human beings and illegal smuggling of migrants, and eco-crimes). More recently, she has been focusing on the process of social construction of otherness and the emergence of new forms of racism at European level and dynamics of identity and recognition within multi-cultural societies. Among her publications on organized crime there are *La Sacra Corona Unita. Potere e Segreto* (Bari-Rome, Laterza 1998), and she is an author with Stefano Becucci of *Mafie nostre, mafie loro. La criminalità organizzata italiana e straniera nel Centro-Nord* (Turin, Edizioni di Comunità 2001) and *Globalizzazione e criminalità* (Rome-Bari, Laterza 2003). She wrote with Cataldo Motta, Anti-Mafia District Attorney of Lecce, *Il Fenomeno dei collaboratori di giustizia nella Sacra Corona Unita* in *Pentiti. I collaboratori di giustizia, le istituzioni, l'opinione pubblica* edited by Alessandra Dino (Rome, Donzelli 2005) and *Women in The Sacra Corona Unita* in *Women and the Mafia. Female Roles in Organized Crime Structures* edited by Giovanni Fiandaca (New York, Springer 2007). Finally, she wrote *Transnational*

Organized Crime Between Myth and Reality: the Social Construction of a Threat in *Organized Crime and the Challenge to Democracy* edited by Felia Allum and Renate Siebert (London, Routledge 2003) and, most recently, she published the outcomes of a research on Mafia armed violence *Guns in the Family. Mafia violence in Italy*, in *Small Arms Survey 2013: Everyday Dangers* (Cambridge, Cambridge University Press).

Andrea Apollonio has a Law degree cum laude from University of Salento. He has collaborated whit JURI Commission of the European Parliament until April 2012, and since October 2012, he is a doctorate student in Criminal Law at the University of Pavia with a focus on money laundering. In December 2012, he was nominated, from the University of Pavia, expert of judiciary subjects [cultore della materia] and began collaborations with different professors. Among his publications, there are *Sacra corona unita: riciclaggio, contrabbando. Profili penali economici del crimine imprenditoriale* (Rome, Carocci 2010), *Critica dell'antimafia. L'avanzare della paura, l'arretramento delle garanzie, l'imperfezione del diritto* (Cosenza, Pellegrini 2013).

Mariano Longo is an Associate Professor of Sociology and Head of the Undergraduate Sociology Program at the University of Salento. The main focus of his scientific activity is connected to the general topic of the relationship between the individual and social structure. He was the first to publish a book on the Sacra Corona Unita in 1997, titled *Sacra Corona Unita. Storia, struttura, rituali* (Pensa, Lecce).

Chapter 1
Introduction

Nicoletta Serenata

The journey to explore the 'Ndrangheta and Sacra Corona Unita (SCU) must start with two dates: March 26, 1990 and August 15, 2007. The latter recalls the well-known Duisburg massacre[1]—a small village in Germany—in which the 'Ndrangheta made its international appearance, although the organization was already well-established and known in Italy and other countries. The other date marks the official presence in Apulia[2] of the so-called Fourth Mafia, the SCU.

Before these dates, the general public ignored the existence of these two criminal organizations, thinking that Mafia was only a criminal organization based mainly in Sicily and Campania. Thus, the general attention was focused on Cosa Nostra and, most recently, on the other well-known Italian criminal organization, Camorra, which operates in Naples and surrounding areas. Therefore, much material was available in the Italian language: books, fictional and nonfictional films, and television programs. However, few of those sources are available for the 'Ndrangheta and SCU, and as one would expect, even fewer in English.

Since the history and development of the 'Ndrangheta and SCU are intertwined, it is natural to present them together. This volume aims to provide a clearer and broader understanding of Italian Mafias. Going *beyond* the regional area of the 'Ndrangheta and SCU, it attempts to compare them with the other Italian Mafia groups, that is, the Camorra and Cosa Nostra. This *interconnected* approach will help clarify how these organizations operate, cooperate, and survive both in Italy and abroad.

This volume is developed within a sociocultural and analytic approach with the aim of delineating the history, growth, structure, culture, and *modus operandi* of the 'Ndrangheta and the SCU. Through different points of view, judicial materials, interviews, and law enforcement dossiers, each chapter—submitted by various Italian scholars—attempts to enhance each reader's knowledge of the phenomenon of Mafia.

---

[1] In this massacre, six young people were killed by the Calabrian Mafia.

[2] Sentence number 878 of the Appeal Court of Lecce.

N. Serenata (✉)
Foreign Languages and Literatures Department, Auburn University,
6061 Haley Center, Auburn, AL 36849, USA
e-mail: serenata@auburn.edu

N. Serenata (ed.), *The 'Ndrangheta and Sacra Corona Unita,* Studies of Organized Crime 12,
DOI 10.1007/978-3-319-04930-4_1, © Springer International Publishing Switzerland 2014

The 'Ndrangheta...

The criminal organization known as 'Ndrangheta, Onorata Società (Honored Society) or Montalbano Family, is settled in Calabria, and today is considered the strongest and oldest Mafia organization in Italy after the Sicilian Mafia. Although it has its roots in one of the poorest regions of the country,[3] over time it has become the richest and most powerful Mafia group, at least in Italy. The *'ndrina* (the basic cell), both in Calabria and abroad, distributes the organization's power through branches or colonies. In Italy, outside of Calabria, the organization is deep-rooted in the North (Piedmont, Liguria, Lombardy, especially in Milan, Friuli-Venezia Giulia, etc.).[4] Abroad, it is present but not limited to countries such as Argentina, Belgium, Canada, Chile, Colombia, Great Britain, Holland, Morocco, Portugal, Spain, Switzerland, Turkey, the United States, and Venezuela.[5] With the resounding event of the Duisburg massacre in 2007, the whole world became aware of how extremely powerful this organization was. The rise and supremacy of the 'Ndrangheta, both in Italy and abroad, occurred thanks to specific features that make it unique.

The capacity to replicate, both from a qualitative and quantitative point of view, the organizational structure in territories far away from the motherland, even outside Europe, is one of the strengths characteristic of the 'Ndrangheta. Colonization is the most common export model. It has been used in the northern regions of Italy as well as outside Italian borders where the exact *modus operandi* has been adopted. The success of colonization facilitated the creation of intermediate structures like

---

[3] According to the data provided by Istat (report 2013), Calabria is the third poorest region of Italy with a poverty index of 27.4% following Sicily (29.6%) and Apulia (28.2%).

[4] The Direzione Nazionale Antimafia (DNA) in its 2012 report estimates that in Lombardy, there are 500 affiliates in 17 locali settled in the cities of Bollate, Bresso, Canzo, Cormano, Corsico, Desio, Erba, Legnano, Limbiate, Mariano Comese, Canzo, Milano, Pavia, Pioltello, Rho, Seregno, Giussano, and Solaro (p. 110). In Piedmont, there are 10 locali in Natile di Careri in Turin, Cuorgnè, Volpiano, Rivoli, San Giusto Canavese, Siderno in Turin, Chivasso, Moncalieri, Nichelino, and Turin (p. 113). In Liguria, there are 4: Genoa, Lavagna, Ventimiglia, and Sarzana (p. 114). In Lazio, there is not yet a locale, but there is a group belonging to the *'ndrina* of Tripodo and Romeo from San Luca that have exported a criminal group in the capital to manage the market of Fondi and invest money in the Café de Paris and the luxurious restaurants George and Federico I (pp. 130–131). In Emilia Romagna, groups are established in Modena, Parma, and Piacenza as well as in the province of Crotone, in particular in the area of Cutro (p. 131). For a full list of 'Ndrangheta diffusion in Italy and its illegal activities in each region, see Grattieri and Nicaso (2007).

[5] The DNA ensures the presence of *'ndrine* in Germany, in particular in Stuttgart, Singen, Rielasingen, Radolfzell, Ravensburg, Engen, and Frankfurt; whereas in Switzerland, they are located in Zurich and Frauenfeld (p. 117). The information regarding Canada is more detailed, where seven families (Tavernes, Figliomenis Cosimo, Coluccios, Commissos, Figliomenis Angelino, Demarias, and Rusos) share the drug market, gambling, forged materials, and extortions in Toronto, especially in the area of Woodbridge—the Italian neighborhood (p. 120). Less information is available for Australia, where the report admits the existence of more than one group, one of which is in Sterling (p. 123).

"lombardia" in Lombardy, "camera di controllo" in Liguria, "crimine australiano" in Australia, and "crimine canadese" in Canada[6] that coordinate the local groups and are in connection with the "Crimine" in Calabria. The second expansion modality, delocalization, is a more silent presence within the social milieu of the city. These Mafiosi, who are not grouped into a *locale*, conduct some "legitimate" business in order to prevent obstacles in their illegal business. An example of this course of action is in Rome,[7] where criminal groups belonging to the 'Ndrangheta have been identified working in commercial activities that cover money laundering and drug smuggling (DNA 2012, pp. 107–108). The prevalence of one model over the other is still not clear as the DNA report emphasizes.

Family is the keystone for the success of a Mafia organization, especially for the 'Ndrangheta. Each *'ndrina* is a family: Fathers, sons, brothers, uncles, and cousins control a village or city. This family structure guarantees secrecy and power, as no member dares to betray his own blood.[8] The homogeneous group—governed by shared and detailed rules and immersed in hierarchical structures—counterbalances the heterogeneous groups of Camorra and their internal feuds, which often lead to wars and internal schisms. This *untouchable* family structure has very few *pentiti* (collaborators of justice).[9] Thanks to this reliability, it was able to attract other criminal organizations, both in Italy and abroad, that enriched its success and power.

The continuous shifts in business (from being an organization that specialized in kidnappings,[10] to later investing in economic and entrepreneurial activities in various sectors: Rural development, health system, tourism, green energies, and sea and ground transportation), allowed the organization to operate simultaneously in a variety of areas and be powerful, trustworthy, and dynamic. Its growth, however, is also due to its current members, who are more *silent* and *educated* compared to the past decades. In fact, nowadays an *'ndranghetista* is no longer illiterate. Indeed, sons of Mafiosi are lawyers, doctors, politicians, and engineers, and they often are

---

[6] The Canadian group has been well-known for about 50 years with a peak of activities during the 1970s and 1980s. The Canadian police named the Calabrian groups the "Siderno Group of Organized Crime" since Siderno, the Italian city, was the starting point for drug smuggling and other criminal trades.

[7] In a 2012 investigation in Rome, the police confiscated € 150 million worth of goods and property belonging to the cosca of Mattiati from Palmi. Among these were the Grand Hotel Gianicolo in Rome, Hotel Arcobaleno in Palmi and 53 real estate properties in Bologna, Rome, and Palmi (Baldessarro 2012).

[8] The national and international success of the organization is in part due to the fact that compared to other Italian Mafia, its structure is more united and, hence, it avoids collaborators of justice.

[9] Some collaborators are Antonio Zagari, Margherita di Giovine, Lea Garofalo, and lately Giuseppina Pesce.

[10] Kidnappings were the first criminal activity of the 'Ndrangheta. It was used to collect money that was partially used to create companies that later will join the legal market, whereas the remaining were invested in drug and cigarette smuggling (Commissione 1998, p. 28). The kidnapping business was in the hands of several *'ndrine* from Platì, San Luca, and Natile di Careri (Commissione 1998, p. 29). In 1982, only Liguria, Valle d'Aosta, Trentino, Friuli Venezia Giulia, Molise, Marche, and Basilicata did not fall victim to any kidnappings. Friuli Venezia Giulia was the only Italian region that from 1965 to 1989 was exempt from this crime (Bellu 1989).

the *clean* face of the organization. Through the education of their sons, fathers are able to penetrate into new areas of legal society, impose their illegal businesses, and thus expand the family business. The result is the *gray area*: A collusion between the legal and illegal world where managers of private and public companies often ask the organization for services and from time to time are also affiliates. An exemplary instance is Domenico Zambetta, regional counselor for the Lombardy region, who paid € 200,000 in exchange for 4,000 votes.[11] The politico-mafioso vote is one of the many trades of the gray area transactions. Others examples are the penetration and manipulation of public offices,[12] as well as stacking contracts for both private and public construction. Although political power has always fascinated and attracted Mafiosi, recently criminal organizations conduct business with white-collars (lawyers, bankers, and accountants). According to Federico Cafiero de Raho, "this 'Ndrangheta is the most dangerous one since with a suit, it enters into the legal economy" (as mention in Baldessarro 2013).

This structural metamorphosis is an important feature in understanding the 'Ndrangheta. The biggest change happened at the end the second Mafia War (1985–1991) when a new structure was created: A federation of clans in which each one is independent in its own businesses. The aim of the federation—where blood relations are always present—is to plan, decide, and organize criminal activities surpassing the isolation and the territorial fragmentation among *'ndrine* (DNA 96). *Operazione Crimine* in 2010 revealed a new structure headed by *Provincia* or *Crimine*,[13] that supervises the whole association, even those *'ndrine* operating outside Italian borders. It exercises total control. The *'ndrina* of San Luca ("the mother" as it is called) governs the whole organization. 'Ndranghetisti, distant from their hometown and the central power, continue to follow and respect the rules of San Luca. Each criminal action is planned and approved by the mother—without its approval, nothing goes further. A new structure was discovered in 2012, the *corona* (crown) that manages all *'ndrine* in the *Ionic mandamento* (DIA 2012, p. 72).

This distinctive structure contrasts with the other important Mafia, the Sicilian Cosa Nostra. 'Ndrangheta branches are not independent like the colonies of the American Cosa Nostra; indeed, the Calabrian colonies respond directly to the headquarters in Italy, highlighting, thus, an intense and supreme control over every aspect of the criminal organization and its components. Another important difference is carried out by the *Provincia*, which distributes power equally among the three *mandamenti* (the Ionic, the Tyrrhenian, and the Center). The *Commissione Provinciale* of Palermo on the contrary had more decision-making power compared to

---

[11] Ferrarella, L. (2012, October 10).

[12] In 2012, the municipality of Reggio Calabria was dissolved due to Mafia infiltrations. It is the first time in 21 years that the law was applied to a provincial capital.

[13] *Crimine* defends the basic rules of the organization, guarantees the general equilibrium, decides the appointment of new *capi-locale*, the opening of new *locali*, the resolution for internal issues, and process affiliates (DNA 2012, p. 96).

the other *Provincie* creating thus an imbalance that damaged the organization itself (DNA 2012, p. 93).

The underestimation by the Italian State and law enforcement of its power and influence allowed the organization to expand easily throughout the rest of Italy, Europe, and then to the entire world. After the murder of two Anti-Mafia judges, Giovanni Falcone and Paolo Borsellino (in the bomb attacks of Capaci and Via d'Amelio, respectively), the law enforcement and the whole of Italy had their eyes on the Sicilian Mafia. Having the entire country focused on another Mafia, the 'Ndrangheta took advantage of this moment and increased its business both in the motherland and outside without much problems. The 'Ndrangheta then adopted a policy of cooperation with the other Mafias, creating, within Italy, alliances with Cosa Nostra and Camorra with which it played a crucial role in the creation of the SCU in Apulia during the 1970s and 1980s. Abroad, it was, and still is, partner— just to name some—with the Colombian, Ecuadorean, and Panamanian cartels for drugs trafficking.

...and the Sacra Corona Unita

The history of the Apulian Mafia is different and rather recent since the first traces of Mafia-type association in the region dates to 1979–1980. The "heel of the boot" was "colonized" by the other historical Mafia groups that saw it as a "happy" choice. The strategic geographical position, the economic, industrial, agribusiness and touristic potential together with the absence of a native criminal organization (Tribunale di Bari 1986, p. 211), made Apulia a fertile environment for new criminal activities. Besides Camorra and 'Ndrangheta, the region already was aware of the presence of Cosa Nostra that promoted local heroin smuggling. According to Sciarrone (1998), Apulia was controlled by the other Italian Mafias: Cosa Nostra was in the Brindisi and Lecce area, the 'Ndrangheta was settled in Taranto, and Camorra operated in Foggia (p. 177). Since the local criminal organization was the result of external influences and colonization, Gorgoni (1995) asserts that Apulia can be considered "the first among Italian regions to develop a new Mafia" (p. 11). Certainly, it is not a proud achievement, but it undoubtedly leads us to think how powerful a criminal organization might be nowadays.

The realization of this new criminal group followed a precise path. At the end of the 1970s, Raffaele Cutolo, a Camorra boss, created the *Nuova Camorra Organizzata* to end Cosa Nostra power in Campania. The Neapolitan boss reached the Apulia region through the *soggiorno obbligato* in which prisoners were sent away from their native regions. Cutolo landed in Apulia. In prison, Cutolo began collecting adherents for his new Mafia group. In 1981, the *Nuova Grande Camorra Pugliese* (New Big Apulian Camorra) was founded, and soon absorbed into the *Nuova Camorra Organizzata* (New Organized Camorra) with the name of *Nuova Camorra Pugliese* (New Apulian Camorra). The 'Ndrangheta approved the new group and baptized Cutolo as an 'ndranghetista. Similarly to the *Nuova Camorra Pugliese*, the

SCU was created to limit the influence of Neapolitan detainees in prison. In fact, Giuseppe Rogoli declared:

> At the time, the whole world knew what they did, how they felt [Neapolitan Mafiosi] [...] they felt they were God Almighty and where they arrived [...] they wanted things with coercion and for a group of us it was not fine. Then a group of us, not me, a group of us decided to create this Sacra Corona Unita to counterpart this excessive power (Tribunale di Brindisi 1994, p. 183).
>
> [All'epoca, lo sa tutto il mondo cosa facevano, si sentivano [...] Dio e Padreterno e dove entravano nei carceri [...] volevano fare degli abusi, delle cose e a noi non stava bene. Allora un gruppo di noi, non io, un gruppo di noi decise di costruire con questa Sacra Corona Unita in controparte a questo strapotere carcerario].

However, according to the collaborator of justice Maurizio Del Vecchio, Rogoli's aim was different:

> When he [Giuseppe Rogoli] created the Sacra Corona Unita his goal was to control all criminal activities in the territory of Mesagne [his hometown]. Clearly, his intent was to gain, under the control of the Sacra Corona Unita, more territorial control in Apulia (Tribunale di Brindisi 1994, p. 182).
>
> [L'intenzione di Pino (Giuseppe) Rogoli nel momento in cui creò la Sacra Corona Unita era quella di controllare tutte le attività criminali che si svolgessero nel territorio di Mesagne. Ovviamente nelle intenzioni di Rogoli vi era quella di acquisire sotto il controllo della SCU territori sempre più vasti sul territorio pugliese].

From Del Vecchio's statement, it is clear that the intention of Rogoli was to expand the SCU power in the whole region and not limit it to the Apulia prisons. In fact, rule number 7 of the Statute clearly affirms: "Do not commit any action or campaign inside or outside the jail without the consensus of the mother," demonstrating that the organization was also active outside prisons. Penitentiaries are in some way an extension of Mafia territories (Violante 1994, p. 142), where important decisions are made about new internal assets, new appointments, and new strategies. For instance, incarcerated members of the SCU decided how to control beach resorts from Lecce to Otranto during the summer season (DNA 2012, p. 156). Criminal activities do not stop at any time and in any place.

If the Camorra was the reason behind the birth of the SCU, the 'Ndrangheta played a crucial role in the foundation and recognition of the SCU as a Mafia organization. On this matter, Del Vecchio affirms: "In order to found the SCU, Rogoli felt the need to be 'baptized' by a Calabrian belonging to the 'Ndrangheta. This Calabrian man was Umberto Bellocchio" [per poter fondare questa associazione lo stesso ebbe la necessità di essere 'battezzato' da un calabrese appartenente alla 'Ndrangheta. Questo calabrese si chiama Umberto Bellocchio] (Tribunale di Brindisi 1994, p. 186).[14] The two groups had formerly collaborated. The Calabrian organization was able to include local Apulian criminal groups in their kidnapping business. The 'Ndrangheta's presence was tolerated and even sought in Apulia, whereas the Camorra was not accepted. Ciconte (1996) explained that "the 'Ndrangheta tries to establish zones of influence to

---

[14] Salvatore Annacondia has declared to the Anti-Mafia Parliamentary Commission that "the father of the SCU was Umberto Bellocchio, a well-known 'ndranghetista, one of the capo-decina of the 'Ndrangheta [...] Bellocchio dictated the rules of the SCU." (Commissione 1993, p. 2458).

conduct their illicit business without hegemony problems [...] and without damaging third-party autonomy. It seems that they establish au-par relations" [la 'ndrangheta nel rapporto con le altre organizzazioni si muoveva lungo una via che era quella di stabilire zone di influenza per portare avanti i propri traffici illeciti senza porsi problemi di egemonia o di predominio ossessivo sulle altre organizzazioni e senza ledere l'autonomia altrui. Sembrano stabilirsi rapporti, per così dire, alla pari] (p. 208). This role-play by the 'Ndrangheta is disclosed via its presence in the original oath of the organization which states:

> The Sacra Corona Unita was founded on May 1st, 1983 by G. R. [Giuseppe Rogoli] and with the help of some rightful godfathers [Calabrian Mafiosi]. In the SCU there are precise rules. Those who disobey those rules will be severely punished. In any situation the founder needs to be informed.[15]
> [La Sacra Corona Unita è stata fondata il 1 Maggio 1983 da G. R. e con l'aiuto di compari diritti. Nella SCU ci sono leggi precise. Chi trasgredisce questi regolamenti sarà punito severamente. In qualsiasi caso si dovrà tenere presente e al corrente il suo fondatore G. R.].

"The SCU lasted from May 1, 1983 until the appeal of the maxi process in September of 1986" (Tribunale di Brindisi 1994, p. 200). The short life of the organization is due to an internal conflict between the founder Giuseppe Rogoli and his right-hand man, Antonio Antonica, who betrayed the organization and its rules.[16] Initially, this break led to a blood feud, and later to a war that saw its peak point in the triennium 1988–1990 (Tribunale di Brindisi 1994, p. 203). In 1990, the SCU was re-founded and named *Nuova Sacra Corona Unita—Rogoli* (N.S.C.U.R.). The presence of Rogoli's name in the organization explained the primary role occupied by Rogoli, whereas the cause of the rebirth was to refine the criteria to affiliate new members (Tribunale di Brindisi 1994, p. 206).

Camorra and 'Ndrangheta were the main influences for the development of the Apulian Mafia. As already mentioned, the support was not accidental; indeed, each organization looked at Apulia with particular interest as the *land of opportunity* for the development of new business. From each partnership, the SCU assimilated hierarchical structure, rites, and formulas that helped the organization to become a more likely Mafia group. However, the SCU personalized them. For instance, the rite for the increase of a rank is repeated three times, and each rank sees the appearance of different personalities, such as Osso, Mastrosso, and Carcagnosso, who are the founders of Cosa Nostra, 'Ndrangheta, and Camorra; Count Ugolino, Florentin of Russia, and Knight of Spain; also Giuseppe Garibaldi, Giuseppe Mazzini, Alfonso Lamarmora, Camillo Benso Count of Cavour, and Carlo Magno.[17] Religious and

---

[15] An Italian original copy of the initial statement of the foundation of the SCU can be found at the end of the volume.

[16] Regarding the rupture between Rogoli and Antonica, Cosimo Capodieci wrote in his cairn: "Rogoli's affiliates were increasing on the territory of Mesagne, and, as part of the association, they wanted their profit, but Antonica did not allow it because everything i.e. contrabands, extortions, gambling, etc. were Antonica's results, thus he did not want to share with all Rogoli's affiliates" (Tribunale di Brindisi 1994, p. 202).

[17] In Appendix VI, there are some Sacra Corona Unita oaths where several of these personalities are mentioned and where an example of a vote is presented.

historical references made the organization more *real* and *authoritative* for the affiliates. The name, in particular, of the organization has a mystical importance:

> SACRED because reading its statutes you can see that when the organization is reunited it consecrates or baptizes someone (like the priest does on the altar); CROWN because it is like a rosary [in jargon called crown]; UNITED because they were to be so united that the crown could not break (Tribunale di Brindisi 1994, pp. 185–186).
> [SACRA perchè la SCU se si leggono i suoi statuti si legge che, quando si riunisce o affilia qualcuno, consacra e battezza (tipo il prete che fa sull'altare) per questo è 'Sacra'; CORONA perchè è come la corona cioè il Rosario e UNITA perchè si doveva essere uniti in modo tale da non spezzare questa corona].

Confusion and contradiction, especially from the Anti-Mafia Parliamentary Commission, led to deny the existence of an Apulian Mafia organization. Despite the uncertainty and the confusion, it was possible—though late—in 1990, with the sentence of the Court of Appeals of Lecce to officially recognize the existence of SCU as a Mafia-type organization. Ideologically, the "Fourth Mafia" ended in 1998 when the *Sacra Corona Libera* (Sacred Free Crown) was created, and which was concentrated in the area of Brindisi and Taranto. Nowadays, in the cities of Brindisi, Taranto, and Lecce, the SCU, as a Mafia organization, is still present although some do not share the same beliefs. On the contrary, Bari and surrounding areas remain under the control of different family clans, which do not belong to the SCU.

The Apulian Mafia is still intensely active in the territory. It is considered a region-based Mafia since its criminal activities do not extend outside the regional boundaries. Nonetheless, the organization has a relationship with other Mafias, Italian and foreign, in particular with the Albanian Mafia for drug smuggling. Heroin, cocaine, and marijuana are not the only business of this Mafia. They deal with gambling, extortions, insurance frauds, slot machines, and recently, investments in supermarkets, toy stores, and real estates. These hidden activities are mere strategies of the organization to operate silently. This technique has allowed the public opinion to believe that the SCU has been extinguished, but the organization worked with the consensus of the local population that even asked for assistance in solving personal issues, such as debt or unemployment (DNA 2012, p. 150).

Although the 'Ndrangheta and the SCU share some pieces of history and development together, they have deep and evident differences that have determined the future of each organization. The absence of cohesion within the organization, together with the lack of a charismatic leader connecting the different clans, made the SCU more of a regional organization. From a hierarchical point of view, Rogoli's vertical structure collapsed under the weight of internal conflicts, leaving space to a conglomeration of clans that spread in the whole region: *Famiglia Salentina*, later named *Nuova Famiglia Salentina*, *Remo Lecce Libera*, *La Rosa*, *La Rosa dei venti* are some of the clans born in Apulia in those years. The high number of pentiti that the SCU has produced also testifies this lack of cohesion. Soon after their arrest, members began to reveal secrets of the organization. Rogoli himself admitted the existence of the SCU, violating one of the main rules of a Mafia group. Yet, through the years, the Apulian Mafia was able to quietly evolve and expand its domain using connections outside the region.

Women and Mafia

"L'unica donna veramente importante per un mafioso è e deve essere la madre dei suoi figli" [the only woman truly important for a Mafioso is and must be the mother of his children] (Falcone and Padovani 1991, p. 76). In a large sense, this sentence contains the very ambivalence on which Mafia bases itself: A male-only society where female presence is prohibited, but constantly present. Although the feminine figure is repudiated, the success of the Mafia relies on a woman, the mother. In fact, she is despised for being a woman, but at the same time accepted as mother and cornerstone of the organization. This double label creates the idealization of the mother as "unicamente buona, una mammasantissima" [uniquely good, a very holy mother] (Siebert 1996, p. 46). This glorification derives from a conflict between the Mafia group and the surrounding paternal society with its restrictive laws. In this context, the mother symbolizes the land and its possession and, hence, she must be protected. According to Renate Siebert, this esoteric Mafia structure is the result of an attempt to hide such duplicity of love and hate for the mother (p. 46), leading her to be seen as a *mammasantissima*.

Analysis on Mafia women has been conducted for decades. Recently, more scholars are exploring the female presence in Italian Mafia groups since, in the last few years, their function is not as passive as for much time it has been believed. On the contrary, their presence both inside and against the organization has increased. Women have always been underestimated in criminal organizations, but through testimonies and judicial documents, women of Mafia's point of view are brought into this volume, showing both continuities with the Mafia tradition and ruptures within it.

Women in the SCU are essential, if not vital for the organization. Pasculli (2009) identifies, in her study, two types of women: The passive woman and the active woman. The passive woman guarantees the male's reputation and serves as an object for his career. The active woman serves as a liaison for Mafia values (pp. 2–3). Women's roles are beginning to increase within the business. With drug trafficking, they become smugglers and manage money as there is no violence involved (p. 5). An excellent model is Domenica Biondi, the wife of Giuseppe Rogoli, known also as "Mimma." While her husband was in prison, Mimma was the bond between her husband (the inside world) and the organization (the outside world), providing guidance to the group.[18] This is a unique feature that has not yet been extinguished. In fact, a more recent police investigation in Lecce reports the presence of Marianna Carrozzo, a woman who assumed the role of lieutenant in managing the drug trade and the clan while her partner was in prison. Compared to other criminal organizations, women in the SCU are more active and involved; in fact, in 1996, the Court of Lecce[19] recognized—for the first time in the Italian judicial history—that women in the SCU can become affiliates through official rite, and be active members of these criminal activities (Pasculli 2009, p. 7).

---

[18] For more information on this matter, see Massari and Motta (2007) where they examine more examples of women involved in the SCU and provide some general theories.

[19] The sentence is from the Juvenile Court of Lecce of April 18, 1996.

Criminal participation of women in the 'Ndrangheta is also prominent. The new generations of women are rather different in the sense that they fight for their freedom and their rights as women and mothers. Through recent documents and testimonies, it is possible to re-discover the basic values of a Mafia culture: Sons' and daughters' education, arranged marriages, honor, and vendetta: All principles and customs assimilated and divulgated by women. Nevertheless, women are usually constrained to a more domestic occupation. In the last few years, those who have escaped from this environment have gone in one of two directions: The first sees them as part of the social and authorial hierarchy of the criminal society occupying important positions (sorella d'omertà), whereas the other is the collaboration with the justice. Both scenarios, and their relative consequences, are discussed in this volume.

Two Unknown Mafia Groups: The 'Ndrangheta and Sacra Corona Unita

Chapter 2 This book opens with a consideration of family, gender, and power. Here, Renate Siebert, who already made a meaningful contribution with a study of women in the Mafia world, presents how Mafia organizations dominate and control the power in their territory. Her essay develops the distinction of two parallel worlds—with sets of rules to follow—and provides a comparison between the *normal* and the Mafia world. Analyzing the supremacy of the organization—which is shown through the control of members, women, children, and people around them—the author highlights how some members seek normalcy and, thus, run away from the organization. As a traditionally masculine organization, the Mafia designates a secondary role to women, although recently, some female figures have gained more power in the organization. Regardless of their promotion among the ranks and new roles (very few), women still have the main duty to *educate* the new upcoming generations of Mafiosi. This restricted duty produces a difference in gender (female vs. male) and in generation (old vs. new). Providing concrete and current examples, the author draws a scenario in which the most powerful Italian criminal organization, the 'Ndrangheta, has developed.

Chapter 3 Enzo Ciconte traces the history of the 'Ndrangheta from the legend of Osso, Mastrosso, and Carcagnosso through the golden ages of the 1960s and 1970s until recent times. The author explains how this organization was able to expand and increase its power without any sort of problem, incentivizing its illegal business. Importance is given to the structural metamorphosis of the organization, enabling it to export branches everywhere. Ciconte's article reveals the true essence of the organization that does not fear anything anywhere.

Chapter 4 This chapter presents the history of the 'Ndrangheta, covering its most important features and emphasizing the family composition and the rituals. Ercole Giap Parini's contribution focuses on the importance of the familiar structure on which the organization sits, enhancing it to the point that it spreads beyond the boundary of their region. Particular interest is paid to rituals and codes that make the organization unique in the members' eyes. The essay also discusses the importance of women in the organization, a topic fully discussed in Ombretta Ingrasci's intervention, and the networking underneath the power of the organization, an argument analyzed in Rocco Sciarrone's essay. Chapter 4 concludes by overcoming some old hypotheses after recent investigations and introducing the new business sector in which the organization operates.

Chapther 5 Ombretta Ingrascì provides a vivid and clear representation of how women are important and vital in a male criminal organization, such as the 'Ndrangheta. Through significant examples, she illustrates women's involvement in extremely active and criminal roles, and how these women represent a symbol of change when they became collaborators of justice. Current investigations have revealed how the stereotype of women dressed in black in constant mourning is replaced with a more active role, such as the *sorella d'omertà* (sister of *omertà*). Although their role has been changed in connection with the evolution of the organization, women are still an object of male's desire. Her analysis establishes that mothers still inculcate to their sons the three fundamental rules of a Mafia organization: Honor, vendetta, and *omertà,* and that young virgin women are still exchanged for peace or to strengthen a family. The contribution concludes with examples of women who have turned their back on the organization and joined the protection program, starting a new life and setting the example for forthcoming generations.

Chapter 6 Rocco Sciarrone discusses how a more modern approach in analyzing the 'Ndrangheta can be misleading. Proposing a closer connection between blood ties, family, and organizational structure, including the hierarchic and reticular assets, he argues how this well-oiled machine created a network of connections in the legal, economic, political, and government institutions. His analysis of the organization is innovative due to the addition of aspects—such as the criminal career of members, the inter-organizational relations, including those with government institutions—that often are not taken into consideration. He further delineates some divergences with Cosa Nostra.

Chapter 7 Monica Massari provides an overview of the origins and evolution of the so-called "Fourth Mafia," the last Mafia organization that was actually created in the southern part of the country, Apulia. The Sacra Corona Unita is different from the other Italian criminal organizations due to its history—marked by sudden changes—but also for its atypical structure of composite criminal groups. The 'Ndrangheta and Camorra played a decisive role in its creation, inspiring their tradition formulas, rites, and symbols of the newborn organization. In describing the evolution of the organization, Massari will define the key factors that determined the downfall of the (initial) organization. Using a comparative approach through a socio-cultural analysis of rituals, norms, and codes of conduct adopted by the SCU, the author delineates differences existing with the other traditional Mafia-type organizations.

Chapter 8 Longo's article initially attempts to delineate the features of an organized crime group. Some of these elements include, but are not limited to, symbolic and cultural elements, rituals, codes, and violence. After the preliminary "theoretical" analysis of criminal groups, the author focuses his attention on the Sacra Corona Unita by analyzing how the internal organization reflects the outside image that the organization displays. In particular, the author examines the role of leadership of the Apulian Mafia by comparing it to the other older groups. The key figure of Pino Rogoli, founder of the newly organization, helped to overcome some major internal issues, and at the same time his charismatic presence balanced the absence of unity, identity, and tradition. In fact, because of its status as a new organization, the SCU felt the need to "create" traditions, rules, and codes that lead an affiliate to join the "new world."

Chapter 9 Andrea Apollonio compares and identifies the current differences between the 'Ndrangheta and Sacra Corona Unita: The first one with its ancient and solid origins, whereas the second is a more recent criminal group. Although they have been defined as "Twin Mafias"—for their territorial proximity and the role the 'Ndrangheta played in the creation of the Apulian group—they have numerous "structural" differences. As Apollonio will explain, these two criminal organizations are two different types of Mafia since they have a diverse *modus operandi*, organizational structure, institutional connections, and social framework.

Supplementary material The last part of the volume contains an appendix with nine sections. Each of them includes data and information collected through this research. The first section reports the hierarchy of the 'Ndrangheta that was extracted from *Operazione Crimine* in 2010 and DIA report of 2012 and the related meaning and function of each rank within the organization. The second part is a map of society in Calabria. Sections III and IV show the Sacra Corona Unita's structure and the various clans in the region. The last five sections contain oaths of the 'Ndrangheta and Sacra Corona Unita, including the founding Statute, and the interesting vocabulary that each organization uses to communicate amongst themselves. These data were obtained through official judiciary documents.

References

Baldessarro, G. (12 November 2012). Sequestri per 150 milioni alla 'Ndrangheta. C'è anche un hotel esclusivo a Roma. *La Repubblica*. http://www.repubblica.it/cronaca/2013/11/12/news/ sequestro_calabria_e_roma_ndrangheta-70795419/?ref=search.

Baldessarro, G. (6 November 2013). 'Ndrangheta, 47 arresti tra i 'colletti bianchi.' A Reggio Calabria il boss gestiva l'azienda sequestrata. *La Repubblica*. http://www.repubblica.it/ cronaca/2013/11/06/news/_ndrangheta_47_arresti_tra_i_colletti_bianchi_-70323241/.

Bellu, G. M. (17 June 1989). In diciassette anni 600 sequestri. *La Repubblica*. http://ricerca.repubblica. it/repubblica/archivio/repubblica/1989/06/17/in-diciassette-anni-600-sequestri.html.

Ciconte, E. (1996). *Processo alla 'Ndrangheta*. Bari-Rome: Laterza.

Commissione Parlamentare d'inchiesta sul fenomeno della mafia e sulle associazione criminali similari. (1993). *Audizioni del collaboratore di giustizia Salvatore Annacondia*. XI Legislatura. Rome: tipografia del Senato, p. 2458.

Commissione Parlamentare d'inchiesta sul fenomeno della mafia e sulle associazione criminali similari. (7 October 1998). *Relazione sui sequestri di persona*. XIII Legislazione, pp. 24–29, Rome.

Direzione Investigativa Antimafia. (2012). *Relazione semestrale al Parlamento. Luglio-dicembre 2012*. Rome.

Direzione Nazionale Antimafia (DNA). (December 2012). *Relazione annuale sulle attività dal Procuratore nazionale antimafia e dalla Direzione nazionale antimafia nonce sulle dinamiche e strategie della criminalità organizzata di stampo mafioso*. July 1, 2011–June 30, 2012. Rome.

Falcone, G., & Padovani, M. (1991). *Cose di Cosa Nostra*. Milan: Rizzoli.

Ferrarella, L. (10 October 2012). Regione Lombardia, arrestato assessore di Formigoni per voto di scambio. *Corriere della Sera*. http://milano.corriere.it/milano/notizie/cronaca/12_ottobre_10/assessore-lombardia-arrestato-2112186707377.shtml.

Grattieri, N., & Nicaso, A. (2007). *'Ndrangheta le radici dell'odio*. Rome: Aliberti.

Gorgoni, R. (1995). *Periferia infinita: storie d'altra mafia*. Lecce: Argo.

Istituto Nazionale di Statistica (Istat). (17 July 2013). *La povertà in Italia nel 2012*. Rome.

Massari, M., & Motta, C. (2007). Women in the Sacra Corona Unita. In G. Fiandaca (Ed.), *Women and the Mafia*. New York: Springer.

Pasculli, A. (2009). Il ruolo della donna nell'organizzazione criminale: il caso barese. *Vittimologia* III.2.

Siebert, R. (1996). *Secrets of life and death: Women and the Mafia*. New York: Verso.

Sciarrone, R. (1998). *Mafie vecchie, mafie nuove*. Rome: Donzelli.

Tribunale di Bari. (1986). *Sentenza contro Romano Oronzo +194*. Bari.

Tribunale di Brindisi, II sezione penale. (20 April 1994). *Sentenza contro Bruno Ciro +28*. Brindisi.

Violante, L. (1994). *Non è la piovra. Dodici tesi sulle Mafie italiane*. Turin: Einaudi.

Chapter 2
Mafia and Daily Life: The Evolution of Gender and Generational Relationships

Renate Siebert

The activities of the Mafia, or to be precise the Mafias, are criminal in nature, but these activities should not be confused with ordinary criminality. For this reason, the Mafia is something different and even more dangerous because its aim is to have supremacy over territories, especially the individuals that live in these territories; over their bodies and souls. Rather than seeking formal control over the institutions of the state, the Mafia aims to have control over the society. Spaces controlled by the Mafia tend to stagnate and decay, turning into hybrid spaces in which citizens become subjects. In places controlled by the Mafia, a type of society is created that combines certain features of dictatorship, based on advanced technologies, with characteristic of pre-modern or feudal subjections. Umberto Santino has developed a theoretical explanation of this socio-historical mixture; he speaks of "signoria territoriale" (territorial domination), defining it as "the aspect of the Mafias that continues over time" (Chinnici and Santino 1991, p. 254).What exactly is the territorial domination of which he speaks?

It consists, first of all, in pervasive personal domination: The organization and its bosses—important or not—pretend to know and decide about matters of life and death, the activities, and even the personal relationships of the people that live in the subjected territory (Siebert 1996a, p. 18). This domination does not stop at the threshold of the house: There is no such thing as privacy where the Mafia rules. Indeed, intimate relations are also manipulated to procure wealth and practical power. Marriage plans between clans require specific "choices," and the risk of Mafia secrets being revealed requires behavioral codes, which are inspired by a hypocritical desire for the appearance of respectability and are imposed by the threat of violence. Bans on divorce and on touching the wife of an honored man are rooted strictly in the rules of predatory enrichment and Mafia command, rather than in the belief related in alleged rules of "honor."

R. Siebert (✉)
Dipartimento di Sociologia, Università della Calabria, Ponte Bucci,
87036, Rende (CS), Italy
e-mail: siebert2011@gmail.com

N. Serenata (ed.), *The 'Ndrangheta and Sacra Corona Unita,* Studies of Organized Crime 12,   15
DOI 10.1007/978-3-319-04930-4_2, © Springer International Publishing Switzerland 2014

Adherence to the parallel social world of the Mafia, for most of its members, is accompanied by a sense of total identification that is expressed in beliefs and the internalization of a system of values often completely opposed to those of civil society and the political environment. The force of this alternative world emerges strongly in the stories of those who collaborate with the justice system, stories that judges uncover in their interrogations. Those who tell their stories feel no guilt for the numerous crimes they have committed. The totalitarian quality of these Mafia criminal organizations, found in the diverse forms of territorial domination, is deeply linked here, in the certainty of the members to be the only ones to declare what is right and what is wrong, who can live and who, on the contrary, must die. Having total power over the life and death of the others, a Mafia boss sees himself as a god, or lifted up to the same level as god. When Antonio Calvaruso asked that the life of an acquaintance who had been sentenced to death be spared, Leoluca Bagarella responded:

> Never again must you allow yourself to make these types of requests for those that I have condemned to be eliminated. Because here, if there is a God, I am He. I have the power to give life, and to take it away (Dino 2008, p. 76).
> [Non ti devi permettere mai più di fare certi tipi di affermazioni su dei soggetti che io ti dico devono essere eliminati (…) Perché qua, se c'è un Dio quello sono io, (…) Io ho il potere di togliere e di dare la vita].

Distancing oneself from this crazed desire for omnipotence, often by collaborating with the authorities, tends to open Mafia adherents' eyes to a puzzling reality: No one is unique, omnipotent, or alone, but everyone interacts socially with each other; the human being, as such, is the result of many relationships that make up a society. Daily life is made of multiple diverse relationships. Having an experience of all these could be traumatic, but it offers new unexpected perspectives. Umberto Ammaturo, a Camorra pentito narrates:

> Being connected with other people and feeling like an ordinary man was strong. I had to learn to control myself, I hear people say no when the answer is no! Indeed, over the years I've discovered something: The real hero in this society is the everyday man: The ordinary man, the family man who works. My eyes were opened up to a new dimension, fraught with difficulties, which are the real things, everyday things, because I had always glossed over society, if I may say so. I had never waited in a line, I had never waited at a ticket window […] Well, today I wait in line […] I had never dwelled on the concept of the corporate body of society. And this was a big mistake as a father. Being a father and not realizing this is a huge mistake […] I had to go through a lot of training. I was not used to having to deal with the public […] It took a lot: A lot of patience (Gruppo Abele 2005, pp. 376–377).
> [L'impatto con la gente e sentirsi un uomo qualsiasi è stato forte. Ho dovuto imparare ad autocontrollarmi, a sentirmi dire no quando è no! Sì, io in questi anni ho scoperto una cosa: il vero eroe in questa società è l'uomo qualunque. L'uomo qualunque, il padre di famiglia che lavora. Ho scoperto una nuova dimensione, irta di difficoltà, che sono le cose reali, giornaliere, perché la società io l'avevo sempre sorvolata, se così si può dire. Io non ho mai fatto una fila, non sono mai stato in coda ad uno sportello (…) Insomma, oggi faccio la fila (…) Non mi ero mai soffermato sul concetto della società costituita. E questo fu un grande errore anche come padre. Essere padre e non avere coscienza di questo è un errore madornale (…) Ho dovuto fare un forte apprendistato. Io non ero abituato ad avere a che fare con il pubblico (…) Ci è voluta tanta, ma tanta pazienza].

Salvatore Stolder, another Camorra pentito, expresses a similar disposition:

Before, if I were to walk into a store, the salesperson would leave everything and come right to me. I had always lived that way, up until I was 37, and suddenly I go to the store and I have to wait in line. I never even went to a supermarket, and now to stand here in line, what an absurdity! Then something happened, once my wife ran into a person with her shopping cart and apologized, but then he came over and said: "Teach your wife how to behave." Nothing like this had ever happened in my life, so I stood there—I am not lying—for five minutes, staring at this man, with him having taken me for a fool [...] I could not react at all. Now I see, and I hope that there is a chance to re-enter a whole different world: I am born again; I am born again under the law. In the past I was in the negative, now I am in the positive. My children make me feel that way. When I speak with them I feel clean. Sometimes I look at my wife and just start laughing because they get into these discussions where they get right to the center of the argument. It kills me the way they talk (Gruppo Abele 2005, pp. 417–420).

[Prima ero abituato che, se andavo in un negozio, il commesso lasciava tutto e veniva da me. Fino a 37 anni ho sempre vissuto così, poi all'improvviso vado al supermercato e sto in coda. Io non ero mai entrato in un supermercato, e sto in coda, una cosa assurda! Poi mi è capitato un episodio, mia moglie con il carrello una volta ha urtato una persona e gli ha chiesto scusa, questo è venuto vicino a me e mi ha detto: "Insegni l'educazione a sua moglie." Non mi era mai capitato un fatto del genere, rimasi – non dico bugie – circa cinque minuti immobile a guardarlo e quello mi avrà preso per un pazzo (...) Ma non ho reagito (...) Ora vedo, spero almeno che ci sia un varco, una possibilità per rientrare in un mondo tutto diverso: sono rinato, sono rinato nella legalità. Mentre prima ero nel negativo, ora sto nel positivo. Me lo fanno sentire i miei figli. Quando io parlo con loro sento un'espressione pulita. A volte guardo mia moglie e mi metto a ridere, perché fanno dei discorsi chiari, vanno subito al centro di una cosa. Mi fanno morire come parlano].

Acting as lords over life, even while imposing death, the Mafia's domination over its territory remains absolute. The Mafia's social control, whether blatant or covert, is everywhere: In daily life, relocations, relations, marriage choices, job market, and investments. Anything from an anonymous letter to threatening calls, from decapitated animals to bombs, from the destruction of victims' gravestones to the defacing of corpses. Destruction of gardens, bombs in stores or under cars, and houses being burnt to the ground. An emblematic case is that of Elisabetta Carullo, a young mayor twice over, of Stefanaconi in Calabria. Attacks began before her election and continued throughout her administration:

During the most severe period, their strategy was clear: Attack. Not the mayor, who was protected, but the lesser-known candidates, on their way home to their families [...] they came at us with small assaults, for example destroying my father's land in the countryside, where they cut down all the trees, the vineyard, destroyed everything that was there. Then, they attacked a counselor, a wheelchair-bound woman with a weak family on her shoulders: They set her house on fire and her parents risked their lives. Such a tragedy. And then there's the former vice mayor, who was the target of thirteen attacks: He also had a weak family, and one night they shot his brother, injuring his arm. These moments are tough to relive. Again, another attack on another counselor: They shot at the front door of her house and the following night they set her car on fire. They also shot the former vice-mayor. Those are the most exemplary instances, but there are many more—over eighty, in fact—that have been reported (Siebert 2001, p. 50).

[Nella fase acuta degli attentati la strategia era chiara: attaccare. Non il sindaco, che era protetto, ma i candidati più deboli della lista, per poi arrivare alle loro famiglie (...) ci hanno colpito con piccoli attentati, per esempio danneggiando il podere di campagna di mio padre, dove hanno tagliato tutti gli alberi, la vigna, distruggendo tutto quanto c'era. Poi, hanno attaccato una consigliera, una ragazza sulla sedia a rotelle con una famiglia debolissima alle spalle: le hanno incendiato la casa, e i genitori hanno rischiato la vita. Un episodio tragico, bruttissimo. E poi l'ex vicesindaco, che ha subito più di tredici attentati: anche lui aveva una famiglia molto debole alle spalle, e una sera hanno sparato nella Proloco ferendo suo fratello al braccio. Momenti drammatici. Ancora, l'attentato a un'altra consigliera: hanno sparato contro la porta di casa e la sera dopo le hanno incendiato la macchina. L'attacco all'allora vicesindaco: gli hanno sparato mancandolo solo per caso. Questi gli episodi più vistosi, ma ce ne sono moltissimi altri, oltre ottanta, tutti denunciati].

Precisely because it is so all-encompassing and pervasive in regard to private and public life (and also because it is deeply rooted in everyday life), territorial dominance represents a form of dominion that requires many people to become involved in illegal activity. Those small, subtle, and nearly unconscious daily habits and routines, like the obvious ones, are clearly criminal in nature. Among the latter illegal activities, there are violent and intimidating acts, but also silence—the refusal, the fear—of testifying. From the former ones, we can count behavior codes, ways of thinking and speaking that legitimize violence and that are passed from one generation to the next, and that play a pivotal role in communication.

By dominating the territory, Mafia assumes power over both illegal and legal activities. Through the monopoly of violence, usually carried out in the form of the death penalty, the Mafia takes on an institutional personality. The importance of Mafioso control over the territory is demonstrated by the fact that even important bosses that became wealthy by smuggling drugs and weapons are not afraid to ask for money (the common pizzo) from the fruit vendor by his house. Of course, it is not because he needs the money, but rather it is to convey a message: We are in charge here. The territory is the space where Mafia power has its roots; it is the material and symbolic place for them to assert, with arrogance, their authority. The territory also represents a shooting ground for their enrichment, a resource to plunder, exploit, and then destroy. Illegal dumping, defacing construction zones, and speculation on water resources: In line with the tendency to waste away industrial society, the Mafia represents a factor of further and dangerous acceleration of environmental destruction.

It is evident how this is important for everyone's daily life and everyone's quality of life. It is in the context of everyday life that citizens gain experience with constraints imposed by the Mafia, and it is on the daily level that citizens exercise freedom and democratic rights or, on the contrary, they are faced with negative criminal powers that suspend the exercise of such rights. Moreover, as shown by the statements from collaborators of justice, even for those who are still involved with Mafia activity, daily life is often the arena for conflicts, choices, and contradictions that lead them to escape from this oppressive environment.

Daily life has another crucial effect on people: Habits—reassuring gestures that help them to reject distressing issues. The sphere of daily life, concerning "territorial domination" in one's personal life, is extremely ambivalent in that truth and falsification are found together. On one side, the Mafia represents a dangerous threat to society, for freedoms and the democratic rights that we can experience from day to day in each of our lives. On the other side, we have the tendency to perceive the

Mafia as something far from us, like something that concerns others, because the Mafia is a phenomenon that generates fear and anguish. The Mafia is death. Imagining it as something far from us heralds a life that is immune from its influences; it falls within the defensive mechanism of the psyche. It is the appearance of the obvious—this is how it is, this is how it has always been, and how it will always be—that represents the core of our daily thinking. The Mafia exists, and certainly is unpleasant. The important thing is that I would not have anything to do with it. The repetition of gestures and daily practices creates mechanism of "familiarization": We tend to integrate facts and unexpected traumatic events into the parameters of our daily routine. The ability to classify these frightening, albeit normal, instances that are remarkable in their cruelty and ferocity tranquilizes us and enables us to stay in our place as passive spectators. We are not called to be part of this cause. After all, these things happen, do not mind them. It is obvious that they happen.

In this respect, daily life represents a privileged sphere of social control; a sphere in which the individual learns how to adapt and conform. Not so much because it was forced by coercive means—institutions acting behind the scenes—but because mechanisms such as "familiarization" help to soften clashes and disputes, and avoid the assumption of ambivalence and contradiction. Everything becomes easier.

Mafia, death, anguish. The difficulty of becoming aware of the danger of the Mafia is this: Daily life and its way of thinking offer grounds for strong mechanisms of removal. Everyday thinking is deeply rooted in our appearance; everyday thinking is comforting and opaque. Everyday thinking acts as an antidote to the agony of death:

> Heidegger got to the root of the specific ambiguity of the daily thoughts and behavior in the suppression of the idea that death is even a possibility. Everyday thinking says, "Someday you will die. But for now, as for me, not yet." It lies, therefore, in the chatter of "yes" [...] For everyday thinking is what truly appears, without further investigation (Jedlowski 1986, p. 41).
> [Heidegger rintracciava la radice dell'ambiguità specifica dell'atteggiamento e del pensiero quotidiano nella rimozione che questi operano dell'idea della morte come possibilità. Il pensiero quotidiano dice: "Un giorno o l'altro si dovrà morire. Ma per ora, quanto a me, ancora no." Esso si adagia, così, nelle chiacchiere del "sì" (...) Per il pensiero quotidiano è vero ciò che appare, senza ulteriori indagini].

The grounds of daily life, thus, turn out to be a crucial place: A symbolic battleground between life and death, Eros and Thanathos. But there, where the Mafias' territorial domination rules, there is also a constant threat of physical violence, even death. "The drama of the Mafia is in the evocative power of primal fears" (Abruzzese 1993, p. 205). On the battleground of everyday life, a bloody war is being fought.

However, as already pointed out, everyday life is not a unique reality. Besides the obvious, the removal of death, out of conformity, daily life is the environment in which an individual lives and grows. The everyday, through strategies and practices connected to the awareness of rights and obligations, through the act of becoming aware of potential freedom, can become a place for civil resistance. Daily practices can become a fertile ground for the construction of a civil and democratic society. In everyday life, every single person develops his or her own personal individuality, experimenting with pleasures and torments of their own choice, creating their own biography.

One can assume that the everyday life of those who live and grow up in a Mafioso environment—in comparison with those in the adjacent society—is "normal," similar to that of everybody else, and in some part significantly different. In the past, such daily aspects were not well-known, and perhaps even of little interest. A significant shift occurred with the phenomenon of collaborators of justice, which was incentivized by specific laws, since the 1980s. Family conflicts, which were created for the decision of one member to become a "pentito," easily led to the breaking of all ties of silence about gender and generational relations among Mafia family members. Nowadays, women and children, mothers, wives, and sons/daughters appear in the spotlight of public opinion and mass media: Sometimes as victims of cross-vendetta, others as an active part of the collaborative process. They often take on the guise of trying to defame the collaborator of justice or pressure him/her to withdraw the testimony. In this regard, scholars and judges spoke about a "new communication strategy" (Principato and Dino 1997, p. 16)[1] of organized crime: If at one time the icon prevailed of the Mafia woman, the whole house, church, and tradition, being unaware about all criminal activities of the male clan, since the 1990s, the Mafia has been sending its women to the front lines, with sensational stunts like press conferences, participation in talk shows, and public smearing of their "pentiti" relatives. Such conflicts, though widely exploited by criminal organizations, still tell us something about their daily life. Likewise, and even more so, the collaborators of justice do.

First of all, these men describe their entire criminal lives, of having killed frequently and brutally, viewed by them as being completely "normal" or, rather, in the same manner as a professional activity. There appears to be an awareness of having lived in a different world: A world, however, equally legitimate, or at least equally "right" as that of society as a whole. Saverio Morabito, a 'Ndrangheta pentito narrates:

> I was a gangster and every day I tried to do it better because I believed it was just a job like any other job, even if it went beyond the limits of the law. And every day I tried to improve myself in my field, like someone who works in a big company as an employee and, over several years, due to his skills, pulls some strings and becomes a CEO. He is successful because he knows how to stay in touch with people, how to treat people, and does not back down when problems arise (Sciarrone 2006, p. 155).
>
> [Io facevo il malavitoso e cercavo di farlo ogni giorno meglio perché la ritenevo una professione come un'altra, anche se andava oltre i limiti della legalità. E ogni giorno cercavo di perfezionarmi nel mio campo, come uno che entra in una grossa azienda da impiegato e negli anni, per la sua bravura, brucia tutte le tappe e diventa amministratore delegato. Ce la fa perché ha saputo mantenere i contatti giusti, ha saputo trattare, non si è tirato indietro di fronte ai problemi].

This perception of normalcy, however, must be the result of a strong influence on the way of thinking and feeling that mark the process of socialization: Both primary, for those who are born and raised in this environment, and secondary, for those

---

[1] The passage said: "In contrasto con questo lungo periodo contrassegnato dall'unica dimensione loro consentita—quella di silenziose e invisibili tutrici dell'ordine e del sistema di valori di Cosa Nostra, uniformate e appiattite sulla figura dei loro compagni—la nuova strategia comunicativa dell'organizzazione le ha sempre più spesso trasformate in decisivo ed efficace veicolo comunicativo nei confronti del mondo esterno."

who become involved through the affiliation process, which is no surprise that it is referred to as a "second baptism." The habit of elitism, of submission to the bosses' authority, of violence, and most of all, of silence. A silence in the communication with others, and presumably, a silence toward one's own deep desires, of one's desire to feel and think. The injunction of non-communication, in the context of contemporary society, undoubtedly marks a division between Mafia society and democratic society.

A sort of paradox, at least for someone who watches this parallel world from the outside, regards the quality of life that seems grotesquely torn between two extremes: On one side, the enormous wealth, at least in the dominant families, and on the other side, the difficulty and the impossibility to benefit from it. Not only for the purposes of going underground, which require a modest lifestyle, even in a cramped underground bunker, but also for a series of impositions from the organization itself, follow the rules of secrecy and of the subordination under the bosses.

Daily life in the Mafia, one could say in conclusion, is marked by a very contradictory quality of life, both on a material and sentimental level. Predominant seems to be the social control that appears as a projection on the territory of a control even more marked which is that over the affiliates and the members of their families. The basic rules are to loyally follow the orders, to be submissive to the hierarchy, to vindicate received offenses without asking the government to help, to not testify against affiliates, to assist fugitives, and to not have any kind of relation with law enforcement and the courts. In the case of transgression (whether of their own accord or that of their family), the efficient trials of Mafia organizations do not hesitate to impose punishments of up to a death sentence.

It is possible to hypothesize that every single individual develops such contexts in significantly different ways according to whether they are young people or adults: The questions of generations; or men and women: The question of gender.

Boundaries, on one hand, and conflicts on the other, between the usual world of civil society and that of the world apart, with their codes and severe hierarchies, appear to be less sharp today, in light of the experiences of collaborators of justice and their families. The horizon of the life of Mafiosi "pentiti" is involved in that affect of personal relations and individual psyche. Through collaborators' testimonies and their families (which look like the tip of an iceberg in movement), we are able to perceive and interpret (with caution) some relevant aspects of these phenomena. From these testimonies, there comes some valuable insight about daily life, about family relations and suffering: Voices that come from "another" world, voices that express dismay, distress—but also relief—for the changes taking place. Voices, which are sometimes silent, are able to be expressed only in the extreme forms of mental suffering.

In the decision to become a "pentito"—and the journey is a long and arduous one—women have a predominant role, both positive and negative. It is often the women who, as the courts say, prevent cooperation at the very last minute. The management of daily life, the mediation between different sectors of the social world, and in particular, the mediation between the one and only past world and the many future worlds are under the domain and the control of women. "Foreign presence" in the Mafia universe, as Alessandra Dino has suggested, women have developed particular communication skills that aid them in crises and changing situations. More open to cultural influences than men—not to mention more educated—women probably, still have a lot to say about this restoration phase in the Mafia world. In particular, wives that come from a non Mafia environment have kept a distance, a change that is helpful in the transition from one status to another. An ambiguous distance, however: Not taking responsibility for their actions through mourning and awareness, they are on the edge, somehow suspended and paralyzed between two incompatible worlds. Among other things, it seems that women tend to hide parental responsibilities from their children more often than men. A Calabrese judge, on this matter, said:

> The first approach is closure, in the sense of not letting everything be known […] But in most cases I've found that the father had a very clear conversation with his children […] wives, conversely […] I noticed closure toward children as to not let them know what the father was doing (Facciolla).[2]
> [Il primo atteggiamento è protettivo e di chiusura, nel senso di non far sapere tutto (…) Ma nella stragrande maggioranza di casi ho trovato il padre che ha fatto un discorso con i figli molto chiaro (…) nelle mogli, viceversa, (…) ho notato una chiusura verso i figli per non far sapere tutto quello che faceva il padre].

This is the course of life in the balance between worlds. On the one hand, the world of the Mafia: One world, a closed horizon, a forced context that does not allow the expression of subjectivity, no dissent allowed. It does not create consistent psychological problems until it appears closed, unique, and intact. A world already beyond those who have decided to "take the plunge"; a world, however, that represents a piece of oneself and that reclaims in some ways a mental domination that these people do not want to give any more. On the other hand: The opening. The promise of subjectivity as an invitation to the dimension of one's choice, as a guarantee to be able to say no, a way of access to democracy, in a way mental and existential, even before institutional and relating to rights.

II.

On the historical level, secular fights for democracy have been fought on several frontlines. I would like to quote, immediately, two that—in a completely negative way—remind us of the Mafia. The first consists of the fact that the democratic system is based on the progressive creation of territorial spaces, which are non-violent on the inside, namely the abolition of private violence (vendetta and justice of itself), in favor of the violence monopoly in the state's hands. Democracy is created in a way that citizens are protected from arbitrary violence and facilitates communication among citizens and between citizens and institutions. Democracy is the opposite of omertà and the threat of violence and death: Both, however, being the fundamental characteristics of the various Mafias.

The second front on which the decisive battle has been waged for centuries, and is one of the columns of the democratic system is the principle of equality. It is notorious that, on the contrary, what we may call the internal rules of a Mafia

---

[2] Personal communication with Eugenio Facciolla. Catanzaro, November 19, 2001.

organization are anti-egalitarian: In the first place because the organization invests itself into an elite superiority ("whoever is a man, I decided it") that is translated in the evocation of life and death over other people, a belief that attracts easily weak and mediocre people. In the second place, the anti-egalitarian Mafia is notorious for its sexism, in the relations with women and feminine in general, but also as multiple testimonies show, in the relations with single women, wives, daughters, lovers, and mothers. Democracy means the guarantee of being able to say no, to have a guaranteed right to dissent, to have the right to choose, both for men and women equally. Mafia means submission, regression from citizen into subject. To women, in particular, it is forbidden to be an individual, lest the consequence be death. Repercussions of those "apart" rules of Mafia world—which is structured in parallel to the "normal" world of the nearby society—are heard from women and men. However, restrictions for women are much heavier:

> Among other things, due to its separate character, the organization is able to preserve ideologies on the inside that have already become obsolete on the outside: I am referring in particular to the control of Mafia women's sexuality, which seems to be static in theory but also in practice, when all around the community where affiliates live (when we also refer to neighbors in Palermo or villages in the rural Sicily) move toward an almost complete liberalization of morality. One of the differences between the inside and the outside is this: The women of Mafia men are not allowed to do what others can do (Lupo 2003, p. 60).
> [Tra l'altro, proprio per il suo carattere separato, l'organizzazione è in grado di preservare al proprio interno ideologie divenute ormai obsolete fuori di essa: e mi riferisco soprattutto al controllo della sessualità delle donne dei mafiosi, che a quanto sembra permanere rigido non solo in teoria ma anche nei fatti, quando tutt'intorno la comunità in cui vivono gli affiliati (quand'anche ci riferiamo ai quartieri popolari di Palermo, o ai paesi della Sicilia rurale) vanno verso una pressoché completa liberalizzazione dei costumi. Una delle differenze tra il dentro e il fuori è proprio questa: alle donne dei mafiosi non è consentito quanto è consentito alle altre].

At this point it is useful to reiterate that the Mafia is a male-only organization. Membership is closed to women. However, in multiple articulated forms, the feminine presence appears to be central for the unleashing of Mafia "domination" over a territory, for the reproduction of domination relations day by day, but also for the illegal management (Siebert 1996b).

For a long time, the role of women in the Mafia world remained in the dark. Silent, unknown, most of the time they become visible during funerals. A widespread social representation is the collective portrait of women eternally dressed in black, in a theatric pose that oscillate between reverential silence of subordination and the supplication of a vendetta. Traditional women, in all regards. The few words that Mafiosi filtrated from this opaque world headed in the same direction: women were completely dedicated to family, to be exemplary mothers and obedient wives; women unaware of the illegal activities of their husbands. Stereotyped women, icons of the common male imaginary. Functional women for the criminal organization precisely due to their invisibility.

Women, however, from time to time were killed or "accidentally" involved in some violent conflict, or because they became an involuntary witness, or because (we may think today) they were involved in some direct participation. Women sometimes "took the plunge" and became witnesses for the prosecution in some trials by testifying, narrating, and accusing.

In order to think about the responsibilities and the effective engagement of women in Mafia criminal organization, it is necessary to distinguish the various level of involvement. Just as the Mafia itself, from the point of view of the social composition of its affiliates, is not homogeneous, even women who are within its range of influence are extremely different from each other. First, there is a distinction between those born and raised in Mafia families (in families where one or more men are affiliates) and those that are connected with the Mafia or for a temporary criminal activity or by a personal relation with Mafiosi.

If women until recently represented a sort of opaque continent and largely unknown—Teresa Principato, at this point, speaks about a "story of submerged centrality" (p. 39)—the phenomenon of the collaboration with justice has opened a dense and invisible veil, showing connections, relations, activities, and responsibilities.

In the moment that the parental family and the Mafia family conflict—like in the case of a repentance of one or more male family members—women stand up, making themselves visible, and earn great importance. The organization, of course, finally decides to give women a voice. But there is more: This sudden emersion of women seems to adhere to a specific strategy that criminal organization follows:

> We do not believe it is by chance that actresses of this new communicative strategy are mainly women who, for the first time, are allowed to speak in defense of the Mafia system—thus implicitly claiming a role within the organization—through the excommunication and the disgust by those who are betrayed and accused. Executing this task, women appear strong, aggressively defending a world of death and suppression, ready to sacrifice their own children, to curse and insult those who try to break free from this lethal commitment, using all necessary means, even going so far as to question family values as sacred as motherhood (Principato and Dino 1997, p. 16).
> [Non riteniamo casuale che attrici di questa nuova strategia comunicativa siano in prevalenza le donne, alle quali viene per la prima volta concesso di prendere la parola in difesa del sistema mafioso – così implicitamente rivendicando l'esistenza di un loro ruolo all'interno dello stesso – attraverso la scomunica e il disprezzo manifestati di chi ha tradito e accusato. E nello svolgimento di tale compito le donne di mafia appaiono dure, aggressivamente tese alla difesa di un mondo di sopraffazione e di morte, pronte a sacrificare i propri figli, a maledire e insultare chi tenta di liberarsi dall'abbraccio mortale del vincolo di affiliazione, servendosi di tutti i mezzi e arrivando addirittura a mettere in discussione valori familiari sacri, come la maternità].

This increasing active involvement of women in criminal activities is undoubtedly incentivized from the fact that several men, following severe prison regulations introduced after the attacks of 1992, cannot exercise their power in the first person. In this context, the women of the family—sisters, wives, daughters, and mothers—are invested with a temporary power to exercise on behalf of men who are either in prison or are on the run. It becomes legitimate, then, to wonder about the prospects of a leadership position in these organizations. I asked Eugenio Facciolla, attorney of the DDA (Direzione Distrettuale Antimafia) of Catanzaro, if it was possible for a woman, after the man was released from prison, to be unwilling to return to her submissive role under the boss:

In my opinion it is unlikely to happen, unless a clan starts to be managed by a woman. However, I believe that it will be extremely hard to find any proof of this in all of Italy, not just in our district. In my opinion, the role of the woman is only temporary in the case of an imprisoned man or fugitive.[3]
[Secondo me questo è difficile che accada, a meno di non trovare una cosca che comincia ad essere retta proprio da una donna. Ma penso che di questo ben difficilmente ne troveremmo traccia in tutta Italia, non solo nel distretto nostro. Secondo me il ruolo della donna rimane sempre quello di reggenza temporanea in assenza del marito detenuto o latitante].

It would seem, then, that the hypothesis of the temporary delegation of power to women in the Mafia and 'Ndrangheta environments is the one closest to reality.

To better understand the intrinsic diversity of Mafia daily life and "normal" daily life and to contextualize the issues for the formative process in the Mafia environment, it is useful to reflect on both the practical and symbolic dimensions of masculine and feminine social constructs within the context of the Mafia. In an environment marked by female submission—where the organization is predominantly male—the image that Mafiosi have of women and of the feminine can be significant and revealing. The Mafia is a secret society of only men (maybe this explains the obsessive female presence in the male imagination in this sort of mono-sexual community). The world of women, in these men's eyes, appears almost like a natural subversive environment compared to the Mafia order. Mafiosi are suspicious about women as concrete people and about everything appearing to have a feminine quality. In this sense, the "feminine" is stigmatized in advance. Women, moreover, are "naturally" considered to be the property of men. Those aspects are explicit in the rites of affiliation, in which the Mafioso candidate offers as a proof of his loyalty, to the organization, the lives of his relatives, mothers, wives, sons, and daughters. Internal rules dictate not to touch the woman belonging to another Mafioso: Those are rules that strengthen the endogamous bond among the members of the clan. It has been emphasized how this prohibition has a strictly instrumental and not moral character: To not compromise the compactness of the group and to keep everything a secret. The apparent, rigid respect for the woman of a Mafioso is that for mother, "the mother of my children." This formal respect is easily connected with the substantial disgust for the figure of the woman.

A reflection on connections and influences between violent and bloody activities, daily life, and intimate relations cannot but touch the sphere of sexuality. Judge Falcone, in an interview with Marcelle Padovani, said: "An extremely famous proverb in Cosa Nostra says: It is better to command than to fuck" (Falcone and Padovani 1991, p. 76). Leadership and power, even desired, exerted, and relished in a very strong emotional way—as it appears in the case of Mafiosi—requires self-control, alertness, and detached coldness that are achieved at the expense of other aspects of intra-psychic life, to the dismay of Eros.

The honored man speaks without showing emotions and sentiments. This attitude, strongly imposed and self-inflicted, cannot have consequences in the way these men express their sexuality. The culture of death—at least one is induced to think—infects the relations with the living, creating boundaries, beyond which

---

[3] Personal communication with Eugenio Facciolla. Catanzaro, November 19, 2001.

there is danger. The danger of getting lost, let go, and becoming weakened: The danger of loving. A "professional ethic" that trains to kill—as the story of totalitarian formations and regimes teaches—requires psychic sacrifices that affect sexual lives and erotic fantasies. In this regard, it is possible to quote a Palermo psychoanalyst, Filippo Di Forti, who in 1982 wrote:

> The Mafioso is not able to love, but only to fuck […] his sexuality is merely genital and consumerist, the imaginary Mafioso is "sexophobic" […] His affective ideology is possessive but his attitude is virilistic and genital-centered, the man must be a "man," no imperfections, and there is no space for erotic communication (50).
> [Il mafioso non sa amare ma fottere (…) la sua sessualità è meramente genitale e consumistica, l'immaginario mafioso è sessuofobico (…) La sua ideologia affettiva è possessiva ma il suo atteggiamento è virilistico e genitalizzante, l'uomo che deve essere "uomo," niente sbavature, non c'è posto per la comunicazione erotica].

In a Mafioso environment—and "pentiti" talk about this—sentimental anxiety is a symbol of unreliability. The sexuality, even commercialized, results in regression, a return to oneself, a surrender to the pleasure principle: Sexuality is life and, as such, it is directly opposed to the Mafia, which is death. "The Mafioso spirit—or as someone once said, the mafiosità—finds its roots and draws its nourishment from this negation of Eros, the negation of life" (Abruzzese 1993, p. 208). Those who are not fully versed in such training of cold detachment, as for instance a Mafia white-collar, become aware of this with great astonishment. A collaborator of justice narrates:

> I, for example, invited them to some evenings that I organized in this place that I had with these G. brothers where I had some beautiful girls (!). These, on the contrary, preferred to stay among themselves, I don't know if you understand, and they had, even if there was a girl that […] "wants to get friendly with these two friends of mine" in brackets because they were never my friends, and they preferred, on the contrary, even if they came to be there with a glass, something, always talking about how they will destroy "the lives" of people! What should I say! They have a repressed sexuality. They never talk about it, beside the rare instance of intercourse, but really rare (!) […] because they were so busy killing people (laugh), what can you do? And then, from the sexual point of view, they have, speaking about sexuality, a sort of taboo (Lo Verso and Lo Cocco 2002, p. 119).
> [Io, ad esempio, li invitai a delle serate che organizzavo io in un locale che avevo con questi fratelli G. dove avevo là una serie di ragazze da favola (!). Questi, invece, preferivano che si stavano tra di loro maschi, seduti, non so se mi sono spiegato, e loro avevano, anche se c'era la ragazza che (…) "Fai amicizia con quei due miei amici" tra virgolette perché amici miei non ci sono mai stati, e loro preferivano, invece, anche se venivano là rimanere appresso a un bicchiere, una cosa, e parlare sempre: di come dovevano distruggere "a vita" a gente! Che le voglio dire? Hanno una sessualità repressa. Loro non ne parlano mai di sesso, a parte il rapporto che poi è pure sporadico, ma sporadico (!) (…) perché era talmente impegnato a andare ad ammazzare a gente (ride), come, come fa? E allora, però, dal punto di vista sessuale, hanno, parlando di sessualità, una sorta di tabù (…)].

Letting one's guard down for an honored man is dangerous; for some reason, it is repeated by everyone. It is the female body that embodies this highly threatening temptation for the discipline and cohesion of this organization. Drastically reducing erotic communication to genital sexuality requires an enormous sacrifice to the individual that is rewarded, at least partially, with the Mafia ideology of manhood. The disgust, for example, that accompanies the expression "to fuck" once again demonstrates the fear of women, the fear of their feminine parts, and the fear of the anarchic power of Eros. The Mafia aversion toward every form of "depraved" sexuality, like homosexuality, and passive homosexuality in particular, is a sign of this behavior.

Giuliano Lo Verso, a clinical psychologist with direct experience of clinical interviews with collaborator of justice, says:

> Contrary to what some American movies have conveyed, the Mafia world is almost asexual. The traditional adage "cummanari è megghiu ri futtiri" (to command is better than to fuck) seems to be taken seriously, in a process of psychoanalytic sublimation. The honored man is worried about power (of death) and money. He does not care much about the feminine. Women, in turn, live their life among themselves with children and this is their power. Certainly, a Mafioso has some sexual relations: Very few with his wife, about which he is unwilling to speak; and with lovers, characterized as loose women whom, instead, he may talk about among other men. However, most reports described relationships as a form of domination and power, not as passionate sex. Something one can brag about among friends, but without any real emotional investment. Relations marked, it seems, by quick eroticism, more or less narcissistic. The honored man must still provide an image of himself as a controlled person, without passion, sober, and loyal to his family and wife (115).
>
> [A differenza di quanto comunicato da una certa filmografia americana, il mondo mafioso è quasi a-sessuato. Il detto tradizionale "cumannari è megghiu ri futtiri" (Comandare è meglio di fare all'amore) sembra essere preso quasi alla lettera, in un processo di sublimazione psicoanalitico. L'uomo d'onore si occupa di potere (di morte) e di denaro. Non ha molto interesse per il femminile. Le donne a loro volta vivono tra di loro e i bambini e questo è il loro potere. Certo, il mafioso ha delle relazioni sessuali: con la moglie, poche e di cui non si parla; con amanti, intese come donne facili, di cui invece si può parlare tra uomini. Relazioni descritte però più come una forma di dominio e potere che non come relazioni passionali, sessuali. Qualcosa di ostentabile tra amici, ma senza un reale investimento affettivo. Relazioni segnate, pare, da un erotismo frettoloso, più di tipo narcisistico. L'uomo d'onore deve comunque fornire l'immagine di sé come di una persona controllata, non passionale, morigerata, fedele alla famiglia ed alla moglie].

It appears, then, that Mafiosi fear the explosive force of Eros, the promise of happiness, amorous regression, and tenderness. Mafiosi fear communication and relationships. Their gloomy duty of "fucking" channels sexuality in a unidirectional path of dominion over the other. A sexuality harnessed, at the principle, of the reality of reproduction—there is also the question of having a male first-born—and the principle of performance of an elusive masculine potency. And thus, the suspicion becomes the behavior that, for all these reasons, prevails against women.

Women do not appear trustworthy for the job of killing: The disgust for the presumptuous inferiority of women is strongly mixed with an admiration and recognition for their difference. Antonio Calderone said:

> Cosa Nostra's men are particularly cautious on what they say to their wives. The starting point is that women think in a certain way, all women, even those who have married Mafiosi or those come from Mafia families. When a woman is hit in her personal affections, she does not reason anymore, there is no more omertà, there is no more Cosa Nostra, there are no more arguments and rules that can stop her [...] The honored Sicilian man knows and tries to keep far from Cosa Nostra wives, sisters, and mothers. He does it to protect them, to defend them, because if a woman knows something he has to order somebody else to kill her (Arlacchi 1992, p. 165).

[Gli uomini di Cosa Nostra stanno molto attenti a che cosa dicono alle mogli. Il punto di partenza è che le donne ragionano in un certo modo, tutte le donne, anche quelle che hanno sposato dei mafiosi o che vengono da famiglie di mafia. Quando una donna viene colpita negli affetti più cari non ragiona più, non c'è omertà che tenga, non c'è più Cosa Nostra, non ci sono più argomenti e regole che la possono tenere a freno. (…) L'uomo d'onore siciliano lo sa e cerca di tenere lontano dalle vicende di Cosa Nostra mogli, sorelle e madri. Lo fa per proteggerle, per salvaguardarle, per salvarle, perché se la donna sa qualcosa finisce che o la deve ammazzare lui o la deve far ammazzare da qualcun altro].

It is dreadful to think that those who become affiliates to a Mafia organization know the consequences: That you have to be on edge, ready to kill close and loved people. Here we are all on a level of reality, and not of mere suppositions. It is confirmed by several homicides that have been carried out by relatives or friends close to the victim because those were the only people that the victim trusted.

III.

A discussion on democratic perspective in our society has to interrogate which are the consequences—for everyone—of twists between legal and illegal spheres, normal and Mafia daily life, rights and oppression for people that grown in those contexts. We cannot but emphasize, in this perspective, the importance of education in contrast with the totalitarian ambitions of the Mafia domain: An education focused on respect and love for one another, on the pleasure of communication, on the game, and on the care of our own subjectivity and critical attention to everything around us. In the family, in the public sphere, in private relations as in public ones. How difficult it is to face psychical and social changes, that family and environmental education in Mafia context have produced in adolescents and young adults emerges from the educational work done by the Istituto di Formazione del Personale di Messina, a service from the Department of Juvenile Justice of the Ministry of Justice. It is evident that the characteristic elements of the Mafia environment—like the obsession with death, megalomania, authoritarianism, total social control, omertà, and negation of subjectivity—deeply influence children and adolescents in those contexts of society. Those who have experience in working with Mafia adolescents in juvenile prisons talk about "halved adolescence":

First and foremost it is important to note the heavy dependence on parental figures. This aspect brings with it a continuous replication of maternal and paternal codes that induce a passive conformation of transmitted values. The strongly vertical structure of the Mafia system determines a censorship and control of emotions that expose the subject to a condition of loneliness and alienation. The adolescent lives without paying attention to him/ herself and with an inhibition of desire that led him to close him or herself off to new information, new beliefs, and new experiences, and to avoid the "risk" of new social relationships outside of the associated environment (Regoliosi 2008, p. 125).

[In primis si deve sottolineare la pesante dipendenza dalle figure parentali. Questo aspetto porta con sé una continua replicazione dei codici paterni e materni, che induce una conformazione passiva ai valori trasmessi. La strutturazione fortemente verticale del sistema mafioso determina una censura e un controllo dei sentimenti che espongono il soggetto a una condizione di solitudine e di estraneità. L'adolescente vive una dimenticanza di sé e un'inibizione del desiderio che lo porta a chiudersi nei confronti di nuove informazioni, nuove credenze e nuove esperienze, e a sottrarsi al "rischio" di contrarre relazioni sociali al di fuori dall'ambiente di appartenenza].

It would be misleading to see a young Mafia man as rebel subject, a young outcast, a teenager "against." Far from it. Analyzing the relationships of the Mafioso adolescent with the current society and comparing this relationship with those characteristics of typical adolescent phase, educators found, in young criminals close to the Mafia, young men extremely determined and aware, with a criminal conduct not at all intended to fill a gap. Organized crime is careful with new recruits, selecting, rejecting, and incentivizing; nothing is left to chance. In the face of social complexity and uncertainty, today's youth, generally tend to reject strong bonds and develop a marked egotistical culture, looking for extreme experiences, depending on consumerism, and developing a strong distance from the adult world, thereby denying authority, whereas on the contrary they prefer peer relations. On the other hand, young people raised in Mafia environments adhere to a strong culture, to the culture of the ego they oppose selflessness and the systematic inhibition of pleasure, to the need for extreme experiences the Mafia replies in an efficient way with its sacred rites, myths, and symbols, the thirst for consumerism is fulfilled with intangible assets like status, honorability, strong identity, adventure, etc. Unlike others, the young Mafioso does not reject authority; on the contrary, he lives in strong submission toward authoritarian figures and merely vertical socialization:

> In fact, the weak image represented today by "regular" society and institutions, contrasted with the perceptions of the Mafia society as a strong, secure, and charming world, able to accompany and give meaning to transition toward adult roles, contributes to strengthening bonds between the adolescent and the Mafia family. Under certain aspects, we could dare to draw a parallel with the condition of the young Islamic fundamentalist that compares the "decline" of the Western world with the "purity" of the Muslim family and who is able to respond comprehensively to the needs of his sense of the sacred, and of belonging (Regoliosi 2008, p. 121).
> [In effetti l'immagine di debolezza oggi trasmessa dalla società "regolare" e dalle istituzioni, contrapposta alla percezione della società mafiosa come un mondo forte, sicuro e affascinante, capace di accompagnare e dare senso alla transizione verso ruoli adulti, contribuisce a rendere ancora più saldi i legami tra adolescente e famiglia mafiosa. Sotto certi aspetti, potremmo azzardare un parallelismo con la condizione del giovane integralista islamico, portato a paragonare la "decadenza" del mondo occidentale con la "purezza" della famiglia musulmana, che sa rispondere in modo esaustivo ai suoi bisogni di senso, di sacro e di appartenenza].

These considerations, which are the result of an educational work experience achieved in close relation with adolescents in the juvenile prison, show the deep dimension of the dynamics to deal with when you seriously want to address the issues of "legal education" and the extremely complex connections between affects and rights. However, what we can deduce from these considerations and observations is the fact that the Mafia family structure and the material and symbolic relations between masculine and feminine that influence children's social processes, from an early age, obtain a fundamental importance, especially in changing perspective.

Much research in recent years, but also the direct knowledge of communication dynamics within Mafia families through the clinical therapeutic work with patients of this environment, defines the strong density of the familiar climate in which the young are raised. Pierre Bourdieu's words about the violence of male dominion can illustrate the vicious cycle in which Mafia family members are entangled:

> When the dominated apply the patterns that are the product of the domain to what dominates them, or, in other words, when their thoughts and perceptions are structured in accordance with the structures of the relations of domination from which they suffer, their acts of knowledge are inevitably acts of gratitude, submission (22).
> [Quando i dominati applicano a ciò che li domina schemi che sono il prodotto del dominio o, in altri termini, quando i loro pensieri e le loro percezioni sono strutturati conformemente alle strutture stesse del rapporto di dominio che subiscono, i loro atti di conoscenza sono, inevitabilmente, atti di riconoscenza, di sottomissione].

Whereas in wider society, historic developments have gradually increased the openness of the family toward other agents of socialization like the different grades of schools and mass media, associations and service structures, and all those initiatives for free time—so that they can assume, in principle, the development toward a "family of individuals"—in the environments connected to the Mafia the familiar horizon appears to be closed, unique, and firmly protected against every temptation of pluralization of emotional needs and extremely vertically structured. The watchwords of believing and obeying completely pervade the family environment, children's education is authoritarian and tends to depersonalize the individual. Indeed, it would be better to never even become an individual. Hierarchic levels do not need to be investigated, what is important is loyalty, to become part of the group, blind obedience to the orders. In this sense, the primary socialization, that familiar, announces the secondary, namely the one that sets up a man to become a potential affiliate, and the woman to aspire a career of being the "mother of my sons," as Mafiosi say when speaking about their wives. Overall, both the aware education and the various forms of communication among components of the family produce an amazing family cohesion in the name of the normalcy. A sense of normalcy that will not be scratched even when heinous crimes often committed by men—fathers, uncles, brothers—come to light. On the contrary, a normality that is claimed aloud. Alessandra Dino quotes a significant interview to Maria Concetta, daughter of Totò Riina, released to "Panorama":

> We never lived with an oppressing fear. We never thought: Oh God, now they catch us, because we were not aware that we were wanted […] I do not know how to explain exactly, it is difficult, but our life was the life of a normal family (216).
> [Non abbiamo vissuto con la paura appiccicata alla pelle. Non pensavamo: oddio ci prendono, perché non avevamo la consapevolezza di essere ricercati (…) Non so come spiegarlo esattamente, è difficile, ma la nostra era la vita di una famiglia normale].

This attitude, often observed within "pentiti" families, denotes a closure in their world beside the "inability to face the reality of the outside world that they refuse to acknowledge not only the rules but also the offenses brought and the suffering caused" (Dino 2002, p. 215). On the other hand, however, there are several clues that point to deep crisis due to the collapse of the omnipotence of the Mafia family, due to arrests, betrayals, collaborations, etc. For the first time, it occurs, for some years now, those relatives—often sons and daughters, never the Mafiosi themselves—make use of public services as a help for their mental health. Usually the mothers take the initiative.

Overall, with attention to both gender and generational differences, we may say that typical relations in Mafia families are represented as vertical, authoritarian, with a father often physically absent, but omnipresent as an authority figure, with a powerful mother, but submissive and with obedient children, very integrated in the familiar group and in the context of a world lived consciously and proudly "apart."

References

Abruzzese, S. (1993). La paura. In F. Occhiogrosso (Ed.), *Ragazzi della mafia*. Milan: Franco Angeli.

Arlacchi, P. (1992). *Gli uomini del disonore*. Milan: Mondadori.

Bourdieu, P. (1998). *Il dominio maschile*. Milan: Feltrinelli.

Chinnici, G., & Santino, U. (1991). *La violenza programmata. Omicidi e guerre di mafia a Palermo dagli anni '60 ad oggi*. Milan: Franco Angeli.

Di Forti, F. (1982). *Per una psicoanalisi della mafia*. Verona: Bertani.

Dino, A. (2002). *Mutazioni. Etnografia del mondo di Cosa Nostra*. Palermo: La Zisa.

Dino, A. (2008). *La mafia devota. Chiesa, religione, Cosa Nostra*. Bari-Rome: Laterza.

Falcone, G., & Padovani, M. (1991). *Cose di Cosa Nostra*. Milan: Rizzoli.

Gruppo Abele (2005). *Dalla mafia allo Stato. I pentiti: Analisi e storie*. Turin: EGA Editore.

Jedlowski, P. (1986). Vita quotidiana e senso comune. *Devianza e emarginazione*. March V(9).

Lo Verso, G., & Lo Cocco, G. (2002). I collaboratori di giustizia. Chi sono oggi, chi erano come mafiosi. In G. Lo Verso & G. Lo Cocco (Eds.), *La psiche mafiosa*. Milan: Franco Angeli.

Lupo, S. (2003). La mafia: definizione e uso di un modello virilista. *Genesis* II(2): 53–66.

Principato, T., & Dino, A. (1997). *Mafia Donna. Le vestali del sacro e dell'onore*. Palermo: Flaccovio Editore.

Regoliosi, L. (2008). Ipotesi per un lavoro di prevenzione e riabilitazione. In Istituto Centrale di Formazione di Messina. (Ed.), *I ragazzi e le mafie. Indagine sul fenomeno e prospettive di intervento*. Rome: Carocci.

Sciarrone, R. (2006). Passaggio di frontiera: la difficile via di uscita dalla mafia calabrese. In A. Dino (Ed.), *Pentiti. I collaboratori di giustizia, le istituzioni, l'opinione pubblica*. Rome: Donzelli.

Siebert, R. (1996a). *Mafia e quotidianità*. Milan: Il Saggiatore.

Siebert, R. (1996b). *Secrets of life and death: Women and the mafia*. New York: London, Verso.

Siebert, R. (2001). *Storia di Elisabetta. Il coraggio di una donna sindaco in Calabria*. Milan: Pratiche Editrice.

Chapter 3
Origins and Development of the 'Ndrangheta

Enzo Ciconte

The word Mafia, as a term, has been very successful and has gone beyond the regional boundaries of Sicily, the Italian region where it was born. Mafia is, without a doubt, the most well-known Italian word in the world. The other Italian organizations, 'Ndrangheta and Camorra, have not had the same amount of international success.

Mafia, 'Ndrangheta, and Camorra are an original Italian criminal product of the nineteenth century, particularly from the Southern regions of Sicily, Calabria, and Campania, respectively. Since their beginnings, they have represented, in the eyes of their contemporaries, a shocking and innovative change compared with other criminal systems from previous centuries. They have built an organization with a precise hierarchy, given a set of rules starting with the most important *omertà*, developed affiliation codes with legends designed to entice and fascinate young people, as well as provided a long-term criminal initiative. For these reasons, such criminal organizations were able to thrive for decades and are still active today, having survived various political regimes, each one different among themselves, whether Bourbon, Liberal, Fascist, or Republican.[1]

Today, the 'Ndrangheta is the strongest and most well-established organization in Italy and Europe, let alone numerous countries outside of Europe. It is the *dominus* of the international drug trade because, in accordance with the big producers, it controls cocaine flows and has not hesitated to commit massacres outside Calabria. This very thing happened in Duisburg, Germany, on August 15, 2007, and has had a remarkable influence not only on the Calabrian political world, but also in some Northern regions like Lombardy, Liguria, and Piedmont.

This is no recent phenomenon. Its history is deeply rooted in the heart of the nineteenth century, even if it was known at the time by other names like *picciotteria*,

---

[1] For those aspects see Ciconte (2008). For the history of Sicilian Mafia, it is useful to see Lupo (1997).

E. Ciconte (✉)
Rome, Italy
e-mail: enzociconte@gmail.com

N. Serenata (ed.), *The 'Ndrangheta and Sacra Corona Unita,* Studies of Organized Crime 12, 33
DOI 10.1007/978-3-319-04930-4_3, © Springer International Publishing Switzerland 2014

onorata società, famiglia Montalbano, maffia (with two f), or *camorra*. The term 'Ndrangheta only came into use during the 1960s.[2]

How could all of this have happened, especially since it has always been considered a "Bush League" version of the Mafia: That is, less important than its Sicilian cousin and, moreover, born in such a poor and marginal region as Calabria?[3] To answer this question, we must travel through time, learning about the legend and observing its organizational structure very closely.

It is not easy to spot *'ndranghetisti* in official documents because among the most important characteristics of the 'Ndrangheta, there is the tendency to work far from the surface, protected, and hidden as much as possible from resounding actions that would attract law enforcement and public opinion. Kidnappings began to attract public attention only during the second half of the twentieth century. But even then, only some were exposed, not all.

In the Italian historiography, the 'Ndrangheta is surely the least studied and least well-known Mafia organization. In an ideal bookstore, books on the Mafia would take up at least three walls of a room. Those regarding the Camorra would occupy one entire wall, while those regarding the 'Ndrangheta would be so few that they could fit on just over two shelves. Only in the past 2 years—following the *Infinito* and *Crimine* investigations coordinated by the courts of Reggio Calabria and Milan—there has been a revived interest of the subject and, consequently, an increase in publications.[4]

For a long time, the Calabrian Mafia was considered by all—not just historians—to be an appendage of Cosa Nostra, like an archaic Mafia: Folkloristic and wrought with occult cruelty. It was thought to be an expression of the underdevelopment typical of Calabria because its organizational structure had the natural family of the *capobastone* as its foundation, as it does to this day. However, a closer analysis of the Calabrian Mafia shatters this image, showing a mature and modern organization similar to Cosa Nostra and Camorra, but with considerably different and peculiar qualities.[5]

One distinctive trait should not go underestimated. The centuries-old history of the 'Ndrangheta has been characterized by a strong sense of anti-statism. This was rooted in the disapproval of the Italian State born during the unification of Italy, which was considered to be far away and hostile. In the years immediately following World War II, a particular phenomenon was produced: The meeting, in certain areas of the province of Reggio Calabria, of 'Ndrangheta groups with left-leaning political parties, thanks to the common experience of being confined during the

---

[2] For those elements, please, see Ciconte (1992). This book is the first book on the history of the 'Ndrangheta.

[3] For a highly interesting description of Calabria, refer to what notable Calabrian writer Corradi (1990) wrote in *Calabria* with a preface of Libero Bigiaretti (see also Corradi (1951)).

[4] For those arguments, see Ciconte (2010, pp. 7–21). The entire events of *Operazione Crimine* have been narrated by the direct protagonists as it is possible to read in Pignatone and Prestipino (2012).

[5] For this problem, it is useful to consult two reports of the Commissione Parlamentare Antimafia (Anti-Mafia Parliamentary Commission) (2000, 2008) in two different legislations.

reign of Fascism. Until the end of the 1970s, the PCI and PSI[6] were supported during elections by Mafiosi. Then the romance ended and the PCI became the most
fervent Anti-Mafia party.[7]

The 'Ndrangheta had the extraordinary capability to make itself invisible; thus,
its presence was generally off the radar to the people of that time. As a result, court
documents and police reports, along with various trial verdicts, hardly contain any
traces of their involvement. After the unification, the Italian government thought
that the main problem was the Camorra, which was the first Mafia organization to
be discovered. Then, attention began to spread to the Sicilian Mafia. Only recently,
with considerable and inexcusable delay, has the government taken up interest with
the 'Ndrangheta.

For a long period of history stretching from the Unification of Italy until nearly
the end of the twentieth century, the 'Ndrangheta has, for the most part, lived in an
informational and investigative darkness that has protected it from the prying eyes
of the forces of repression. While it became stronger and more extensive, the mass
media did not see it and police did not investigate with much attention.

This precise lack of attention, on both local and national levels regarding the
expansive force of the 'Ndrangheta, has been one of the factors that allowed this organization to grow and extend its power over new territories. The spotlight of public
interest was pointed at Cosa Nostra since the beginning of the nineteenth century
and, thus, the attention of the State was also on the Sicilian Mafia.

Then, as time passed by, the tide began to turn. Following the massacre of 1992
that killed judges Giovanni Falcone and Paolo Borsellino, the Sicilian Mafia took
a severe blow by the Italian State with the help of the numerous testimonies of collaborators of justice that followed Tommaso Buscetta's example.

The voids that the repressive actions of the State had created in the Sicilian
Mafia were quickly filled by the 'Ndrangheta. Today the Calabrian organization
has a monopoly on the Italian regions of Piedmont, Valle d'Aosta, Lombardy, and
Liguria; and has a significant presence in Tuscany, Emilia-Romagna, and Lazio.
It also maintains a solid presence in other foreign countries—both in and outside
of Europe—where it has its own colonies, such as France, Belgium, the Netherlands, the United Kingdom, Portugal, Spain, Switzerland, the Balkans, Australia,
the United States, Argentina, Chile, Brazil, Colombia, Venezuela, Mexico, Ecuador,
Bolivia, Dominican Republic, Morocco, and Turkey.

Its real strength is represented by an organizational structure based on blood
family relationships of the *capobastone*, which is the boss of the *'ndrina*, the basic
cell. Nearly all-immediate relatives of the *capobastone*: Children, siblings, cousins,
and grandchildren are members of the organization.

This family and parental net, extended by arranged marriages with daughters or
sons of other Mafiosi, allows the 'Ndrangheta to be present in every Italian region,

---

[6] PCI stands for Partito Comunista Italiano (Italian Communist Party), while PSI is Partito
Socialista Italiano (Italian Socialist Party).

[7] For this argument, see Ammendolia and Frammartino (1975); Manfredi (1981); Ciconte (1992);
Ciconte (1996).

as well as in European and extra-European countries. If one were to draw a map of 'Ndrangheta presence around the world, he or she could see that the same surnames are found in Calabria, in the other Italian regions, and in foreign countries.

A structure that exhibits these characteristics has prevented the uprising of the collaborators of justice. While the Mafia and Camorra have been shaken by so-called *pentiti*, the 'Ndrangheta has had very few because a Calabrian Mafioso who decides to collaborate would have to denounce his father, children, siblings, uncles, grandchildren, cousins, and in-laws. To be clear, not all close relatives of the *capo-bastone* are Mafiosi, but this is the case more times than not. For various reasons, some of them do not participate in 'ndrina life, nor are they ritually affiliated with it (Ciconte 1996, pp. 17–40).

'Ndrine (plural of *'ndrina*) increase in size by following the institution of cross-marriage between families, a practice used by European nobility in past centuries. The only difference is that this time it is not aristocracy, but Mafiosi. Thus, it is very common for a woman from one *'ndrina* to be forced to marry a man who belongs to a Mafia family; and so, she ends up being incorporated into the main clan.[8]

Often the most solid and long-lasting alliances between *cosche* had—and still have—cross-marrying as the basis. The crossings are dense and the tangle of relationships is difficult to untangle. Mafia families tend to be very large, and in them the ones who have more male members carry the most weight. A *cosca* with more men is a more powerful *cosca*, from a military point of view. This is very important in Mafia wars where the number—like in all wars—has significant importance; nonetheless, the number is also important for the territorial expansion of the 'ndrina itself. In fact, the 'Ndrangheta's method for expansion in Northern Italy is based on what we might call "colonies" or "branches."

In the 'Ndrangheta and in the Mafia subconscious, the very notable legend of Osso, Mastrosso, and Carcagnosso have played a key role. Terrible names, but at the same time captivating; so intriguing that, since the nineteenth century, they have stirred curiosity and ignited fantasies in young people wishing to become affiliated.

Who were these mythical characters that had such unlikely names? Osso, Mastrosso, and Carcagnosso never existed except in the legend that tells of three Spanish knights—probably young, though their age remains unknown—belonging to a secret society in Toledo named *Garduña*, who arrived in Italy around 1412.

Their trip was not for pleasure, nor was it of free will. In fact, they were fleeing from their own land—today they would be defined as fugitives—because they defended the honor of their own family, vindicating with blood the offense committed against their sister.

Legend has it that they stayed on the island of Favignana for 29 long years. No one knows why the Spanish knights chose that mysterious and fascinating island, nor does anyone know if someone had suggested this location to them. All that is known is that, while they were hidden from everybody and working underground in the island's abundant caves, they prepared the social rules for the largest Mafia organizations. No islander had noticed their presence and, until just a few years ago, the legend itself was unknown to the island's very inhabitants.

---

[8] For the role of women in different Mafia organizations, see Siebert (1994).

When they reemerged, Osso went to Sicily and founded the Mafia; Mastrosso headed to Campania to organize the Camorra; and Carcagnosso, having passed through the Strait of Messina, landed in Calabria to give birth to the 'Ndrangheta.

A ritual from the 'Ndrangheta affirms that Osso represents Jesus Christ; Mastrosso, Saint Michael the Archangel; and Carcagnosso, Saint Peter, who is seated upon a white horse at the front door of the Society. Other sources entrust the protection of Saint George to Osso, that of the Virgin Mary to Mastrosso, while Saint Michael the Archangel, or the Archangel Gabriel, would be under the protection of Carcagnosso.[9]

It is a fairy tale, of course, but it has played a decisive role in the construction of the culture and ideology of the 'Ndrangheta and for young Mafiosi. It is fraught with extraordinary symbolic elements: The reference to Spain as the base myth of all three criminal organizations, validated by noble origins—a fact of crucial significance for the identity to be transmitted to new affiliates—and, finally, it has been built purposefully to reclaim honor, family, secrecy, and rules. There is also an allusion to the importance of jail in the formation and mythology of the Mafia as is easily understood by the reference to the island of Favignana, location of a Bourbon penitentiary.

And finally, there is a mix between the sacred and the profane: The will, at all costs, to cling to the cloaks of the Catholic saints and to every Madonna in order to gain strength and authority under their protection. All the principal ingredients to create a good Mafioso are there. The rest will be created by experiences and daily practices that, for an 'ndranghetista, begin very early, right from adolescence.

Someone, upon hearing this legend, would probably either smile or just shake their head in disbelief that it could have been so important in the training of *picciotti* (young boys). And yet it was, and still is, the case.

This aspect clearly emerges in the baptism—that is to say, the affiliation rite—of a young man who is becoming a member of the organization. More than in the other Mafia organization, the rituals that articulate the life of the organization have always played a crucial role in the 'Ndrangheta for new affiliates.

One enters the 'Ndrangheta through the rite of baptism, a term analogous to the similar rite in the Catholic religion. It was the custom for the son of the *capobastone* to receive a double baptism in his crib: One by the Catholic Church and that by the 'Ndrangheta, thus elevating the baby to a *giovane d'onore* (honored youth). Obviously, this symbolic baptism would find an official and ritual confirmation only when, in due time, the young boy had proven himself worthy after having committed crimes of blood.

Since this is an absolute ritualistic ceremony, it is of enormous importance to the young affiliate. For the first time in his life, he is crossing the invisible threshold from the legal to the illegal world, which will transform him into a *picciotto* at the exclusive service of the 'ndrina.[10]

---

[9] For the importance of the fable, see Malafrina (1986); Ciconte and Macrì (2009); Ciconte et al. (2010).

[10] Judge Saverio Mannino (1997) has observed how rituals in the 'Ndrangheta are "instruments of an ideology that is used to give to the associative relation a legitimation, based on presumption of sentiments of honor and superiority" (p. 372).

It has already been said that the structure of the 'Ndrangheta rests upon the family of the *capobastone*, but the use of formal rituals among relatives should not be a surprise. Mafia ceremonies, in which non family members of the *capobastone* also participate, are highly symbolic and full of grandeur.

Among other things, the ubiquitous allegorical figures of rituality and symbology serve to solidify relationships and connections. The ritual is a celebration, just like a birthday party, Saint's day, baptism, first communion, or a wedding. Like the others, it is a reason to get together, to celebrate, to be recognized, and to affirm supremacy and hierarchies.

Collaborators of justice have recounted the moment of the affiliation and waiting for the ritual, which stirs up emotions and even anxiety. Many witnesses that were baptized have confirmed that the rite of baptism was never taken for granted. The young candidate-to-be is full of mixed emotions. It is a memorable day that will be etched in his memory. The Calabrian collaborators of justice said this, and it has also been well-represented in the works of some Calabrian writers like Saverio Strati and Don Luca Asprea.

Before the baptism there is a ceremony that decontaminates the room from external presences. In one such ceremony, these words were uttered:

> I baptize this room as our three Spanish knights did […] our three Spanish knights that departed from Spain […] if they baptized using chains and iron, with chains and iron so do I baptize it (Ciconte 2011, p. 3).
> [Io lo battezzo come lo hanno battezzato i nostri tre cavalieri di Spagna (…) i nostri tre cavalieri che dalla Spagna sono partiti (…) se loro hanno battezzato con ferri e catene, con ferri e catene lo battezzo io].

These words were intercepted during an electronic eavesdropping in a bar in Singen, Germany, on December 20, 2009. This formula is similar to a Calabrian version from the mid-twentieth century. Other examples have been recorded in lands as far away as Australia whose rituals closely resemble this very example.

The 'Ndrangheta is an organization that swims like a fish in water in the wake of modern globalization; yet, one cannot fully comprehend its expansive force if there is no reference to these ancient rituals. It very well may seem like a paradox, but it is a reality, like it or not.

It may seem obsessive to read about wiretappings of honored men who often talk about affiliation rituals, or about *doti* (endowments), or rather, the ranks that each member possesses within the organization.

Throughout the entire second half of the nineteenth century and during the Fascist period, the 'Ndrangheta grew without finding any major obstacles in its path. But during the early 1950s, the organization started its upward phase. This period represents a real about-face to the history of the Calabrian organization. During those years, the 'ndrine entered the arena of trafficking "foreign tobacco," a term donned by police for cigarettes imported from foreign countries. At that time they were precious goods and were offered in illegal circuits at lower prices compared to the Italian cigarettes sold legally through the State's monopoly on tobacco shops.

The smuggling of foreign tobacco was favored by the presence of Anglo-American forces in Italy, particularly in Naples. That port hosted the first ships full of cigarettes. There were men belonging to the Allied Forces that gave way to this lucrative criminal activity, which favored criminal groups of the area that at the time were not Mafiosi; but in a couple of years, they would be affiliated enough to have an influence on them.

This period set the pace for the decades to come. The ascent of the 'Ndrangheta was becoming refined by the second half of the 1960s, predominantly with the construction of the *Autostrada del Sole* (Highway of the Sun), in the section that connects Salerno with Reggio Calabria. Building the highway meant overcoming a historical setback, thus unifying Calabria with the rest of Italy. This had a positive effect on many aspects of Calabrian society.

There was, however, also a negative side. In fact, the largest firms in the North, winners of the contracts, contacted the *capibastone* and made veritable agreements with them; in particular, they established the payment of the "pizzo" in exchange for protection of their construction site, the employment of 'ndranghetisti as watchmen, the integration of Mafia firms in subcontracts, the supply of building materials, and the transportation thereof.[11]

At that time, there was a construction of a real business model between the Northern firms and the 'Ndrangheta. All parties made pacts of non-violence. This model would be adopted in the following years. We will see in relation to the construction—which never came to fruition—of the fifth iron and steel center in GioiaTauro,[12] in the construction of road linking the Ionic and the Tyrrhenian seas, in the construction of the airport and industrialization of Lamezia Terme, in the coal-burning power plant of ENEL in Gioia Tauro—which was also never finished—in the contract for the still-under-construction NATO base in Crotone that should have hosted F16 planes—another unfinished job—and in many more public activities, big or small that they may have been, including a recent amplification of the *Autostrada del Sole*.[13]

For all those endeavors, even in those that were not carried out, the work was launched and the 'Ndrangheta found a way to insert itself and earn huge amount of money. The question of economic income was very important, but the possibility of gaining prestige also weight heavily on the organization because it was forced to work side by side with important national firms. People saw Mafiosi arm in arm with managers of firms and with politicians. It was a real leap forward for the honored men during that time.

---

[11] For the history of Calabria in this period is useful to see Cingari (1982).

[12] The decision to build a new iron and steel center had an outstanding effect on the 'Ndrangheta during that time, consecrating the power and prestige of the Piromallis. For those aspects of the event, it is crucial to see Arlacchi (1983). For the further development of the 'Ndrangheta in Gioia Tauro see Forgione (2012).

[13] For those aspects, see Forgione and Mondani (1993). Regarding the power plant of ENEL, see Commissione Parlamentare (1990).

The expansion of the economic intervention of the Italian State in the *Mezzo-giorno* (Southern Italy) would last throughout the 1970s. In Calabria—from the so-known Colombo Block onward—the distribution of State funds was considerable, but its concrete management got out of the hands of the state. The Italian government began to finance the 'Ndrangheta, although indirectly, thus contributing to its growth and power. The State provided money, but could no longer manage the majority of it. The State often appeared evanescent, and intervention instruments—from *Cassa per il Mezzogiorno* to different agricultural authorities and consortia for industrial development—often folded to the interests of clientele, whether illegal or partial. Its action was substituted by a veritable illegal control of the economy.

The 1960s and 1970s were the "magic" years for the 'ndrine because they "de-provincialized" themselves, dispersing all over the world in search of new business. The 'Ndrangheta would no longer be locked in the narrow confines of its origins, in the recesses of rural society, in the badlands of Aspromonte; but it would have made the choice to extend beyond national and international boundaries.[14]

This was, without a doubt, a pivotal turning point that would propel the Calabrian Mafia into far and unknown lands.[15] With its many transnational connections solidified throughout the preceding decades, the 'Ndrangheta worked like an enormous magnet, attracting drug markets as well as weapons and explosives dealers with its criminal reliability. The drugs, at first heroin, but soon followed by cocaine, represented the most lucrative trade in the entire history of the criminal organization.

Having already laid the foundation in previous decades, during the 1970s and 1980s there was a huge transformation within the Calabrian Mafia. It went beyond regional borders, exporting its activities to the North with kidnappings, consequently gaining a leading role in international weapons and drug trades; and in the 1990s, it demonstrated itself to be equipped with an organizational and action capacity similar to its Sicilian sister, Cosa Nostra.[16]

Surely taking advantage of the underestimation and misunderstanding that continued to surround it, its dynamic development would fully unfold within the framework of cultural and economic trends, and in political conditions existing at regional and national levels. Those years were characterized by a cohabitation—or coexistence—of the State with the various Mafias, which, since the beginning of the Cold War, had entered the complex and diverse anti-communist block that had characterized the Italian post-war movement, becoming an important component in a short time. This period in history, dominated by blocks and the impossibility of political change, meant that the fundamental task of the institutions and the State apparatus was to maintain in power of a given social and political block.

Throughout the 'Ndrangheta's history, there are two distinct periodical moments: First, the relations with the Fascist world and, secondly, that of the legitimization that led the Calabrian Mafia to become a structure of economic and political power.

---

[14] For the 'Ndrangheta of Aspromonte, see the classic and ever-useful Stajano (1979). The description of Africo facilitates the understanding of social change and the particular reasoning of the 'Ndrangheta. Also regarding the Aspromonte, see Bianco (1959).

[15] For those arguments see Gambino (1976, 1986). See also Malafrina (1981).

[16] For the kidnapping season see Ciconte (1997).

The two phases are not clearly distinguished because they partly overlap temporally. In the same period some 'ndrine chose the path of subversive corruption, rather than that of power. Then, the former leveled their behavior to the latter (De stefanos and allies) and put themselves to the service of the local and national power without exception.

The 'Ndrangheta is perhaps the Mafia organization that had the most contact with the subversive world. While the crucial period happened between the end of the 1970s and the beginning of the 1980s, the 2-year period from 1969 to 1970 were the most significant. Looking back at the town of San Luca, in the heart of Aspromonte, the *Montalto* Mafia meeting took place on October 26, 1969. This meeting, which included the most influential 'ndrine leaders, was apparently held the same way every year for time immemorial.

The Montalto meeting that year was very different from previous meetings throughout the 'Ndrangheta's history. It was distinct because some of the honored men, the Nirtas from San Luca and the De Stefanos from Reggio Calabria being among them, wished to discuss the possibility of the organization endorsing the political project having survived the Fascist regime—Prince Junio Valerio Borghese—who had proposed a coup d'état. The choice was difficult because it would require an imminent and direct political dislocation of the 'Ndrangheta. A providential interruption by the police, who were informed of the meeting, prevented the project from being carried out.[17]

Another meaningful event happened in July of 1970, with the revolt for the state capital in Reggio Calabria, named "boia chi non molla" (executioner who does not give up) as its famous slogan.[18] It was a revolt with subversive traits, led by the Fascist right and recruiting a wide participation of 'Ndrangheta men. In those episodes, relationships were formed between some 'Ndrangheta groups and men of the subversive right wing.

At that time, two more events took place: On one hand, some people of the subversive right were affiliated with the 'Ndrangheta. On the other hand, however, the secret services also came into contact with certain men of the 'Ndrangheta, not to mention the extreme right-wingers. Some of these men had a double position because they were both honored men and representatives of the extreme right.[19] But an important development was afoot: The workers for the State were taking advantage of both parties. The failing of the coup d'état in the 2-year period of 1969–1970 does not interrupt the relations between the 'Ndrangheta and the subversion world that will continue for the following years.

By the middle of the 1970s a significant new development occurred. The most influential *capibastone* decided to join the freemasonry. They were, however, covered lodges and did not actually have anything to do with official freemasonry. The decision came from the necessity to build relationships with the professional

---

[17] About Montalto, see Marino (1971) who describes the events of the memorable day.

[18] More information on that historical period has been narrated by Cuzzola (2007). *Storie e memorie della rivolta.*

[19] See Misiami (1994). The article summarizes the internal debate of the PCI of Reggio Calabria.

world—in which freemasonry has a substantial presence—in order to maintain a direct connection with those circles and find a fast track for business.

The *'ndranghetisti* who maintained close relationships with the subversive right wing were mainly the ones who orchestrated this operation. This [thing] was facilitated with tools provided by the government and with secret services.

The decision to join the freemasonry warranted a modification of the 'Ndrangheta structure; a superior command level named *Santa* was introduced which involved the elite members of the Mafia, known as *santisti*. The *santisti* were authorized to build relationships with sectors whose prior contact had been strictly prohibited, starting with the *Carabinieri* and police officers. Many *capibastone* became informants for law enforcement, which created chaotic and ambiguous relations. This explains the recurring "confidential source" theme in police and *Carabinieri* records.

Being protected by covered lodges made it easier to develop relationships with state officials. Beginning with magistrates, these connections would prove to be vital components in determining the course of legal proceedings. But in the meantime, they were still able to make direct contact with politicians, freelance workers, and managers of public companies that were able to ensure, or procure, new business ventures.[20]

The 1980s were characterized by the ideological conviction that the huge expansion of the market and of the companies themselves would result in a process of modernization, thus bringing the "questione merdionale" to an end. However, by the end of the century, the 'Ndrangheta would come to be portrayed as one of the causes of the warped and corrupt modernization of the current Mezzogiorno region.

During those decades, the Mafia had a profound influence on the economy. It created a sort of double market, one legal and the other illegal; the first undergoing heavy intervention and conditioning by the second. Mafia companies, or at least those dealing with Mafia funds, penetrated the legal market, altering the rules, destroying healthy companies, and preventing the creation of new economic enterprises. Violence, especially of the organized variety, thus became not only a problem of public order, but it also became a new economic entity capable of acting on the open market and making economic choices. These selections lead to the failure of many companies and, in turn, the promotion of Mafia entrepreneurs. These are the essential and warped aspects that have represented the so-called modernization in Calabria and other parts of the Mezzogiorno.

The Mafia was quickly gaining control of the economies of many areas within the region. This was possible through the inadequate and incompetent management of power by the local ruling classes. In Calabria, the formation of the ruling classes had a distinctive feature because it was marked by the historic weakness of society and the Calabrian middle class, which—having lived in the shadows of large estates—had internalized certain behavioral patterns and ambitions by the agricultural upper class, above all the acquisition and ownership of land.

---

[20] See Fantò (2007).

The middle class later became clerical and bureaucratic, daughter of urban growth and public service, attracted in the cities by the flow of public funds, fascinated by occupations that were once considered liberal; primarily the legal profession. That explains both the political and economic dependence from the domestic power centers and the particular formation of the Calabrian political class. This also explains the frailness of the civil society, whose historical and structural weakness left a void. Throughout the 1980s, this void was filled by politics, which was the true mistress of the region's development and destiny.[21]

An extraordinary turning point was the decision of nearly all *'ndrine* to settle in Northern Italy, a strategic choice that would allow the 'Ndrangheta to become rooted in places that the Mafia and Camorra were never able to achieve over the long term.

Using Milan and Lombardy as the central location to conduct the organization's business matters was no accident. Milan is not only a big industrial and financial city (considering that in 1990, there were 8,000 financial societies and 173,000 commercial societies), but it is a vital center for the Italian economy and strategically located with regard to the rest of Europe.

It was, therefore, a very attractive geographical position for the Mafia strategic interests. In May 1991, Giovanni Falcone highlighted the importance of Milan as the "center of the international heroin trade from the Middle and Far East" and as well as a "hub for cocaine trafficking in Central Europe" (1). The most significant element that demonstrated Milan's centrality was the fact that "the most important illegal money laundering base" was located there due to its proximity to Austria and Switzerland (1).

When Falcone made that diagnosis, he could not have predicted the subsequent developments that would lead to the decline of the presence of Cosa Nostra in the North, let alone could he imagine the impetuous development of the 'Ndrangheta.

The Lombard metropolis offered ideal conditions for the use and reemployment of illicit capital; for that reason it has long been a true hub for money laundering.[22] The 'Ndrangheta's economic activities went in several directions. Shortly after their arrival in the North, the 'ndranghetisti began buying bars, pizzerias, garages, Italian Treasury Bonds (BOT), Treasury Credit Certificates (CCT), commercial activities operating in the field of clothing, home furnishings, so-called "earth moving," (excavation) gas stations, car washes, gyms, financial and real estate agencies, construction companies or property management, demolition companies, auto scrap trades, and transportation companies; moreover, they also formed real estate and financial companies and bought several properties in an effort to hide through using dummy corporations.

Some 'ndranghetisti began using some relatives who voluntarily had been left out of the cocaine smuggling to reduce the risk of being arrested and identified. Their main task was to be holders and managers of those properties obtained

---

[21] For the transformation of the middle class in Mafia, see Casaburi (2010).

[22] More information about Milan as a criminal place for money laundering may be found in Draghi (2011).

illegally. They were named "blockheads" and had been a central role in covering up Mafia funds.

The warning about the danger of the 'Ndrangheta in the North was given in good time. In fact, the Anti-Mafia Parliamentary Commission created by the Italian Parliament had pointed out in 1990 that:

> In the municipality of Vimercate, Calabrian families operated with members integrated into construction companies as small or medium business owners who also had political activities in the local area that allowed them to gain influence over the sizeable Calabrian colony that was established there (pp. 9–11).
> [Nel comune di Vimercate operano famiglie di origine calabrese, con elementi inseriti nell'attività edilizia come piccoli e medi imprenditori, le quali svolgono, a livello locale, anche attività politiche che consente loro di avere influenza sulla numerosa colonia calabrese ivi insediatasi].

Vimercate was hardly an exception. And, in fact, the Commission continued:

> Similar situations are found in the municipalities of Saint Angelo Lodigiano, Lodivecchio, Solerano and Bareggio, where the establishment of Calabrian people in public administration was more copious. Mayors of the outer suburbs of Milan reported incidents that proved highly significant in terms of dangers faced by the local government (pp. 9–11).
> [Situazioni analoghe si registrano nei comuni di S. Angelo Lodigiano, Lodivecchio, Solerano e Bareggio, dove l'insediamento nelle amministrazioni comunali di personaggi di origine calabrese è più numeroso. Taluni sindaci dell'hinterland milanese hanno riferito di episodi altamente significativi sotto il profilo dei pericoli cui sono esposte le amministrazioni locali].

During the time that the events took place, the situation continued to change. In fact, in Vimercate:

> Two Calabrian men who had been working for a construction company were killed. They turned out to have links with political circles. In Segrate, certain companies that had been granted contracts during the previous administration were replaced by a single firm that succeeded in obtaining all public contracts (Commissione Parlamentare Antimafia 1990, pp. 9–11).
> [Sono stati uccisi due calabresi che svolgevano attività edilizia e risultavano avere collegamenti con ambienti politici. A Segrate alcune ditte affidatarie di appalti concessi dalla precedente amministrazione sono state sostituite da un'unica impresa che riesce ad aggiudicarsi tutti gli appalti pubblici].

Extortion was a very common practice. Such a practice finally brought the covert practice of *omertà* to the forefront. A real master in the field of extortion was Giacomo Zagari, an 'ndranghetista who had arrived in Lombardy in the 1950s. His son, Antonio, described the particular technique used by his father. The men of his 'ndrina called some industries asking for a large amount of money in exchange for protection, asserting their ability to protect industries from damage of any kind.

Zagari was very well-known in his area and he had a very bad reputation because people knew about his criminal past. The meaningful thing is that victims turned to Zagari himself asking protection from extortionists. Zagari offered himself as a mediator faking a negotiation with his same men. It was evident that in a short span of time an agreement for the amount was reached. The "fake" negotiation made by Giacomo Zagari always had a positive outcome. The system was truly ingenious and proved to be effective: The extortionists' boss introduced himself to the on-call victims, acting as a protector and a mediator!

The main interest of the story lies in the consequences that the extortion produces. Antonio Zagari continues:

> This industrialist would have offered also to my father a figurative employment in this company, paying him a regular monthly salary. Of course, all this in exchange for not having troubles of any kind. The important thing was that people knew that there were Zaragis in his company (Ciconte 2010, pp. 41–42).
> [Questo industriale avrebbe offerto anche a mio padre figurativamente un posto all'interno della sua ditta pagandolo regolarmente ogni mese. Tutto questo, ovviamente, per non andare incontro a noie di qualsiasi genere. L'importante era che si sapesse in giro che nella sua fabbrica c'erano gli Zagari].

The origins of this ancient way of protection can be traced back to nineteenth century in southern Italy.

In the North, the 'Ndrangheta is strong[23] and its authority has grown in recent years, especially since 1993. But the strength of the 'Ndrangheta continues to remain stable despite some recent events that have put it in the national and international spotlights.

In order to understand the transformation of the 'Ndrangheta in recent years, it is imperative to analyze two events that mark discontinuity with the history, with the tradition, and with the ancient inclination, of the Calabrian Mafiosi to not emerge and remain hidden. The first such event happened in Locri on October 16, 2005, with the homicide of Francesco Fortugno, who was the President of the Regional Council of Calabria at the time of the event.[24] The second event was the massacre of Duisburg in Germany on August 15, 2007, by 'ndranghetisti coming directly from San Luca—a village of one of the most important Calabrian writers, Corrado Alvaro, and of the *Madonna di Polsi*, a sanctuary venerated by all inhabitants of Reggio Calabria, which 'Ndrangheta had chosen as a symbol of its power.

This crime was a politico-mafioso message and certainly could not have been brought to fruition and decided in Locri alone. It is possible to arrive at this conclusion by examining the blatant arrangements that have characterized it and by considering the objectives for which it was executed. Fortugno was killed in front of a polling place and in the presence of other people. He could have been killed in other different ways, perhaps less clamorous and resounding compared to what actually happened. So why was he killed in such a manner that inevitably drew national attention?

The safest way to kill him would have been to encircle his house, which always happened in similar cases. They would spread rumors of his death in order to muddle the truth of what actually happened, whether it was the vendetta of a betrayed husband to that of someone who could not keep his promises. Or, he could have perhaps been eliminated during a hunt since the politician was a hunter himself.

---

[23] On the dynamics of settling in the North, see Sciarrone (1998).

[24] See Fierro (2007); Ciconte (2013).

The way in which the homicide was committed confirms the intent to send a clear message to Calabrian politicians, to the Regional Council, and particularly to its President. As was later discovered, President of the Regional Council Agazio Loiero knew in advance that Fortugno would be elected because he had accumulated the majority of the votes of the province of Reggio Calabria, whereas Fortugno's direct opponent Domenico Crea was not elected because he was not helped by the President.

Everything indicates that the homicide had not been decided in Locri, but that the decision was made in a politico-mafioso environment that oversaw big business and 'Ndrangheta strategies. Those who had decided to kill him in such a theatrical way did so on purpose. The real instigators did not live in Locri. It is also possible that the decision was made by more *'ndrine*, by an assembly of men that make up an informal inter-cosche adjustment that is activated when making necessary choices that have a more general value in economic terms or a very strong impact outside.

There is a higher level than the territorial 'ndrine; this has been known for a long time, even though it has no specific name or even a provable existence due to the chronic lack of collaborators, especially in the highest positions. Only in 2012 were the *Carabinieri* able to immortalize a *capibastone* meeting that occurred under the Statue of the *Madonna della Montagna of Polsi*, capturing it on film. The meeting made the appointment of Domenico Oppedisano official as the new head of *crimine*, which had just happened the night before.

The choice to elect Oppedisano fell on an elderly person, respected by his past which he reminded to those present: "There were more than a thousand people present that night in the mountains" (Minniti 2011, line 1). Neither did he say when it happened, nor did he specify the year. He only remembered, however, that "they put me in between Peppe Nirta and 'Ntoni Nirta and there they gave me the rank of Santa" (Minniti 2011, line 24–25). It is probable, even if it is not certain, that he was referring to an event that happened during the years of the Borghese coup d'état, when as collaborators of justice have narrated, on the Aspromonte, there were more than a thousand people ready to take up arms when the call were to be made. Luckily for all, the much-awaited signal never came.

It is important to specify that Oppedisano was not elected boss of the 'Ndrangheta, but rather he represented a figure of balance and guarantee, perhaps because the choice to elect younger person to a high level position at that moment in history would not have been possible (Ciconte 1996, p. 40).

The newness of the whole event rests in the fact that the *locali* of the 'Ndrangheta reached an agreement to elect a top legal entity that would be able to settle disputes, end or prevent blood feuds, and undo intricate knots that the contestants could not solve on their own. One thing seems clear: His personality did not even remotely resemble or compare to that of those who oversaw the fate of the provincial commission of Cosa Nostra in Palermo, bosses like Riina and Provenzano. He was not the *il capo dei capi* (boss of bosses) to repeat an expression used in some newspapers. He was a figurehead chosen in a short period, chosen perhaps because he was older and did not have much time ahead of him, thus rendering him anything but a threat.

And yet, many expressed their concern for that choice. Is it possible, they wondered, that the fate of the 'Ndrangheta would be entrusted to a man like Oppedisano, an old man who could frequently be seen on the streets of Reggio Calabria driving an *ape* (a type of small, three-wheeled Italian truck). People wondered the same thing when Riina was captured, which lead to doubts and bewilderment. There are some substantial differences between the Calabrian *Crimine* structure and the so-known *Cupola* of Cosa Nostra. For the Calabrian one, we might talk about an informal level, not structured, more agile and sophisticated, and probably not only comprises affiliates, but also of people not belonging to the organization.

The homicide was committed while taking into account the strong State reaction that, as a matter of fact, was there with the arrival of prefect Luigi De Sena in Reggio Calabria. Those who decided to hit were aware of the State's reaction and could even afford the luxury of sacrificing someone in Locri. For that reason the message to the politicians was very clear.

It is only possible to comprehend what has become of the 'Ndrangheta nowadays if we understand the many different refined and superior levels that participate in the decision-making process. Yet not even the Fortugno homicide, after the numerous speeches of the immediately following days, had the strength to make the nature of the 'Ndrangheta and its power comprehensible. Other resounding events would be necessary; indeed, much louder than the Fortugno homicide.

The moment of Duisburg finally arrived and caused quite an uproar. The public opinion and European commenters discovered the 'Ndrangheta during the Feast of the Assumption's massacre of 2007 and had the opportunity, the strength, and the arrogance of those who felt strong enough to kill far away from home. That massacre, which was so devastating and so unusually out scheme drew international attention. Six deaths in a place far away from San Luca had piqued the attention of many reporters that did not indulge in folkloristic and vivid interpretations, neglecting the evaluations of the reasons of that massacre and the consequences that would come of it.

The 'Ndrangheta, which operated in far-away Duisburg is a modern and dynamic organization that knew how to intertwine the ancient and post-modern, recalling its ancient origins as well as its globalized economy, rituals, bank accounts, and the strict dialect and languages of different countries where they have lived for years now.

With Fortugno and Duisburg there was a new unexpected and fast change in the tradition of the history of the 'Ndrangheta. Should we expect more changes of this type, even more violent? It is not easy to answer this question. Of course, it is striking that the surge of criminal events has manifested itself in Locri who has appeared as the most unstable of the entire Calabrian criminal system.

The instability is a detriment to all Mafiosi, as the experience tells us. Therefore, it is true that bosses of the different families—not only those from San Luca, but also from those other important and respectful 'Ndrangheta families—have rushed to settle a meeting and call for peace. A new balance had to be found and was found indeed, with a rapidity that embarrassed peace mediators that often work, with no success, in war zones and in different international arenas. In San Luca nobody else was killed after peace was reached.

According to the DIA, a profound change is being undergone in the 'Ndrangheta:

> The illegal cocaine market allows the 'ndrine to entertain relations, through brokers and money launderers, with big South American criminal cartels. The bosses of the Calabrian cosche that manage big international trades of illegal narcotic and psychotropic substances are no longer living exclusively in the Mezzogiorno, but elsewhere, often abroad. The tendency is to control the illegal market less and less from the province of origin, and this is reflected in the judicial investigation of law enforcement, since in recent years there have been so many 'Ndrangheta fugitives, weavers of the drug market, under arrest in foreign territories (pp. 6–7).
> [Il mercato illegale della cocaina permette alle 'ndrine di intrattenere rapporti, attraverso broker e riciclatori, con i grandi cartelli criminali sudamericani. I capi delle cosche calabresi che gestiscono i grandi traffici internazionali di sostanze stupefacenti e psicotrope non vivono più, solo ed esclusivamente, nel Mezzogiorno d'Italia, ma altrove, spesso all'estero. La tendenza è quella di pilotare il mercato illegale sempre meno dalle province di origine e questo trova un immediato riscontro nelle investigazioni giudiziarie esperite dalle Forze di polizia, giacché negli ultimi periodi sono stati diversi i latitanti affiliati alla 'ndrangheta, tessitori della rete del commercio di droga, tratti in arresto fuori dal territorio nazionale].

The DIA reports can be misleading. It is not impossible to imagine that 'ndranghetisti are on the verge of leaving Calabria to relocate themselves in some vague area to manage illegal and criminal trades in utter peace. Calabria, and particularly Reggio Calabria, continues to be the command center where most decisions are made. The reason is simple: Calabria controls the territory; and without this control, there would be no Mafia criminal organization.

The territory is the symbol of power and command; it will never be abandoned, save for extenuating circumstances. One of the bosses of Nirta-Strangio use to control his neighborhood of San Luca directly from his home, where he had installed a big screen. He was a fugitive, but supervised and saw everything without being seen.

As for the other considerations made by the DIA, it is necessary to add that the *locali* of the 'Ndrangheta spread everywhere in Italy and abroad, acting—today more that yesterday—as investment centers for the enormous funds collected throughout the years. And now—more than ever—the economic crisis, affecting the capitalist economy like a heavy storm, can meet the demand for money that comes from the world of enterprises and banks with the liquidated supply, which the Mafia undoubtedly controls.

This is the time for economists, investors, recyclers, and brokers: Men that know the clefts of the finance. This is their moment, for they are the backbone of the 'Ndrangheta's future. In essence, the 'Ndrangheta is no longer a thing of the past, because it is not only concentrated in the province of Reggio Calabria or on the Ionian side where we saw the aforementioned turmoil. The Tyrrhenian side is also of crucial importance, especially for the port at Gioia Tauro that plays a strategic role in the trafficking of illegal goods of every imaginable nature. The Piromalli family has been there to oversee the territory for the longest time.

It is possible to find the 'Ndrangheta's *locali* in the municipalities of Crotone, Lamezia Terme, Vibo Valentia, and Cosenza. No province should be considered immune, even if the diffusion is not equally proportionate in all these areas.

The 'Ndrangheta has occupied spaces that once were empty. If we compare the police's 'Ndrangheta *locali* maps from 10 or 20 years ago with current ones, we can clearly see a dramatic progression of 'ndrine development and conquest of new territories. Some of the old 'ndrine are in decline, but none have completely disappeared. On the contrary, there are many new self-motivated and determined men.

This is the current situation in Calabria; yet, it is important to keep in mind that when speaking about the 'Ndrangheta, one talks about the only Italian Mafia organization that has stable and ancient branches in all Central-North regions of the country as well as abroad, and in all continents without exception. And it does business and money laundering in those far away localities, interweaving social relations and exhibiting a gaining interest in politics.

In many municipalities of Lombardy, Liguria and Piedmont, there is a heavy presence—ancient and well established—that is not well-understood because the public is not aware of its presence. It is the silent 'Ndrangheta, its only noise being the rustling of money, which allows business deals to take place. But, as it is well-known, the faint rustle makes a noise that only trained and attentive ears can perceive. The rest of the population is distracted by other, more deafening noise and words that put fear and anguish in people's hearts, whether it is illegal immigration, security, rape, armed robbery, or theft.

In recent years, the themes of security and street crime have been at the forefront of the Italian government's policies, whereas the Mafia has been confined to a corner as if it were now a resolved issue.

The 'Ndrangheta, in Calabrian everyday life, surpassed Fortugno and Duisburg, continue to operate with absolute power that heavily influences daily life, the economy, the actual conditions of the working class, and tries to undertake some kinds of commercial or entrepreneur activities that have to do with politics or administration of some small municipality or city. At the same time, it continues to occupy a large portion of territories in the North of Italy and in foreign countries.

References

Ammendolia, I., & Frammartino, N. (1975). *La Repubblica rossa di Cauloria. Il sud tra brigantaggio e rivoluzione*. Reggio Calabria: Casa del Libro.

Arlacchi, P. (1983). *La mafia imprenditrice. L'etica mafiosa e lo spirito del capitalismo*. Bologna: Il Mulino.

Bianco, U. (1959). *Tra la perduta gente*. Soveria Mannelli: Rubettino.

Casaburi, M. (2010). *Borghesia mafiosa. La 'ndrangheta dalle origini ai giorni nostri*. Bari: Dedalo.

Ciconte, E. (1992). *'Ndrangheta dall'unità ad oggi* (pp. 9–20). Bari-Rome: Laterza.

Ciconte, E. (1996). *Processo alla 'ndrangheta*. Bari-Rome: Laterza.

Ciconte, E. (1997). Un delitto italiano, il sequestro di persona. In L. Violante (Ed.), *La criminalità*. Turin: Einaudi.

Ciconte, E. (2008). *Storia criminale. La resistibile ascesa di mafia, 'ndrangheta e camorra dall' Ottocento ai giorni nostri* (pp. 8–13). Soveria Mannelli: Rubettino.

Ciconte, E. (2010). *'Ndrangheta padana*. Soveria Mannelli: Rubettino.

Ciconte, E. (2011). *'Ndrangheta*. Soveria Mannelli: Rubettino.

Ciconte, E. (2013). *Politici (e) malandrini*. Soveria Mannelli: Rubettino.

Ciconte, E., & Macrì, V. (2009). *Australian 'ndrangheta. I codici di affiliazione e la missione di Nicola Calipari.* Soveria Mannelli: Rubettino.

Ciconte, E., Macrì, V., & Forgione, F. (2010). *Osso, Mastrosso, Carcagnosso. Immafini, miti e misteri della 'ndrangheta.* Soveria Mannelli: Rubettino.

Cingari, G. (1982). *Storia della Calabria dall'unità ad oggi* (pp. 341–357). Bari-Rome: Laterza.

Commissione Parlamentare Antimafia (Parliamentary Anti-Mafia Commission). (4 July 1990). *Relazione sull'esito del sopralluogo a Milano di un gruppo di lavoro della Commissione* (pp. 9–11). X legislatura XXIII (19).

Commissione Parlamentare Antimafia (Parliamentary Anti-Mafia Commission). (26 July 2000). *Relazione sullo stato della lotta alla criminalità organizzata in Calabria.* Relatore Figurelli, Michele. XXIII. (42).

Commissione Parlamentare Antimafia (Parliamentary Anti-Mafia Commission). (19 February 2008). *Relazione sulla 'ndrangheta.* Relatore On. Forgione, Francesco. XXIII, 23(5).

Commissione Parlamentare. (24 October 1990). *Relazione sulle vicende omesse alla costruzione della centrale termoelettrica di Gioia Tauro.* X Legislation, 23(4).

Corradi, A. (1951). Gente di Calabria. *Alamanacco Calabrese.*

Corradi, A. (1990). *Calabria.* Vibo Valentia: Qualecultura Jaca Book.

Cuzzola, F. (2007). *Reggio 1970. Storie e memorie della rivolta.* Rome: Donzelli.

Direzione Investigativa Antimafia (DIA). (June 1995). *La criminalità organizzata in Lombardia* (pp. 6–7).

Draghi, M. (11 March 2011). *Le mafie a Milano e nel nord: aspetti sociali ed economici.* Milano: Università degli studi di Milano.

Falcone, G. (24 May 1991). Ma quella del Nord non è mafia. *La Stampa* (pp. 1–2).

Fantò, E. (Ed.). (2007). *Massomafia: 'ndrangheta, politica e massoneria dal 1970 ai nostri giorni.* Rome: Koinè.

Fierro, E. (2007). *Ammazzàti l'onorevole. L'omicidio Fortugno. Una storia di mafia, politica e ragazzi.* Milan: Baldini Castaldi Dalai.

Forgione, F. (2012). *Porto franco.* Milan: Dalai.

Forgione, F., & Mondani, P. (1993). *Oltre la cupola. Massoneria mafia politica.* Milan: Rizzoli.

Gambino, S. (1976). *La lunga notte della Calabria.* Reggio Calabria: Edizioni Quaderni Calabria-oggi.

Gambino, S. (1986). *'Ndranghita dossier.* Chiaravalle: Frama sud.

Lupo, S. (1997). Le mafie. *Storie dell'Italia repubblicana* (Vol. III, tome 2). Turin: Einaudi.

Malafrina, L. (1981). *'Ndrangheta alla sbarra.* Rome: Dimensioni 80.

Malafrina, L. (1986). *La 'ndrangheta. Il codice segreto, la storia, i miti, e i personaggi.* Rome: Gangemi.

Manfredi, G. (1981). Mafie e società nella fascia jonica della provinciale di Reggio Calabria: il "caso" Nicola D'agostino. In S. Di Bella (Ed.), *Mafia e potere: società civile, organizzazione mafiosa ed esercizio dei poteri nel Mezzogiorno contemporaneo.* Soveria Mannelli: Rubettino.

Mannino, S. (1997). Criminalità nuova in una società in trasformazione: il Novecento e i tempi attuali. In A. Placanica (Ed.), *Storia della Calabria moderna e contemporanea.* Rome: Gangemi.

Marino, G. (1971). *La mafia a Montalto, sentenza 2 ottobre 1970 del Tribunale di Locri.* Reggio Calabria: La voce di Calabria.

Minniti, C. (9 March 2011). "Quando diventi Santista…" *Calabria Ora* 9 March 2011. https://lh3.googleusercontent.com/-PprVs5_TJCM/TXffKxmU0LI/AAAAAAAACnk/bs6BdKZf9z4/s1600/santista.JPG. Accessed 9 March 2011.

Misiami, S. (1994). La crisi interna del PCI reggino nel secondo dopoguerra. *Rivista storica calabrese* X(V).

Pignatone, G., & Prestipino, M. (2012). In G. M. Savatteri (Ed.), *Il contagio. Come la 'ndrangheta ha infettato l'Italia* (pp. 24–28). Bari-Rome: Laterza.

Sciarrone, R. (1998). *Mafie vecchie, mafie nuove. Radicamento ed espansione.* Rome: Donzelli.

Siebert, R. (1994). *Le donne, la mafia.* Milan: Il saggitore.

Stajano, C. (1979). *Africo.* Turin: Einaudi.

Chapter 4
'Ndrangheta. Multilevel Criminal System of Power and Economic Accumulation

Ercole Giap Parini

In their traditional territories, the *'ndrine* (the cells of the *'Ndrangheta*) practice a kind of "territorial domination," (Santino 1994; Siebert 1996) which is maintained via a network of corrupt politicians and other clients. In many areas of Calabria, this network involves substantial portions of society in the exploitation of public resources, which assures for the *'ndrine* a deep reservoir of consensus and, consequently, social and political protection.

The role women play inside *'Ndrangheta* families is crucial; women are responsible for the reproduction of the Mafia's values and are engaged in the daily management of illicit trafficking. Nevertheless, the peculiar condition of women inside the *'Ndrangheta* families leads a number of them to collaborate with justice.

The *'Ndrangheta* has recently become active in Central and Northern Italy and in other European countries; in these areas, it has replicated its organization and practices.

The Calabrian Mafia groups have also become actively involved in the worldwide black markets. Particularly in the cocaine trade, the *'ndrine* are supposed to be among the most important agents worldwide, operating as intermediaries between the groups involved in production and those trafficking the drug.

I will try to show how these activities, far from being separate faces of the same phenomenon, are closely linked together. I will also describe the effort of the *'ndrine* to attain a kind of legitimacy in the global economy by providing legal businesses with illegal services crucial for the competitive strategies, such as the illegal disposal of hazardous waste.

E. G. Parini (✉)
Dipartimento di Scienze politiche e sociali, Università della Calabria,
Ponte Bucci, Cubo 0/B, 87036 Arcavacata di Rende, CS, Italy
e-mail: g.parini@uinical.it

N. Serenata (ed.), *The 'Ndrangheta and Sacra Corona Unita,* Studies of Organized Crime 12,   51
DOI 10.1007/978-3-319-04930-4_4, © Springer International Publishing Switzerland 2014

Preliminary Remarks

Calabria is a region of Southern Italy, separated from Sicily by the Strait of Messina. In official statistical reports, it is usually described as characterized by economic marginality and social vulnerability;[1] a condition that persists despite a large amount of public resources that the region has received in order to stimulate the economic and social development since the 1950s. This has produced the counter effect of the phenomenon called "welfarism," that is, a degeneration of a safe welfare state, with the intromission of corruption and the build of a patronage system (Fantozzi 1993; Sciarrone 2011; Costabile and Fantozzi 2012). This represents one of the weakest points that facilitate the infiltration of the Mafias in the public life.

Starting from this brief sketch of the Calabrian profile, I will try to give evidence of a paradoxical condition in which one of the most important Mafia groups in the world has born and is still deeply rooted in such a weak region.

Like the *Camorra* (the organization based in Naples and in the surrounding areas) and the Sicilian *Cosa Nostra*, the *'Ndrangheta* is an ancient Mafia organization, since its origins go back at least to a couple of centuries ago though its mythological birth is rooted in the Middle Ages (Malafarina 1978; Ciconte 1992).

Despite its strength and rootedness in the original territories, and the fact that it has long been able to move its activities in territories very far from Calabria, for a long time, it has been considered to be a local organization playing a secondary role in the Mafia system. This under-evaluation has facilitated the *'Ndrangheta* in becoming one of the strongest Mafia groups in Italy and a well-known criminal organization in the international spotlight.

Since 1991, the *'Ndrangheta* has collaborated closely with the Sicilian Cosa Nostra[2] and, partly due to the crisis of the 1992 massacres and the subsequent State reaction, it has become one of the most relevant criminal groups worldwide with very strong ties to Colombian, Bolivian and Mexican ones.[3]

---

[1] On a land of a little more than 15,000 km^2 of extension, around 2 million inhabitants live with an average individual income € 4.000 less than the Italian one (€ 12.700 vs 17.028), the third-to last position of the Italian regions. The gross domestic product per capita is € 16.655 (the second last in Italy), about € 9.000 less than the national average (25.725); 8.1 % of the value added comes from industry, 7.1 % from real estate, 3.9 % from agriculture, and the remaining portion from the service sector (of a public type in particular). The total unemployment rate is 4 % points more than the national one (12.73 vs. 8.41 %); these data become even more impressive if only the young male or female population is considered (Istat data 2010-2011-2012 collected and elaborated by Unioncamere in the database available at http://www.unioncamere.gov.it/Atlante/).

[2] In 1991 the so called *'Ndrangheta war* stops (an internal conflict of the 'ndrine of Reggio Calabria, that lasted more than 5 years starting in 1998, in which the powerful Imerti-Condello's and De Stefano's families were opposed—number of the deaths estimated at around 1,000 during those years). A state witness said that the reconciliation was fostered by Cosa Nostra that obtained in exchange of the murder of the judge Antonino Scopelliti, Supreme Court's State prosecutor during the mass trial against Cosa Nostra (as mentioned in Ciconte, 1996, p. 150).

[3] "In the global spotlight, the drug traffic management still remains the prominent and most profitable criminal activity for the Calabrian Mafia organizations. These have strengthened the ability to maintain relationships with the South American narcos organizations and managed to put

This focus on offshore strategies is nothing new in its behavior. The history of the Siderno Group of Organized Crime begins in the 1950s, when the boss of Siderno sent his young friend Michele Racco to Toronto in order to set up a little pasta factory that soon become the headquarters of an important criminal network devoted to gambling and extortion (Minuti and Nicaso 1994). A couple of decades after, in the 1970s, a number of families of the Ionic Coast were sent to Australia to carry out criminal activities such as extortion and drug trafficking. This movement of Mafiosi out of Calabria had been decided following an agreement between Albert Anastasia and Frank Costello (Ciconte 1996, pp. 172–173).

Organization and Rites

For a long time, judges and scholars have been debating about the morphology of the *'Ndrangheta* organization.[4] A characteristic traditionally ascribed to the *'Ndrangheta* is the horizontality and the substantial autonomy of the individual groups (*'ndrine*) (Ciconte 1992, 1996; Gratteri and Nicaso 2006).

Nowadays, this model has changed and some elements of monitoring have been introduced in various judiciaries' models. This happened for two reasons: In the last decade, the courts have collected more pieces of evidence about the inner functioning of the *'Ndrangheta* due to the evolution of the investigations and the contribution of the state's witnesses.[5]

The *'ndrine*—usually groups of people belonging to the same family—represent the cells that make up the organization and have a supremacy over the territories where they become established. (Parini 2008). When the total number of affiliates succeeds 50, *'ndrine* in the same territory can meet collectively in a *locale*; the chief of the *locale* exerts a hierarchical power over the affiliates.

The last inquiries point out the existence of an upper level, called *crimine* and constituted by the chiefs of the most important *locali* (the ones on the three districts of the Reggio Calabria area: The city, the Ionic coast, and the Gioia Tauro plain). This is a monitoring body of the rules, though the autonomy of each *locale* in its respective territory is guaranteed.

---

themselves among the most important in the control upon the cocaine's import flows (Bolivia and Colombia upon all) and routes from the production places to Europe" (Direzione Investigativa Antimafia Second semester 2007, p. 104).

[4] By considering the Mafias in general, for a long time, there was no knowledge about them as an organization, since many preferred identifying Mafiosi with people who shared cultural values and practices in a wide sense (Sciarrone 2009). However, something has changed with the systematic use of the state's witness who shed light over the inner nature of the Mafias organizations.

[5] The evidence brought by the three steps of the "Crimine" inquiry—carried out by the Reggio Calabria Direzione Distrettuale Antimafia (DDA) starting 2004—are particularly relevant to describe the current assets of the 'Ndrangheta.

When the *'ndrine* move to other territories, they tend to replicate this structure and all the *locali*, in Calabria, in Italy and outside Italy are under the monitoring of the *crimine*.

This structure is fostered by a set of ritualistic practices and "codes" based on myths, defining the secret identity of the association. These are particularly vivid while deciding on the new pledge's entry into the *'ndrina*. The initiation rites are described in the "codes," pieces of paper—often written in a naïve Italian—usually found during police inspections in fugitive hideouts (Malafarina 1978; Ciconte 1992).

These elements, permeated with a mythological aura, are not folkloristic nor are they linked to the past. The DNA specialists, in the last report on the *'Ndrangheta*, state that they are crucial for maintaining unity within the organization by fostering the respect of shared rules and giving the idea to affiliates to operate as a community (Direzione Nazionale Antimafia 2012, p. 96). In fact, they have the duty of defining the strengths of the organization over the adepts and to swear the pact to secrecy (Paoli 2000). Besides that, in Calabria these elements also become a true "ornament" of the organization since they lure a number of youngsters. In other words, these apparently backwards rites play a specific functional role in providing a new, trusty workforce (Parini 2003). Esoteric rites[6] of affiliation may be truly attractive to potential affiliating people living in the poor surroundings of a problematic Calabrian town such as, for instance, Reggio Calabria and used to living in a cultural context where the *'Ndrangheta* is glorified through these rites and myths.

Creating Networks for Power

In certain areas of Calabria, the *'Ndrangheta* is not only a criminal phenomenon since it aims at pervading the economic, social, and politic fabric. This is a twofold strategy. From one hand, Calabrian Mafiosi are able to pervade social life by presenting themselves as benefactors who solve minute people's necessities in a way that makes the bosses the true "masters" of the communities, since any little decisions has to pass through them. In the middle of the 1990s, scholars Umberto Santino and Renate Siebert have called this kind of power "territorial domination," an expression that focuses on a power characterized by pervasiveness and of a totalitarian attitude: The boss is who has the control over the main resources available on "his" territory. Siebert writes that territorial domination is:

---

[6]As a sample of that, this is an excerpt of the affiliation codes reported in a memory book of an 'Ndrangheta man, Serafino Castagna. As you can see, myths and affiliation practices are mixed together: "In the name of the organized and sacred society, I consecrate this place in the same way our ancestors Osso, Mastrosso, and Carcagnosso consecrated it, through irons and chains. I consecrate it through my faith and through my long words. If until now I used to know this place as an obscure one, since now I know it as a sacred, holy, and inviolable place, where it is possible to set and to dismantle this honored society." "Thanks!" the others said together" (Castagna 1967, p. 33).

A form of personal and widespread domain: The organization, its bosses—important or otherwise—claim to know and even decide about matters regarding life or death, activities, and especially the personal relationships of their subservient citizens (Siebert 1996, p. 18). [Una forma di dominio personalizzato e capillare: l'organizzazione, i capi—piccoli o grandi che siano—pretendono di sapere e di decidere, in linea di massima, su tutto ciò che concerne la vita, le attività, le relazioni delle persone che vivono nel territorio sottomesso].

The effectiveness of this kind of power is based on the fact that it is not a mere act of violence. The bosses and their families base their power on the ability to build up a network of widespread convenience where the victims somehow become accomplices. In other words, it is a system in which everyone has something to gain.

In order to repress the entrepreneurial fabric of society, the *'Ndrangheta* operates as a protective type of organization (Gambetta 1993): Entrepreneurs and shopkeepers have to pay the so-called "pizzo" or *squeeze*, a tax for an "imposed" protection. The little more than 200 cases of extortion denounced yearly represent a very small part of an increasingly widespread phenomenon in which the victims are very reluctant to denounce. A number of Calabrian entrepreneurs have interiorized that practice to the point that they consider the "pizzo" a balance-sheet item, that is, a given element of the system. Besides that, the *'ndrine* usually transform their victims into accomplices when they set up money laundering networks through the same shops and farms.

In order to strengthen its local power, the *'Ndrangheta* constantly tries to combine alliances with politics, pieces of the legal economy, professional men, and exponents of the public administration as well;[7] this is truly useful for the Mafiosi in order to consolidate a network capable of providing them with easy access to public contract as well as protection of the *'Ndrangheta*'s affairs.

The importance of the links with the politics is so great that the men of *'Ndrangheta* always try to get acquainted with politicians, even if they are reluctant: The enquirers claim that at a local level: "The goal is achieved through pre-electoral agreements with prospective candidates […] or through threats against local public authorities" (Direzione Nazionale Antimafia 2012, p. 546).

The level of infiltration in the local political system is supported by the overturning of the law by the President of the Republic, due to Mafia infiltration, of more than 50 city councils and two ASLs (Local Health Offices) beginning in the 1990s when the dismantling was decided by law.

There are a number of reasons why the men of *'Ndrangheta* are involved in this strategy aimed at the control over a number of municipal councils and public services.

First of all, easy access to public economic resources[8] is surely important for the daily reproduction of the local *'ndrine* and for financing their further activities (it is

---

[7] Starting the 1970s, the *'Ndrangheta* has come into contact with the Masonic lodges, particularly strong in the Calabria professional and political goods. Through this alliance, the *'Ndrangheta* seeks full social legitimacy and a stronger integration in the economy and politics (see Forgione 2009, p. 25).

[8] In the autumn of 2012 two Cosenza county council members were arrested and charged with favoritism of a public service contractor owned by a boss settled in Rende, one of the most important towns in Calabria.

an unusual practice to reinvest the resources achieved locally in the drug traffic in order to promote the *'ndrina* to more distinguished level of importance).

Controlling public resources is also crucial in order to get consensus through the daily management of municipal affairs. In fact, many citizens' rights are determined within this context:

> The city council is a "crossroads" where the everyday needs of the citizens, both small and large, are known to intersect. In territories where doing favors (as opposed to having rights) is the law of the land, and where, when a citizen has a problem, he thinks about who he can call, as opposed to being able to go directly to the police (Mete 2009, p. 58).
> [L'amministrazione comunale è un crocevia dal quale transitano le piccole e le grandi esigenze quotidiane dei cittadini. In territori in cui vige la regola del favore e non del diritto e nei quali quando un cittadino ha un problema pensa a chi potere telefonare e non a quale ufficio rivolgersi].

This is a condition of citizens' subjugation that confirms the "territorial domain" by which the Mafia power is defined and where citizens are reduced to *subjects*.

Another reason why *'Ndrangheta* is focused on politicians' alliances is because of the possibility, through the acquaintances with a mayor or city council member, to keep in contact with the highest levels of the Italian political system. Even from the local branches, made up of municipal councils and local politicians, the *'ndrine* can exert influence over Parliament and the rest of the government, for instance when the laws against money laundering or the condition of imprisonment of bosses are discussed. The so called Mafia-State agreement is a very controversial ongoing investigation of a dark period (1992–1994) when highest-level politicians were suspected of negotiating with the Mafia in order to stop the use of general violence against people as well as pieces of the artistic patrimony of the State in exchange for better prison conditions for a number of bosses belonging to the *'Ndrangheta,* Cosa Nostra, and Sacra Corona Unita.

On December 16, 2005, the Vice President of the Calabria Regional Council, Francesco Fortugno, was killed and investigations pointed to *'Ndrangheta*. In particular, the investigative activities were oriented toward the affairs of the ASL (Local Health Office) of Locri where the victim used to work. Through this investigation, a thick system of interests emerged. At the center of that, the interests of the local "cosche" were linked to the large economic resources stemming from the activities related to the managing of the healthcare system in that area—that is, expenses for the plant modernization, supplying contracts for tools, food, bed linen, and so on: Many of the suppliers were firms directly associated with the Mafia or headed up by the Mafia's straw men.

Beside the relevance of economic resources, even more relevant is the possibility of acquiring social consensus through the control of a basic right such as health, having great influence over a number of physicians in order to help a boss in prison.[9]

---

[9] The role of complacent physicians in lightening the type of punishment for bosses in jail is a crucial resource for the *'ndrine*. In 2012, inquirers have discovered two private clinics in the Cosenza area where the bosses in jail used to go after the testifying by compliant physicians to be in a false state of mental illness (Badolati and Sabato 2012).

The twofold Role of Women between Order and Reaction

Since the organization formally excludes women, it remains largely masculine in nature, and represents what Siebert calls "social capital" available to the "cosche":

> Just because Mafia women, on one hand, used violence in characterizing the relations among the affiliates and between them and the surrounding world, on the other, due to their condition of subjugation and because they are compelled to speak out against some types of violence and not others, represent a truly social capital available to the criminal organization, while they exert their territorial mastery (Siebert 2003, p. 27).

First of all, women play a traditional role inside the *'Ndrangheta*'s family by attending to the domestic duties as mothers, wives, sisters, and daughters of the Mafiosi and by reproducing the Mafia's cultural code (Ingrascì 2007).

Moreover, Siebert in "*Le donne, la mafia*" recalls the important role women have played at least since the 1980s, when wives, sisters, and daughters of bosses were entrusted with important roles in the Mafia business. Giuseppa and Caterina Condello—wife and sister, respectively, of Reggio Calabria boss Nino Imerti—used to carry out criminal negotiations when the boss was on the run, in particular by blackmailing shopkeepers. Another case that attests the employment of women in the *'Ndrangheta*'s business is the one denounced by collaborator Giuseppina Pesce—daughter of the Rosarno boss Salvatore—who testified that her mother and her sister were at the head of an extortion ring and used to help the organization communicate with the boss while he was in jail.[10] If this is not evidence of women's emancipation (their role is still aimed a reproducing a masculine power), the changes regarding gender relations in the context of the Mafia are not to be underestimated in the least.

Another notable aspect of the woman's role is the potential disorder they represent and the instability that they bring to the *'Ndrangheta* system. In a Mafia family, women are torn between two opposed sets of values: As mothers, wives, daughters, and sisters in traditional families, they are the caretakers; as relatives of Mafia affiliates, they have to accept their death (or even promote it in the case that Mafia cultural codes such as revenge are leaked). However, even in their role, they have a vivid perception of multiple contradictions, which make them the vulnerable part of the Mafia system due to their ambivalent centrality. In other words, they surpass their male counterparts in perceiving the contradiction between the well-being potentially allowed through the accumulation of power and economic resources, and a style of life daily pervaded by the true possibility of death (Siebert 1997, p. 127).

Giuseppina Pesce has decided to collaborate with the justice by denouncing her Mafia family. She has explained her decision through a letter:

> I have expressed my will to start this experience due to the fact that I am a mother and by the wish to have a better life, far from my familiar context, where we were born and raised. I am still convinced that this is the right choice since, due to the style of life chosen by our

---

[10] This is what has emerged from the judicial operation called *All inside* 2 executed by the DDA of Reggio Calabria in 2010.

relatives, our life has ever been dominated by suffering and other difficulties and by the lack of courage due to the fear for the consequences.[11]

[Ho espresso la mia volontà di iniziare questo percorso, spinta dall'amore di madre e dal desiderio di poter avere anche io una vita migliore, lontano dall'ambiente in cui siamo nati e cresciuti. Ero e sono convinta che sia la scelta giusta, dal momento che per scelte di vita di familiari e congiunti, siamo sempre stati segnati da una vita piena di sofferenza e difficoltà e soprattutto mancanza di coraggio per paura delle conseguenze].

The women who denounce represent a true threat to the organization, since they know almost everything about how it works: This is why they are often destined to an ill fate. Titta Buccafusca, wife of Limbadi boss Pantaleone Mancuso, after her decision to collaborate with authorities, was allegedly forced to commit suicide in the summer of 2011. Maria Concetta Cacciola, daughter of a member of the Bellocco 'ndrina, one of the most important in the Rosarno's plain, committed suicide by poison on August 22, 2011, after her decision to cooperate with the authorities. Lea Garofalo, wife of a Mafioso in the Policastro area, in 2002 had started to collaborate with the judges, shedding light on the drug trade and public contracts managed by the 'ndrine in Northern Italy: She was subsequently kidnapped and killed right outside Milan, where her remains were discovered at the end of 2012.

Moving Strategies

The 'Ndrangheta has a long tradition of moving beyond the borders of its original territories. For a criminal group, the decision to move is a multifactorial one: The 'ndrine can move out of the necessity for protection (in order to escape from internal revenge or from police) or swayed by the possibility of gaining more resources from the black market.[12] Nevertheless, as we have seen with the Siderno Organized Crime Group, there is a kind of traditional trend in the 'Ndrangheta agenda that involves strategically planning their moves outside in order to build up new illicit markets.

In Northern Italy, there is an old tradition for bosses to move there because they had been banished from their territories by authorities, and this happened at the same time of maximum emigration from Southern Italy in general, and from Calabria in particular (Ciconte 1996, pp. 160–168). In accordance with Ciconte, these two processes have fostered the uniqueness of transplanting stable groups there, which are strictly related to the families of origins.

If in the beginning, it is reasonable to assume that unforeseen factors had an important role, the transplanting of stable groups outside Calabria has become a planned strategy throughout time (Ciconte 1996, p. 162).

In Milan and in its surrounding areas, the 'ndrine' colonization started during the 1960s, when Calabrian Mafiosi (in particular the Mazzaferro's family) began to

---

[11] Excerpt from a letter addressed to the Chief of the Procura dei minori di Reggio Calabria on August 23, 2011.

[12] To view the debate about Mafias' moving strategies, see Varese (2011); Campana (2011); Silverstone (2011).

show interest in the building sector and public contracting, by exporting illicit and violent practices there that had been previously carried out in Calabria. Nowadays, the courts denounce that in this region, which is one of the richest and most competitive in Europe, the *'Ndrangheta* strategy aims to hide itself in the entrepreneurial structure of society more than show its predatory violence (Direzione Nazionale Antimafia 2012; Direzione investigativa Antimafia, First semester 2010). Alliances with politicians and representing the so called "gray area" are important in order to consolidate a system in which the men of the *'Ndrangheta* take advantage, for instance by acquiring contracts inside crucial public sector. According to the DIA:

> Investigations have provided evidence about the existence of true criminal systems, aimed at the exploitation of social and economic fabrics; in that practice corruption is reliant on the acquisition of market sectors and to the infiltration into the stable economy (Second semester 2011, p. 100).

In order to do that, the *'Ndrangheta* needs professional men: On September 20, 2011, a financial consultant was arrested and charged with illicit international financial operations geared toward protecting firms led by the *'ndrine*.[13]

In Liguria and Piedmont, the level of penetration of the *'ndrine* is so deep that some city councils have been dissolved by the government. This is the case of Bordighera, in Liguria; three in Piedmont in 2011 were kept under close observation by public authorities to decide about their dissolution.

In Lazio, there is a mix of traditional illicit markets controlled by the *'ndrine* (drug trade and extortion) as well as activities aimed at taking control of licit markets (Direzione Investigativa Antimafia, Second semester 2011). The attempt to control the fruit and vegetable wholesale market of Fondi, one of the biggest in Europe, is particularly significant (Direzione Investigativa Antimafia, First semester 2011). With regards to Rome, it is noticeable that the Calabrian are investing in the real estate market as well as in the restoration sector, and also by acquiring places of excellence such as the Caffè Greco in Via dei Condotti in the truly historical downtown of Rome.

'Ndrangheta's groups play a crucial role in the network of international crime by controlling crucial points of the drug trade as well as other illicit markets. This became particularly true after the 1990s when, as a consequence to the Cosa Nostra crisis following the 1992 massacres, Calabrian groups gained a reputation of thrusting among other criminal groups, in particular Columbian narcos and Mexican cartels. One of the most pressing facts, demonstrating the role of the *'Ndrangheta,* emerged through the three steps of the "Decollo" inquiry carried out by Catanzaro's District Anti-Mafia Office (DDA) between 2004 and 2011. In particular—according to the courts—the *'ndrine* of Rosarno and Reggio Calabria carried out a huge cocaine trade in alliance with the paramilitary terrorist organization Autodefensas Unidas de Colombia (AUC) based on interest for financing their own activity through it.[14]

---

[13] This person had excogitated a system to transfer *'Ndrangheta's* firms in the USA in order to hide capital in case of bankruptcy (Direzione Investigativa Antimafia, Second semester 2011).

[14] With the 2004 *Decollo* investigation, a huge traffic of cocaine emerged that involved Italy, Spain, Germany, France, Colombia, United States, Australia, and Venezuela. During the police operation 5,000 kg of cocaine were confiscated. At the head of the organization was the powerful Mancuso *'ndrina,* together with other families of the Reggio Calabria area and of the Ionic coast.

In order to manage trades like these, the role played by a series of men of the *'Ndrangheta* who have established in Colombia and in Venezuela is absolutely crucial; apart from that, the network of affiliates in different countries who are involved in the laundering of "dirty" money is also crucial. As a result, these practices put a significant part of Europe's black market in jeopardy ("Zappa" investigation).

In recent years, worldwide public opinion has been moved by the "Duisburg massacre": Six members of a family coming from San Luca, little town on the Ionic Coast in Calabria, were killed by members of another San Luca family in a restaurant belonging to the victims. This fact and its subsequent investigations have shown that Mafiosi's strategies and practices have been rooted in territories that stem very far from the original ones. In the last report of the DNA, a strong presence of the *'ndrine* was denounced in Germany, as well as their ability to export their organization and their practices. Based on a series of wiretappings, investigators claim that *'Ndrangheta*'s rituals, rules, and behavior in Germany are not different from the ones, which are widespread in Calabria. The *'Ndrangheta* in Germany is present and active in various sectors. In 2011, the Bundeskriminalamt (the German police also known as BKA) reported the presence of 29 *locali* involved in drug trafficking and smuggling as well as in money laundering by investing in real estate and in shops or restaurants. In 2008, the German Secret Service decried that the *'ndrine* were able to influence even the Frankfurt stock exchange by investing conspicuous financial resources.

Conclusion: An Integrated System of Crimes that Is Going to Be Even Further Legitimated

Far from considering the different expressions of the *'Ndrangheta*'s activities as separated strategies performed by different groups, we are facing an articulated but widely unitary strategy. This is more than a hypothesis since we now have evidence of the existence of a level of coordination settled in Calabria, the so called *crimine* that exerts a kind of monitoring over all the *locali* in Calabria, in Italy, and abroad. Besides that, the replication of the same structure and the same rites foster this interpretation, and it makes possible to hypothesize that the consensus, the availability of trustworthy workforce, the political backing, and the possibility to control the economic goods are resources that are so crucial for protecting and endorsing the activities in the global illicit arenas, where the *'Ndrangheta* produces the majority of its revenues.

An overwhelming amount of the *'Ndrangheta*'s global activities is the drug trade. Nowadays, it has at its disposal, as a competitive advantage, a network for illicit traffic, which is well-articulated and effective in facing the security system of different countries. For attentive observers, *'Ndrangheta's* interests converge more and more toward illicit services for a licit economy. In fact, in the last few years, the *'Ndrangheta*, together with other criminal groups, has often been at the center of a number of investigations into so-called "eco-crime," that is, trafficking of hazardous industrial waste, and by doing this, they are poisoning the sea and the soil of large areas in Southern Italy.[15] This is particularly dangerous since the *'Ndrangheta* is becoming the dirty face of the licit economy.

References

Badolati, A., & Sabato, A. (2012). *Codice rosso. Sanità tra sperperi, politica e 'Ndrangheta.* Cosenza: Pellegrini.
Campana, P. (2011). Assessing the movement of criminal groups: Some analytical remarks. *Global Crime, 12*(3), 207–217.
Castagna, S. (1967). *Tu devi uccidere.* Milan: il Momento.
Ciconte, E. (1992). *'Ndrangheta. Dall'Unità a oggi.* Bari-Rome: Laterza.
Ciconte, E. (1996). *Processo alla 'Ndrangheta.* Bari-Rome: Laterza.
Costabile, A., & Fantozzi, P. (2012). *Legalità in crisi. Il rispetto delle regole in politica e in economia.* Rome: Carocci.
Direzione Investigativa Antimafia (DIA). (2007–2011). *Relazione semestrale:1st and 2nd semester.* Rome.
Direzione Nazionale Antimafia (DNA.). (2012). *Relazione annuale sulle attività svolte dal Procuratore Nazionale antimafia e dalla Direzione Nazionale antimafia.* Rome.
Fantozzi, P. (1993). *Politica Clientela Regolazione Sociale. Il Mezzogiorno nella questione politica italiana.* Soveria Mannelli: Rubbettino.
Forgione, F. (2009). *Mafia Export. Come 'ndrangheta, cosa nostra e camorra hanno colonizzato il mondo.* Milan: Baldini Castoldi Dalai.
Gambetta, D. (1993). *The sicilian mafia.* Cambridge: Harvard University Press.
Gratteri, N., & Nicaso, A. (2006). *Fratelli di sangue.* Cosenza: Pellegrini.
Ingrascì, O. (2007). *Donne d'onore. Storie di mafia al femminile.* Milan: Bruno Mondadori.
Legambiente. (2010). *Rapporto ecomafia.* Rome: Edizioni Ambiente.
Legambiente. (2012). *Rapporto ecomafia.* Rome: Edizioni Ambiente.
Malafarina, L. (1978). *Il codice della 'Ndrangheta.* Reggio Calabria: Parallelo 38.
Mete, V. (2009). *Fuori dal comune. Lo scioglimento delle amministrazioni locali per infiltrazioni mafiose.* Rome: Bonanno.
Minuti, D., & Nicaso, A. (1994). *'Ndranghete. Le filiali della mafia calabrese.* Vibo Valentia: Monteleone.
Paoli, L. (2000). *Fratelli di mafia. Cosa Nostra e 'Ndrangheta.* Bologna: il Mulino.
Parini, E. G. (2003). Miti e ritualità dell'affiliazione alla mafia. Note per una definizione del fenomeno mafioso a partire dalla sua segretezza. *Ou, XIV*(1), 125–131.
Parini, E. G. (2008). 'Ndrangheta. In M Maresu & L Pepino (Eds.), *Nuovo dizionario di mafia e antimafia* (pp. 373–381). Turin: Edizioni Gruppo Abele.
Santino, U. (1994). La mafia come soggetto politico. Ovvero: la produzione mafiosa della politica e la produzione politica della mafia. In G Fiandaca & S Costantino (Eds.), *La mafia, le mafie.* Bari-Rome: Laterza.
Sciarrone, R. (2009). *Mafie vecchie, mafie nuove.* Rome: Donzelli.
Sciarrone, R. (Ed.). (2011). *Alleanze nell'ombra. Mafie ed economie locali in Sicilia e nel Mezzogiorno.* Rome: Donzelli.
Siebert, R. (1996). *Mafia e quotidianità.* Milan: il Saggiatore.
Siebert, R. (1997). *Le donne, la mafia.* Milan: il Saggiatore.

---

[15] For more information see Legambiente, *Rapporto ecomafia* (2010, 2012).

Siebert, R. (2003). Donne di mafia: affermazione di uno pseudo soggetto femminile. In G Fiandaca (Ed.), *Donne e mafie. Il ruolo delle donne nelle organizzazioni criminali* (pp. 22–45). Palermo: Università degli Studi di Palermo.

Silverstone, D. (2011). A response to: Morselli, C., Turcotte, M. and Tenti, V. (2010): The mobility of criminal groups. *Global Crime, 12*(3), 189–206.

Varese, F. (2011). Mafia movements: A framework for understanding the mobility of Mafia groups. *Global Crime, 12*(3), 218–231.

Chapter 5
'Ndrangheta Women in Contemporary Italy: Between Change and Continuity

Ombretta Ingrascì

There was a difference between women and men during my grandmother's time when we were in Calabria. Men were separated from women: Men ate, while women stayed in the kitchen. When the men finished, then the women were allowed to eat. This division, however, did not prevent women from knowing and seeing what went on. My grandmother was there, and she knew everything; all women know everything about everything. However, my grandmother was subjected to her husband. My grandfather drank. He beat my grandmother. He was naughty and unruly, like all men are. All women in the 'Ndrangheta are subjected—they have no say when others are present—but the husband always follows the wife's suggestions. And then, it just depends. Women are the ones who, when their husbands are in jail, always stand in their husbands' stead; however, in the context of the family—because the 'Ndrangheta is family-run for the most part—they are structurally connected with the family, that is, the Mafia family as well as the family of origins, the parental family (Ingrascì 2013, p. 67).

The tale of collaborator of justice, Emilio Di Giovine, offers a vivid description of gender dynamics inside his maternal family, the Serrainos, an historic 'Ndrangheta family in the area of Reggio Calabria. This scene sheds light on the contradictions of the female condition in the 'Ndrangheta, which goes from victimization to responsible participation.

Women play many roles in the 'Ndrangheta. In the household, they transmit the Mafia's cultural code, encourage vendetta, act as guarantors of honorary men's reputations, and are objects of exchange in prescribed marriages. In the criminal sphere, they often bring messages from prison, transport weapons, manage the money of the family, cash in extortions, and sometimes, they actually lead the cosca.

As shown by judiciary investigations, criminal organization does not officially recognized this variety of participation as far as women cannot be formally affiliated through the initiation rite. Indeed, women do not have an official position in the

O. Ingrascì (✉)
Altre. Atelier di ricerca sociale, via Settembrini 33,
20124 Milano, Italy
e-mail: o.ingrasci@gmail.com

N. Serenata (ed.), *The 'Ndrangheta and Sacra Corona Unita,* Studies of Organized Crime 12,   63
DOI 10.1007/978-3-319-04930-4_5, © Springer International Publishing Switzerland 2014

'Ndrangheta organizational chart. Their membership is due to their family connection. This is not surprising, given that the 'Ndrangheta's central core (the 'ndrina) and the blood family overlap.

Compared to the past, female participation is now more consolidated, and is becoming ever more systematic. It has changed so much that women have employed roles beyond the private sphere, becoming more and more involved in the criminal environment. Giovanni Musarò, magistrate of the DDA of Reggio Calabria observed: "Nowadays there is no 'Ndrangheta investigation in which women are not arrested" (Musarò 2012). This new scenario is the result of a new attitude of the police and magistrates that have weakened their chivalrous outlook toward Mafia women,[1] and at the same time, it shows a real transformation, as a consequence of the female emancipation of the wider society. However, the female emancipation has been a pivotal impact on the 'Ndrangheta not only to its advantage, but also against it, as shown by the growing number of women who turned state evidence.

In other words, 'Ndrangheta women act as agents of a double change: A change in continuity, taking on roles that were exclusively male in the past, yet without transforming their subordinate condition; and a transformative change, rebelling against the Mafia by collaborating with the State.

This essay will explore both directions of change by using judiciary materials and, above all, by "listening" the voices of those directly involved. First hand testimonies give an internal in-sight, allowing analysts to go beyond both the old stereotype of Mafia women being unaware of their male relatives' activities and the new cliché of the lady boss, according to which women would hold an equal or even superior power to their male counterparts.

The Private Sphere: Vendetta, Marriage, and Honor

Education and Vendetta

As much as in other Mafia-like criminal organizations, in the 'Ndrangheta, women play a traditional role in the private sphere resulting in both active and passive functions. The first function is educational: Women actively instill in their sons and daughters a mentality based on a series of beliefs, informing the ideology of the criminal group. A woman once belonging to a 'Ndrangheta family who turned state evidence said:

> She is [last name of the woman] my mother. Are you kidding? Not at all [...] It is deeply rooted in her; she was born and raised, and even raised my son, in that way. She instilled in his mind what she was unable to do with me; in fact, if my son sees me, he will kill me (Ingrascì 2007, pp. 10–11).

---

[1] For more information regarding the change of view from the court toward women, see Ingrascì, O. *Donne d'onore. Storie di mafia al femminile,* pp. 108–121.

[È una [cognome della donna] mia madre. Stai scherzando? È mica una (…) è radicato in lei, lei è nata e cresciuta e lei ha fatto crescere mio figlio così, lei gli ha inculcato in testa quello che non è riuscita a inculcare in me, tanto è vero che se mio figlio mi vede mi ammazza].

Her mother taught her, like she did with her sons and grandsons, omertà, the law of silence:

> We grew up with an oafish mentality: Never bring yourself to say: "That person stole something." Never say anything; you must remain silent. Oh, but I was unable to. In fact, once when I saw my brother stealing one thousand lire, I soon told my mother. I was beaten severely and told: "Why did you tell me? You must keep quiet!" (Ingrascì 2007, p. 11).
> [Noi siamo cresciuti nella mentalità balorda: mai venire a dire «quello ha rubato una cosa»", mai venirlo a dire, devi stare zitta, guai, ma io non ero capace, tante è vero che a volte vedevo mio fratello rubare mille lire e subito lo dicevo a mia mamma. Erano tante di quelle botte che prendevo «perché me l'hai detto? Devi stare zitta!»].

She transmitted gender discrimination, the superiority of male compared to female:

> They [the bothers] were gods; I was the whore and they were kings. I, to do a favor for my brother, had to sell everything: My dowry, my gold, everything. Do everything for them […] If her son told her: "Give me a million!" his mother would go around to find the million and she would end up finding it. I asked her: "Mom, I need a pair of shoes." "Regardless, you can do without them" she responded. This is the type of mentality that you carry with you for generations (Ingrascì 2007, p. 14).
> [Loro (i fratelli) erano gli dei, io ero la puttana e loro erano i re. Io per fare un piacere a mio fratello dovevo vendere tutto, la mia dote, il mio oro, tutto. Fare tutto per loro (…) Se suo figlio le diceva «Mi serve un milione» sua mamma andava in cerca del milione e tanto lo cercava che poi lo trovava. Le chiedevo io «mamma mi servono un paio di scarpe», «nonostante tutto»- mi diceva- «puoi farne a meno. Questa è una mentalità che ti porti da generazioni in generazioni»].

Generational transmission of Mafia principles is fundamental in the 'Ndrangheta families as described by Giuseppina Pesce, a pentita who belonged to one of the most important families of the Tyrrhenian 'Ndrangheta (on the west coast of Calabria). In her confession, released in 2010, she declared that her children's destiny would have been predetermined by the family, had she not decided to change course:

> If I don't change my ways now and take my children with me when I get out of jail, my son could already be in a juvenile detention center, and they will put a gun in his hands anyway. My two daughters, on the contrary, will have to marry two 'Ndrangheta men and they will be forced to follow them around. I want to try to create a different future for them. […] When my son once said that when he grew up he wanted to be a policeman, his uncle beat him, and then he promised to give him a gun as a gift (Abbate 2013, pp. 71, 61).
> [Se io non cambio strada e non li porto con me, quando uscirò il bambino potrebbe già essere in un carcere minorile, e comunque gli metteranno al più presto una pistola in mano; le due bimbe invece dovranno sposare due uomini di 'ndrangheta, e saranno costrette a seguirli. "Io voglio provare a costruire un futuro diverso per loro." E continua "(…) Quando il mio bambino, una volta, ha detto che da grande avrebbe voluto fare il carabiniere, suo zio l'ha preso a botte, poi gli ha promesso che una pistola giel'avrebbe regalata lui"].

Women are particularly active in the "pedagogy of vendetta." One of the mother of some children separated by the Juvenile Court of Reggio Calabria kept her educational activity by visiting her son, reminding him of the future shoes he would have to fill as a member of a 'Ndrangheta family: "You are a Facchineri and like a black falcon you have to fall on your enemies; you are from a strong and important family that no one can put under" [Tu sei un Facchineri, e come un falco nero dovrai piombare sui tuoi nemici, tu sei di una famiglia importante e forte che non si fa mettere sotto da nessuno] (Siebert 2003, p. 27). The study reporting this episode underlined that:

> By using the association between the last name and the falcon, the woman proposed to the child a violent image with which he has to identify himself. The child has to imagine that he is a predator, a member of a strong family, with no fear, ready to fight (Siebert 2003, p. 27). [Utilizzando l'associazione tra il cognome e il falco nero, la donna proponeva al bambino una immagine violenta con cui identificarsi. Il bambino doveva immaginare di essere un predatore, membro di una stirpe forte, senza paura, pronto al combattimento].

Women teach the principle of vendetta and are agents of private violence: Stimulating, encouraging, and reminding their male relatives to execute vendettas to regain lost honor. Women carry out this function especially during times of bloodshed. This function dated back to the so-called prefiche (mourners) and has been structurally modernized, as demonstrated by recent criminal investigations. In 2009 the *Operazione Artemisia* carried out by the DDA of Reggio Calbaria ended the bloody feud in Seminara—a small village of 3,500 inhabitants of the plain of Gioia Tauro, in province of Reggio Calabria—which took place between 2006 and 2009.[2] Court records illustrate the significant role that women on both sides of conflicts, and belonging to different age groups, have played in order to continue the chain of vicious retaliations that fueled the conflict. In particular, wiretappings and environmental interceptions show the perspective of those who had a role in the war by revealing their practices and behaviors. Interviews recorded by law enforcement show the impressive daily life of women regarding death and the vindictive dynamics typical of a Mafia system. Women converse about different topics that range from recipes and doctor appointments to the desire to eliminate their adversaries. They do not seem intimidated. On the contrary, they even proved aggressive, "calling to arms" all members of the family. For example, the capobastone's wife of the 'ndrina of Seminara, in the aftermath of the attack on her husband, calls her daughter living in northern Italy, and with a threatening voice, forces her to come back to Calabria, otherwise she will be disowned by the family:

> This is the last thing I will tell you […] this morning we left for work and they shot at […] your dad, but thank God they didn't get [him]; now your brothers are around. If you want to come, come; otherwise be aware that you do not have anybody else […] without eating or drinking (Tribunale di Reggio Calabria 2008, p. 250).
> [Vedi che questa è l'ultima cosa che ti dico, vedi che questa mattina siamo partiti per lavorare, ed hanno sparato a (…) e al papà meno male che non li hanno presi, ora i tuoi fratelli sono tutti in giro, se volete venire venite altrimenti fate conto che non avete più a nessuno (…) senza mangiare o bere].

---

[2] For a full reconstruction of the blood feud and the role of women in the event, see Ingrascì, O. (2011) Donne, 'ndrangheta, 'ndrine. Gli spazi femminili nelle fonti giudiziarie. *Meridiana* 67, pp. 35–54.

In the face of the numerous recordings that show this familiarity and cultural acceptance of violent death advanced by conflict between 'ndrine, the judge that produced the order for custody notes: "More than fear or sorrow for what has happened, the talkers, who are often women, only think about the next move: To revenge what happened" [più che la paura o il dolore per ciò che è accaduto, i colloquianti, spesso donne, pensano esclusivamente alla prossima mossa, per vendicare ciò che è accaduto] (Tribunale di Reggio Calabria 2008, p. 250). One of the women, after the attempted murder of her brother, protests against her relatives who are hypothesizing a possible reconciliation, stating that the bloody feud should not end and that the hatred will last until the seventh generation. The taped conversation showed the conspiratorial behavior of families from both sides. Women, relatives of victims, not only do not denounce the killings or injuries to the police, but even offer conflicting and unreliable statements in order to set investigations on the wrong track. Justice for them is a private matter, which must be compensated for only by an act of revenge showing the will—as written in the order for custody—"to exclude the state and its institutions from the dispute that they intend to solve with their barbaric methods" [di escludere lo Stato e le sue istituzioni dalla contesa che intendono risolvere con i loro barbari metodi] (Tribunale di Reggio Calabria 2008, p. 179).

Commodity Exchange in Arranged Marriages

In Mafia societies, arranged marriages constitute, even today, a fundamental part of the politico-military strategy of the families. They serve to form alliances between 'ndrine or make peace after a feud. In a criminal context, dominated by insecurity and distrust, blood alliances are crucial to the survival of a clan. They make it possible to expand the network of trust between families that share the same values and criminal objectives, and enhance the size of the cosca via connections with groups territorially close to them. The alliance of 'Ndrangheta families, Condello, and Imerti was sealed by a marriage, which allowed them to become stronger in the event of a clash with the De Stefano family.

Pentito Salvatore Morabito, regarding the practice of establishing relationships and alliances between clans through marriages in his home town of Platì, says:

> [...] Families often intersect through marriages. Crossed marriages are used to keep the peace in Platì, which is actually the only village where there has never been a feud. It is more or less the same thing that happened with royal families. By now the families of Platì—Sergis, Papalias, Barbaros, and Perres—are all related to each other: Sons and daughters get married and become godparents, and distant relatives become first, second, and third cousins. So all of them know that if a feud would happen to break out, they would all be involved; and then, before getting revenge they'd have to think three times (Colaprico and Fazzo 1995, p. 100).
>
> [(...) Spesso le famiglie si incrociano con i matrimoni (...) I matrimoni incrociati sono serviti a mantenere la pace a Platì, che infatti è l'unico paese dove non è mai scoppiata una faida. È un po' la stessa cosa che succedeva con le famiglie reali. Ormai le famiglie di Platì – i Sergi, i Papalia, i Barbaro, i Perre –si sono imparentate tutte con tutti: le figlie e i figli si sposano, si fanno compari, diventano parenti tra cugini, secondi cugini e terzi cugini.

Quindi tutti sanno che se dovesse scoppiare una faida, in un attimo li coinvolgerebbe tutti, e allora prima di vendicarsi su qualcuno ci pensano su tre volte].

In addition, wedding ceremonies are privileged places to carry out attacks on enemies. Collaborator of justice, Rita di Giovine sheds light on this: "Usually when they want to kill someone they do at weddings, funerals, or baptisms" [di solito quando vogliono ammazzare qualcuno lo ammazzano o nei matrimoni o nei funerali o nei battesimi] (Terza Corte di Assise di Milano 1998). These words were comments on the attempted murder of her brother, Emilio Di Giovine; the attack was carried out during the wedding of her daughter, Marisa Di Giovine, but it was not successful because he was a fugitive (Ingrascì 2013).

During weddings, the organization takes fundamental decisions. The wedding between Elisa Pelle, daughter of Giuseppe Pelle (better known as Gambazza), and Giuseppe Barbaro, son of the deceased Pasquale Barbaro of the family "u Castanu," celebrated on August 19, 2009 was held—as trial documents report—as important:

'Ndrangheta summit to decide the awarding of the new position for Crimine [...] the result of a complex "negotiation" that saw the opposition of Tyrrhenian, Ionic, and Reggio Calabria cosche, which was solved with a painstaking agreement (Tribunale di Reggio Calabria, 2010).
[Summit di 'ndrangheta per decidere il conferimento delle nuove cariche del Crimine (...) in esito ad una complessa "trattativa" che ha visto contrapposte le cosche della tirrenica al mandamento reggino ed a quello jonico e che è stata risolta in base ad un faticoso accordo].

The endogamy of class and the parental hermeticism guarantee the closure of the group, useful for reducing the risk of defections. The mating of close relatives within the same family tree have created many difficulties for investigations, especially in municipalities of the Ionic coast of Calabria where people, besides the same physical resemblance, often have the same last name (Gratteri, 2003). Judge Michele Prestipino explains:

In some places it is true that a Mafia family has a well-known name, but behind that name it is possible to identify a number of family units with the same last name. To untangle among people that not only have the same last name, but also the same first name, a specialized study on genealogical tree is necessary to understand the dynamics, alliances, and contacts that often conflict with each other (Pignatone and Prestipino 2012, p. 49).
[In alcune località è vero che la famiglia mafiosa ha un nome noto, ma dietro a quel nome spesso sono identificabili una pluralità di nuclei familiari con lo stesso cognome. Per districarsi tra soggetti che portano non soltanto lo stesso cognome, ma in molti casi anche lo stesso nome di battesimo, occorre uno studio specialistico sugli alberi genealogici per capire dinamiche, alleanze, contatti a volte contrastanti].

Women, in most cases, are pawns in these arranged marriages. The role of the bride of a man belonging to a 'ndrina is not always well-accepted to her. In such cases, she is, however, obliged to submit to the family's will. Being a passive object of marriage exchange causes great suffering, above all, when the goal of the union is to reconcile two rival families after a feud. To confirm the end of the conflict, the virginal blood spilled during the wedding night is symbolically offered as compensation to the one shed in warfare. In the case of conciliation weddings, women are forced to marry killers of their own loved ones, namely those who, before the peace agreement, were from the opposite side.

Rebelling against the family choice is, in most cases, impossible. The passive role of women within the marriage practices of the 'Ndrangheta is closely intertwined with the code of honor.

The Code of Honor

Women are registered in the cultural regime of honor, which decides which behavior and attitudes are male and female, prescribes how one should act, and what one should not do. In the 'Ndrangheta, the code of honor does not only do this, but it is also a military control system reducing the woman to an object that belongs to the man and the family.[3] Women are subjected to segregation from adolescence onward. A collaborator of justice confesses:

> I was born and raised in a very strict family, and I was not allowed to go out. They did not let me study; when I reached the second grade they told me that it was not necessary to continue because, fittingly, the most important thing was to be at home, work in the home and, thus, school was of no use. But if I didn't need school, I didn't need to smuggle cigarettes, but I had to do it (Ingrascì 2007, p. 11).
> [Nata e cresciuta in una famiglia molto ristretta, io non potevo uscire, non mi hanno fatto studiare, arrivata alla seconda elementare mi hanno detto che non valeva la pena andare avanti perché giustamente non serviva a niente continuare perché l'importante è che io stavo in casa, lavoravo in casa quindi non mi serviva a niente la scuola; però se non mi serviva la scuola non mi serviva neanche andare a fare il contrabbando di sigarette (…) invece l'ho dovuto fare].

Women of man in prison are controlled not only by the family, but also by the entire cosca. The witness Maria Concetta Cacciolla, smothered by the continuous control of the entire organization, wrote to her husband Salvatore Figliuzzi of the Bellocco cosca of Rosarno, in prison convicted with Mafia association, to complain on her lack of freedom. She could only go out to drop off her children at school, but even in that situation she must be with a trusted person:

> How can I live this way if I cannot even breath […]? I go out in the morning to drop off my children at school […] I cannot have any contact with anybody […] What good is my life when I cannot have contact with anyone? (Abbate 2013, p. 111).
> [Come posso campare così se non posso nemmeno respirare (…) Esco la mattina per andare a portare i figli a scuola (…) Non posso avere contatto con nessuno, a cosa mi serve la mia vita quando non posso avere contatto con nessuno?].

Moreover, women have also been the subject of theft in cases where they refuse to get married. The boss Francesco Pesce (alias u Testune), successor of the Pesce family of Rosarno, had appropriated his fiancée by force against her will. The frequent kidnappings seem to suggest that there is a return of ancient practices, such as that of abduction.

Women are beaten and, in some cases, even mortally punished, often along with their beloved, in case it is discovered that they are having an extra-marital affair.

---

[3] For an analysis of the exploitation of the code of honor in the Mafia, see Ingrascì, O. *Donne d'onore. Storie di mafia al femminile,* pp. 26–38.

Thanks to women's testimonies, judges have been able to shed light on old cases of missing women that were actually killed by their brothers, husbands, or fathers because they were guilty of relations outside the marriage and, thus, had violated the code of honor.

During 2011 investigations, collaborator Giuseppina Pesce shed light on the case of a missing woman archived by the police. The 'Ndrangheta court rules the death penalty for women who drift from the code of honor. The solution of the honor killing is a path used to restore the reputation after an event has tarnished the family name. In other words, deviant female behavior has dishonored the family, which now needs to prove to the entire community that it can defend its own pride at whatever cost, to the point of scarifying its own daughters, sisters, or wives.

The same codes of honor do not apply for men of the family that are allowed not only to have chaotic love lives, but, as we have also seen, brutal and violent behavior toward women.

Female Participation in Criminal Activities

The lack of a formal female presence in the 'Ndrangheta has not prevented women from active participation. The prohibition of women from participating in the organization through the initiation rite is a norm with very few exceptions throughout the criminal organization's history. There are, in fact, historic documents proving a formal structure of female involvement: In the minutes of some court documents from the beginning of the 1900s, there are cases of women not only tried for criminal conspiracy, but also affiliated with the so-called picciotteria. In the conviction of members of a criminal organization based in Palmi and its surrounding areas, there is a specific reference to women, in which the court says:

> In this association of evildoers […] women were also admitted, dressed as men, that took part in thefts and other crimes—women admitted to having to take an oath while pricking the little finger of their right hand to produce blood, and swearing the aforementioned secret. Everybody went out carrying pistols and daggers (Archivio di Stato di Catanzaro 1892, p. 336).
>
> [Nelle associazioni di malfattori (...) furono pure ammesse delle donne, che vestite da uomini, prendevano parte alla perpetuazione dei "furti" ed altri reati e le donne ammesse dovevano pur esse prestare giuramento facendosi uscire il sangue dal dito mignolo della mano destra e promettendo il segreto, come si è detto di sopra. Tutti andavano armati di pugnale e rivoltella].

According to the police sources from the early 1900s, the picciotteria of Santo Stefano D'Aspromonte even had a female section, and in Nicastro, the boss' sister-in law, "armed and dressed as a man," went with him to the night criminal activities (Ciconte 1992, p. 81).

More recently, the presence of a specific position for women has emerged—the so-called sorella d'omertà. The trial documents relative to *Crimine-Infinito* investigation, directed by the DDA of Milan and Reggio Calabria in 2010, described positions and ranks within the criminal organization, including the sorella d'omertà. This position was first mentioned by collaborator of justice Antonio Zagari during a judicial hearing in 1995 for the process regarding the *Isola Felice* investigation. The pentito described the symbolic depiction of the 'Ndrangheta, its positions, ranks, hierarchy, and other issues regarding ritually symbolic matters. Zagari had already talked about sorella d'omertà in his autobiography, asserting that:

> 'Ndrangheta rules do not consider affiliating female elements a possibility; but if a woman is particularly deserving, she can be associated with the title of sorella d'omertà; without taking an oath, which is obligatory for men. However, it is difficult to recognize the title to those who are not already wives, sisters, fiancées, or related in some way to honored men (1992, p.12).
>
> [Le regole della 'ndrangheta calabrese non contemplano la possibilità di affiliare elementi femmina ma se una donna viene riconosciuta particolarmente meritevole può essere associata con il titolo di sorella d'omertà; senza però prestare giuramento di fedeltà alla organizzazione come è obbligatoriamente previsto per gli uomini; ma difficilmente si riconosce il titolo a chi non è già moglie, figlia, sorella, fidanzata, o comunque imparentata con uomini d'onore].

The Case of Maria Morello: Sorella d'Omertà

Other collaborator of justice mentioned the figure of sorella d'omertà, like Calogero Mercenò:

> Such a position, which exists in every region, is committed to a woman. In the case of the region of Lombardy, we have Morello Maria, who has the task of helping fugitives within the organization. In the case of Morello [...] I can say that she is, with full rights, a member of the organization with the rank of santista—which is the highest a woman can have within the 'Ndrangheta. I want to point out that, in the region, there can be only one woman in the clan that assumes the rank of santista and, thus, has the role of sorella d'omertà (Gratteri and Nicaso 2006, p. 31).
>
> [Tale carica, che esiste in ogni regione, è affidata ad una donna, che nel caso della Lombardia è Morello Maria, che ha il compito di dare assistenza ai latitanti dell'organizzazione. Nel caso della Morello (...) posso dire che la stessa è inserita a pieno titolo nell'organizzazione e ha la dote di santista che è la più elevata che una donna può avere all'interno della 'ndrangheta. Faccio presente che nella regione può esserci una sola donna componente del clan, che assume la dote di santista e svolge per l'appunto le funzioni di sorella d'omertà].

Maria Morello is the only concrete case of sorella d'omertà that studies and magistrates know, and concerns the 'Ndrangheta in Lombardy during the 1970s and 1980s. Originally from Cosenza, but living in Como for many years, Morello performs a variety of functions for the Mazzaferro's cosca: Hiding weapons, individuating targets to rob, and creating protective nets for affiliates. Foti, in the trial relating to the investigation *Fiori nella notte di San Vito* of the DDA of Milan, calls her sorella d'umiltà (humility sister), meaning a woman who serves the society and "could be defined as a source of support in roles that are not exclusively military" [che potrebbe definirsi come un fiancheggiamento in ruoli non prettamente militari] (Ingrascì 2011, p. 45). Maria Morello is not related to any affiliates, but she has a significant criminal past:

> Bad checks, misappropriation of foreclosed homes, forging credit instruments, threats, resisting arrest, smuggling, and, in 1968, conviction for attempted bribery for helping a smuggler avoid the intervention of the Guardia di Finanza (financial police) (Ingrascì 2011, p. 46).

[Assegni a vuoto, sottrazione di cose pignorate, falsità in titoli di credito, minaccia, resistenza a pubblico ufficiale, contrabbando, e nel 1968 condanna per istigazione alla corruzione per aiutare un contrabbandiere ad evitare l'intervento della Guardia di Finanza].

Her specialization, being an informant to the police in exchange for favors, did not prevent her from joining the group and thus assuming the position of sorella d'omertà, although keeping secrets is a fundamental prerequisite of this role, as the name itself implies. The woman continued to act as an informant, adapting this activity to the new function: If called by the police regarding activities of affiliates, she maintained confidentiality while handling fabricated information against rivals of the 'Ndrangheta to the benefit of her criminal group. In the conviction magistrate wrote: "The informant Morello [...] could have said more to the Warrant Officer if she wanted to, but she instead handpicked information to pass on to police, following the logic of helping the honored society" [La confidente Morello (...) avrebbe potuto dire di più al maresciallo, se avesse voluto, ma in realtà selezionava le informazioni da passare alle forze dell'ordine, secondo una logica di favore verso la "onorata società"] (Ingrascì 2011, p. 46). As some collaborators have pointed out, the member of 'Ndrangheta did not like her activity of informer; however, they accepted it because it could have worked in their favor.

In 1976, at her restaurant in Laglio, on Lake Como, there was an important summit of 'ndranghetisti who had moved northward with the aim of creating, on the initiative of Mazzaferro, a "control room" for rank assignments in Lombardy's 'Ndrangheta. In the conviction, it is highlighted that "reserving the restaurant for the meeting had required particular confidence for the sensitivity of the topics discussed" [riservare il ristorante per la riunione, comportava particolare fiducia, per la delicatezza degli argomenti (...) trattati] (Ingrascì 2011, p. 46).

Morello proceeds like a woman that reached a high level, so that she not only entertains close relations with Mazzaferro, the boss, but she can even express her dissent for the assignment of ranks; showing, thus, the high amount of knowledge and respect she had within the organization. In judging her position, the court evaluated the following elements of danger: "Her closeness to previous offenders, her numerous criminal records, her loyalty to the code of omertà, and typical values of the 'Ndrangheta" [quali elementi di pericolosità la frequentazione di pregiudicati, i numerosi precedenti e la fedeltà al codice di omertà e di valori tipico della 'ndrangheta] (Ingrascì 2011, p. 46).

Apart from the rank of sorella d'omertà, of which little is known, women do not reach high-command or leadership positions in the 'Ndrangheta. This indicates a total formal absence in the organization. Nevertheless, they play an important role in the criminal sphere, especially in the absence of men.

Female Ambassadors, Cashiers, and Bosses

Female participation is particularly accentuated during the absence of men, when they are fugitives or in prison. As told by a collaborator of justice:

[…] Men were always fugitives or under house arrest, because they forced themselves—that is, locked themselves—at home, and women were the ones who always worked […] Everything that happened, happened through us women […]. My aunt and cousin do all the work. I, too, when I was in Calabria, not the weapons, but I took my uncle somewhere in the car, or I went to get little notes to bring to my uncle, he called them "ambasciate;" […] When weapons arrived, it was my aunt who acted as a relay, she delivered them; or my cousin went to take, I don't know, the gun, the shotgun, whatever was needed, and brought to her father (Ingrascì 2007, p. 78).

[Gli uomini erano sempre latitanti o erano agli arresti domiciliari forzati, perché si arrestavano da soli, cioè stavano chiusi in casa, e chi lavorava erano tutte le donne (…) Cioè tutte le cose che si svolgevano erano sempre tramite noi donne (…) Mia zia, mia cugina fanno tutto. Anch'io quando ero giù in Calabria, non le armi, ma portavo mio zio, lo accompagnavo in macchina da qualche parte, oppure andavo a prendere i bigliettini da portare a mio zio, lui le chiamava "ambasciate" (…) Quando arrivavano le armi era mia zia che faceva da staffetta, mia zia che le consegnava, oppure mia cugina andava a prendere, non so, la pistola, il fucile, quello che serviva e lo portava a suo padre].

These roles also emerge from the analysis of the case of Seminara feud, identified in *Operazione Artemisia*, aforementioned. Women of clans in conflict had the role of "custody and concealment of weapons, external surveillance, acquiring information, and transmitting messages" [di custodia e nascondimento delle armi, di vigilanza esterna, di acquisizione di informazioni, di trasmissione di messaggi] (Tribunale di Reggio Calabria 2008). According to magistrates, these seemed to be simple activities, but they were extremely significant, in order to maintain the group cohesion and strength, and resisist to the attacks coming both from institutions and from their rivals, and finally to organize for winning the struggle that had been unleashed, by committing new bloody crimes.

The women involved in the 'Ndrangheta are always women belonging to the family nucleus at the base of the criminal organization, the 'ndrine. They go outside the domestic threshold when it is needed.

In April 2012, the *All Inside* and *Califfo 2* investigations shed light on the role of women in the Pesce cosca of Rosarno. According to the arrest warrant, the "bacinella"—the common fund of the groups—was in the hands of Maria Grazia Messina, mother in-law of Antonino Pesce and grandmother of Francesco Pesce. Other women, on the contrary, acted merely as figureheads. The collaborator Giuseppina Pesce told about this active feminine presence, emphasizing particularly the role of messenger:

[…] Our role was just that of carrying messages. We went to the prisons and could not escape when our family members, brothers, husbands, fathers, asked us to do this, in short, to relay messages (Tribunale di Reggio Calabria 2012).

[(…) il ruolo nostro era proprio questo, di portare i messaggi, andavano al carcere e non potevamo sottrarci quando i nostri familiari, fratelli, mariti, padri, ci chiedevano questo, insomma, di portare i messaggi].

The female role emerges even more in the other powerful cosca of Rosarno, the Bollocco. Judge Giovanni Musarò defined Aurora Spanò, partner of Giulio Bellocco, as "an authentic boss" (Musarò). Previously involved in *Operazione Tasso* and sentenced to 6 years for criminal association aimed at loan sharking, Aurora Spanò was struck again by *Operazione Tramonto*, which, in March 2013, hit the Bellocco cosca. The woman was even accused for the leadership position she shared with her partner. According to the indictment:

> Bellocco Giulio, class 51 and Spanò Aurora in the role of management of the cosca, with the task of deciding, planning, and identifying criminal activities to be carried out, targets to pursue, and victims to hit, gave directives which were implemented by the others members (Tribunale di Reggio Calabria 2013).
>
> [Bellocco Giulio cl. 51 e Spanò Aurora nel ruolo di direzione della cosca, con compiti di decisione, pianificazione e di individuazione delle azioni delittuose da compiere, degli obiettivi da perseguire e delle vittime da colpire, impartivano direttive alle quali tutti gli altri associati davano attuazione].

The hardening of authoritative head is also evident from the way she relates with her cellmates. Two of them denounce that fact that—as reported in the order for custody:

> By relying on the importance of her criminal family, Aurora Spanò put authoritarian and oppressive behaviors in place towards them, demanding that the bed be made or that the bathroom of the cell be cleaned after she used it, or that the breakfast be served. Even during the two women's grieving periods, there were threats of retaliation once their sentences were served. (Don't you dare talk to me that way [...] Do you not know who I am?! [...] If you do not know who I am, it means I'll be seeing you outside [...] I'll make her pay, too) (Tribunale di Reggio Calabria 2013, p. 150).
>
> [Aurora SPANÒ, facendo leva sullo spessore criminale della sua famiglia, poneva in essere nei loro confronti comportamenti autoritari e vessatori, pretendendo che le venisse rifatto il letto o che venisse pulito il bagno della cella dopo che la stessa ne aveva usufruito o che le fosse servita la colazione. Davanti alle rimostranze delle due donne scattavano le minacce di ritorsioni da consumare una volta scontato il periodo detentivo ("(....) non permetterti di parlarmi in questo modo....non sai chi sono io!" "(....) se non sai chi sono io vorrà dire che ci vedremo fuori (...)" "(...) gliela faccio pagare anche a lei")].

She showed a strong and criminal attitude when one of her cellmate insulted her calling her "miss" to point out that Aurora was not married to Giulio Bellocco. To exact her revenge, she ordered her son to punish the husband of her cellmate who, soon after, would be brutally beaten. The judge defined her behavior toward the other inmates as "dictatorial."

Agents of Change

Female turning state's evidence is a novelty for the 'Ndrangheta, although the first case can be traced back to 1993. It is interesting, therefore, to wonder about the motivations and processes that have triggered this transformation.

One of the factors that undoubtedly facilitated the beginning of this new role of women as agents of change has been the process of female emancipation in the Italian society. Though incomplete and imperfect, it has been able to offer different and alternative female models to women enclosed in traditional and patriarchal families.

Another contributory factor has been the diffusion of an Anti-Mafia spirit and action recently developed in Calabria. Since 2008, the arrival of judges Giuseppe Pignatone and Michele Prestipino at the DDA of Reggio Calabria, and later the arrival of Alessandra Cerreti, has strengthened the work of colleagues that had already been working against the 'Ndrangheta, like Judge Nicola Gratteri, leading to a long list of successful investigations.

The Anti-Mafia affected other institutions, such as the municipalities of Monasterace and Rossano and Decollatura, each with a high concentration of Mafia infiltration and run by women mayors, respectively, Maria Carmela Lanzetta, Elisabetta Tripodi, and Anna Maria Cardamone. All have determined to enforce the rules and laws. This has also joined the efforts made on behalf of civil society, comprising mainly young people who, in recent years, have organized various types of events and initiatives against the 'Ndrangheta.

Turning state's evidence has made the work of magistrates more effective since it has enabled to break the secrecy of the Mafia organization and, therefore, to carry out new investigations. Such investigations had negative impacts on organized crime, and positive effects on the perception of public opinion about the effectiveness of Anti-Mafia state's actions.

In 2007, there were 97 collaborators of justice that previously belonged to the 'Ndrangheta, and in 2008, another four were added (101); three more in 2009 (104); in 2010, the number grew by ten (114), and in the first half of 2011, another four collaborated, reaching a total number of 118.[4] The women who turned state's witness have doubled from 2008 to the first half of 2011 (from four to eight).

The collaboration proceedings have brought the legendary impenetrability of the organization into question. The family structure of the association led many analysts to believe that the blood relations at the core of linkage between the members of the association explain the lower number of collaborators in comparison with other Mafia associations. There is no doubt that accusing relatives is difficult and, therefore, in many cases, it was indeed the constraint of blood that prevented a falling-out within the association. However, as hypothesized by sociologist Rocco Sciarrone, other factors, there exist in order to explain the lower tendency of informants within the 'Ndrangheta, including the type of structure of the organization, solid and flexible at the same time, and with a hierarchy of the knowledge based on the model of the Carbonari society at the end of the 1800s; and the anti-pentiti strategy implemented by the organization grounded more on offering informants money, rather than implementing revenge actions. In other words the "lost sheeps" are not killed, but rather contacted one by one, being promised better opportunities than those offered by the government. Women have been pawns of this reconquering technique, playing a very valuable role in getting their deviant men back on track. The reaction of women, when faced with their relative's choice to collaborate, is of great importance for the success of the collaboration itself. Supporting the man obviously facilitates the process of collaboration. Conversely, if not endorsed, or even disowned by his wife and family, he can sometimes retract his statements.

Women who turned state evidence show to be vulnerable and, at the same time, firm in separating themselves from the criminal organization. Yet, some cases of

---

[4] Data received from "Relazione del Ministero dell'Interno al Parlamento" regarding special protection measures.

women who offered their testimonies to the state ended in tragedy. Lea Garofalo, 35 years old, was killed by her husband, Carlo Cosco, 'Ndrangheta boss from Crotone. In 2011, Maria Concetta Cacciola, 31 years old, mother of three, became collaborator of justice, but soon after retracted and left the protection program. After returning to the oppressive environment of her original family, she committed suicide by drinking muriatic acid. Even Titta Buccafusca, 38-year-old wife of Pantaleone Mancusi, boss of Vibo Valentia, and mother of a child, was not able to keep testifying against the 'Ndrangheta. In 2011, she decided to speak out, but after a few days she changed her mind and committed suicide by drinking muriatic acid.

Other female collaborations continued, despite the numerous emotional, logistical, and organizational difficulties that the decision to testify implies. Rita Di Giovine turned herself over to the police in 1993, when she was 36. Her declarations not only helped the judge Maurizio Romanelli to carry out *Operazione Belgio* against the Serraino-Di Giovine clan—one of the most powerful criminal organizations in Milan in the 1980s—but also provided the first insight into the role of women in the 'Ndrangheta, revealing its oppressive features. Rita was able to start a new life despite the assassination plans by her relatives belonging to the 'Ndrangheta. She did not only finish high school, fulfilling the dream of learning how to write, but she also met a man with whom she could share her life. Giuseppina Pesce, from a historic 'Ndrangheta family on the plain of Gioia Tauro, has kept collaborating with judges, showing great courage. She also offered as Rita Di Giovine did 20 years ago, a representation of Mafia women that went beyond stereotypes. The fear of being killed, especially by her brother, never leaves her. Nevertheless, she has kept to testify in front of the court.

When looking at women who turned state witness, it is no doubt that one of the main aspects of their stories is the relationship with their sons and daughters. According to many observers, children are the main cause of their change: Maternal love would push these women toward the state, previously considered as an enemy. Redeeming the future of sons and daughters is undoubtedly a fundamental incentive; however, it is necessary to deconstruct the myth that maternal love is the sole motive behind turning state evidence or becoming a witness.

First of all, a mother's love is not the discriminating factor that makes the difference compared to those who do not rebel against the 'Ndrangheta. On the contrary, maternal love is the root of the behavior of women who do not collaborate and continue teaching their daughters to obey the men of the family. This could be a coping mechanism in order to survive in a sexist and violent environment. Indeed, in relation to the "survival techniques" of Mafia women, sociologist Renate Siebert wrote:

> Women themselves tend to become spokeswomen of male superiority, adjusting themselves to the prescribed female role in order to secure a space where they can act without being disputed, to exercise power over objects, people, and relations that are not formally recognized to them (Siebert 1998, p. 58).
> [Le donne stesse tendono a farsi portavoce della superiorità maschile, adeguandosi formalmente al ruolo femminile prescritto – al fine di garantirsi uno spazio incontestato per agire, per mettere in atto un potere su cose, persone e relazioni che formalmente non viene riconosciuto loro].

In addition, maternal love pushes women to perpetrate the vendetta system. Women accused in the *Artemisia* investigation, described previously, hope for the death of the rival clan's young guys in the name of their children.

Finally, attributing the reasons for collaboration merely to maternal love risks to reduce the femininity to an ahistorical and universal role tied with maternity, like the 'Ndrangheta does.

Instead, it seems to be mainly the fatigue and exasperation of experiencing segregation, family, and male control that can bring 'Ndrangheta women to the choice of collaborating with justice. More than motherly love, it is vulnerability that makes them strong and ready to make such a brave choice as rebelling. And not surprisingly often is the love for another man who offers them the opportunity to escape or to dream to run away from her overbearing husband. Giuseppina Pesce met a worker in the factory where she worked, while Maria Concetta Cacciola glimpsed her freedom just virtually, as she knew a man by a social network.

In other words, witnesses decide to start the meandering and difficult route of collaboration with justice because they are moved by a desire concerning them as women. It is important to represent witnesses as women, subjects, and persons that choose consciously, since it permits to counterbalance the attempts of lawyers, families, and, sometimes, journalists to depict female witnesses and collaborators as affected by mental disorders, and, thus, to contribute to highlight their reliability as witnesses in trials. The judge for the preliminary investigation regarding *Operazione Tramonto* based on Maria Concetta Cacciola's own testimonies defines them as "intrinsically credible, logical, and held up under scrutiny" [intrinsecamente credibili, logiche e riscontrate dagli accertamenti compiuti] (Tribunale di Reggio Calabria 2013). Maria Concetta Cacciola died in 2011, whereas *Operazione Tramonto* was carried out in 2013. Surviving, her words still have a devastating effect on the 'Ndrangheta's cosche. This is a clear example of the power of collaborating and becoming a witness.

Having deconstructed the rhetoric of "the mother witness," it is however important to emphasize that it is their maternal status that produces a long-term liberating effect that continues for generations to come. It is a choice of freedom, first of all, for themselves, but also has important effects on their sons and daughters; and, moreover, the fact that these women distance themselves from 'Ndrangheta—because women and not just because mothers—makes their testimony a real opportunity to produce a new transmission bringing discontinuity.

Giuseppina Pesce, in her first meeting with judge Alessandra Cerreti, affirmed: "I have wanted to see you because I feel like I'm a victim [...] of this family context that does not belong to me" [io l'ho voluta vedere perché mi sento vittima di questa (...) di questo contesto familiare che non mi appartiene] (Abbate 2013, p. 55). At the same time, Giuseppina is aware that her choice will guarantee a different education for her own children, as seen previously.

The role of agent of change played by Giuseppina as a mother is evident in the words entrusted in a letter that explains her reasoning:

> On October 14, 2010, I expressed my desire to start this process, driven by love as a mother and also by the desire to have a better life, far from the environment in which we were born

and raised. I was—and am still—convinced that this is the right choice. Due to lifestyle choices of family and relatives, we have always been marked by a life of suffering, hardship, and above all, a lack of courage for fear of consequences; when, however, each one of us should be able to do and choose what is right and wrong (Prestipino and Pignatone 2012, p. 146).

[Il 14 ottobre 2010 ho espresso la mia volontà di iniziare questo percorso spinta dall'amore di madre e dal desiderio di poter avere anche io una vita migliore lontano dall'ambiente cui siamo nati e cresciuti. Ero e sono convinta che sia la scelta giusta dal momento che per scelte di vita di familiari e congiunti siamo sempre stati segnati da una vita piena di sofferenza e difficoltà e soprattutto mancanza di coraggio per paura delle conseguenze. Quando invece ognuno di noi dovrebbe avere la facoltà di fare e scegliere ciò che è giusto e sbagliato].

At the trial for the death of Lea Garofalo, her daughter Denise Cosco sued her father. The gesture is in continuity with her mother's breach as a demonstration that Lea's choice had an impact on the transmission of a female model of liberation from 'Ndrangheta oppression.

Giuseppina Pesce, finally, aims to be a positive example for women with a life similar to hers. In her letter to judges, she wrote: "I also hope that many people like me who find themselves in these situations find the courage to rise up" [spero anche che molte persone come me che si trovano in queste situazioni trovino il coraggio di ribellarsi] (Prestipino and Pignatone 2012, p. 147).

The aspect of the emulation effect is not to be neglected. Giuseppina has led the way for her cousin Maria Concetta Cacciolla, just like Piera Aiello did for her sister-in-law Rita Atria in Sicily in 1991. Giuseppina has shown that it is possible to escape from the 'Ndrangheta unashamedly, acting as a concrete example of the possibility of abandoning the criminal family.

Conclusion

Exploring the role of women in the 'Ndrangheta is difficult because researchers have to deal with a secret criminal organization and with a subject that operates primarily in the private sphere. It is, therefore, a doubly hidden object of study. The knowledge gap can be filled only by listening to former men and women of honor that, due to law number 82 of 1991, have decided to cooperate with the justice system.

Through testimonies of women that publicly took a step against the organization, it has been possible to reconstruct the different facets of the female universe in the 'Ndrangheta, and, especially, to overcome stereotypes, according to which Mafia women are not aware of their husband's activity and are respected as women. Grasping the internal insight is undoubtedly effective, thus, confirming the importance of using oral sources in the study of the Mafia in order to integrate the representation offered by trial sources (Ingrascì 2013).

Women who belong to the families of 'Ndrangheta are women who, on one hand, understand, know, and act criminally in the name of family; work as watchmen in homicides; transmit sensitive information; take positions that are heard; and have conspiratorial attitudes. On the other, they leave the spheres of formal power to men and, on the private level, are subjected to severe male control. On the one side, they act independently; on the other, they are dependent on men of the family or even suffer from abuse. In the 'ndrine, their presence, often strong, is certainly aware and, at the same time, marked by extreme vulnerability.

'Ndrangheta women are the protagonists of a double transformative course movement influenced by the emancipation process of society: One is the result of a pseudo-emancipation process; the other is the result of a path of liberation.

In the first process, women have taken tasks that in the past were exclusively male, yet they kept suffering to male oppression: They seem to "left over," but in reality, they continue to perpetuate the chauvinist system of the 'Ndrangheta.

In the second type of change, on the contrary, women who turned state witness have undertook a liberating track. This change is a positive transformation not only for themselves, but also for the society, and, therefore, it must be understood in terms of innovation and not, like the first type, as a change that masks continuity. When Mafia women are able to break the chains of subordination, affirm their will-power, and teach their sons and daughters the value of words against the Mafia's law of silence. Women who collaborate demonstrate their ability to capitalize on the emancipatory influences acknowledged by the whole of society, being agents of change on two levels: One of self-determination and the other of transmission. For this reason, they may be defined as free and emancipated women, as opposed to those women who remained caged in the 'Ndrangheta's family networks, conformed to the male model.

References

Abbate, L. (2013). *Fimmine ribelli. Come le donne salveranno il paese dalla 'ndrangheta*. Milan: Rizzoli.

Archivio di Stato di Catanzaro. (9, Sept 1892). *Corte d'Appello delle Calabrie, Marino Francese + 147*, p. 336.

Ciconte, E. (1992). *'Ndrangheta. Dall'Unità a oggi*. Bari-Roma: Laterza.

Colaprico, P., & Fazzo, L. (1995). *Manager calibro 9. Vent'anni di criminalità a Milano nel racconto del pentito Saverio Morabito*. Milan: Garzanti.

Gratteri, Nicola (16, Sept 2003). Interview.

Gratteri, N., & Nicaso, A. (2006). *Fratelli di sangue*. Cosenza: Pellegrini Editore.

Ingrascì, O. (2007). *Donne d'onore. Storie di mafia al femminile*. Milan: Mondadori.

Ingrascì, O. (March 2011). *Donne 'ndrangheta, 'ndrine. Gli spazi femminili nelle fonti giudiziarie. Meridiana. Rivista di Storia e Scienze Sociali, 67*, 35–54.

Ingrascì, O. (2013). *Confessioni di un padre. Il pentito Emilio Di Giovine racconta la 'ndrangheta alla figlia*. Milan: Melampo.

Musarò, G. (13, Sept 2012). Interview.

Prestipino, M., & Pignatone, G. (2012). *Il contagio. Come la 'ndrangheta ha infettato l'Italia*, In G. Savatteri (Ed.), Bari-Rome: Laterza. http://www.laterza.it/index.php?option=com_laterza&I temid=97&task=schedalibro&isbn=9788842098348.

Siebert. R. (1998). Donne di terra di mafia: i riflessi del processo di emancipazione femminile. *Il Mulino* XLVII(375), p. 58.

Siebert. R. (2003). *Donne di mafia: affermazione di uno pseudo-soggetto femminile. Il caso della 'ndrangheta. In Donne e mafie. Il ruolo delle donne nelle organizzazioni criminali internazionali.* Palermo: Dipartimento Scienze Penalistiche, Università di Palermo.

Terza Corte di Assise di Milano. (29, Sept 1998). *Sentenza n. 20.* Milan.

Tribunale di Reggio Calabria. (March 2008). *Ordinanza di custodia cautelare, procedimento penale n. 5503/07, RGNR DDA, n. 3926/08 RGIP DDA.* Reggio Calabria.

Tribunale di Reggio Calabria. (July 2010). *Direzione distrettuale antimafia. Decreto di fermo di indiziato di delitto, Agostino Annamaria + 155.* Reggio Calabria.

Tribunale di Reggio Calabria. (2012). *Verbale di udienza del 08/06/2012, procedimento penale 819/11– R.G.N.R. 4302/06 a carico di ARMELI SIGNORINO + 63.* Reggio Calabria.

Tribunale di Reggio Calabria. (2013). *Ordinanza di custodia cautelare, procedimento penale n. 891/12 R. G. N. R. D.D.A, n. 452/13 R. G.I.P. D.D.A.* Reggio Calabria.

Zagari, A. (1992). *Ammazzare stanca. Autobiografia di un 'ndranghetista pentito.* Cosenza: Edizioni periferia.

Chapter 6
'Ndrangheta: A Reticular Organization

Rocco Sciarrone

A Long Underestimation

The development of the Calabrian Mafia was followed by the historical underestimation of its dangerousness, that had consequences in terms of lack of attention both in terms of law enforcement strategies and research and analysis strategies.[1] Until recently the 'Ndrangheta was considered a minor criminal organization, residual expression of an underdeveloped society, thus more "primitive" compared to the Sicilian and Neapolitan Mafias (Cosa Nostra and Camorra). This vision was extensively diffused in the public discussion for a long time shared by politicians, scholars, and judges.[2]

A different reading approach was proposed in a report approved in the 2008 by the Anti-Mafia Parliament Commission, in which the 'Ndrangheta was defined "liquid Mafia." It is a striking metaphor that was borrowed from a successful work of sociologist Zygmunt Bauman that actually spoke about "liquidity" to try "to grasp the nature of the present, in many ways *novel*, phrase in the history of modernity" (Bauman 2002, p. 2). In my opinion, the metaphor risks of being misleading if it is applied to the 'Ndrangheta or, more generally, to the Mafia. As well as inadequate are other analogies used in the report of the Anti-Mafia Parliament Commission when the Calabrian Mafia is compared to the "big fast food chains" and to the "tentacular structure" of Al Qaida, but also to the vitality of the "neoplasm" (Commissione Parlamentare Antimafia (CPA) 2008, p. 23). In this way, a true association of

---

[1] The status of the knowledge of the 'Ndrangheta—despite recent increased interest—continues to be very unsatisfactory. Among the "historical" Mafia, the Calabrian remains the least studied.

[2] For more information, see Violante (1994, p. 89); Becchi (2000, p. 101). Furthermore, Eric Hobsbawm (1971, pp. 29–52) had already mentioned the 'Ndrangheta as a primitive form and a pre-political social revolt, of which shepherds, farmers, and small artisans were protagonists that were trying to defend themselves from feudal and State power.

R. Sciarrone (✉)
Culture, Politics and Society Department, University of Turin,
Lungo Dora Siena, 100, 10153 Turin, Italy
e-mail: rocco.sciarrone@unito.it

N. Serenata (ed.), *The 'Ndrangheta and Sacra Corona Unita,* Studies of Organized Crime 12,   81
DOI 10.1007/978-3-319-04930-4_6, © Springer International Publishing Switzerland 2014

different phenomena very different among themselves for organizational structure, modality of action, and operation, is made.

An interpretation of this nature can lead to distorted information also in terms of policy and contrast strategies. If the peculiar character of the 'Ndrangheta was liquidity, it would follow that countering and would require being equipped with special tools, or with "containers" that can "contain" it. The "modern liquidity" that Bauman talks about is characterized by "transience," "friability," "brittleness," and "until-further-noticeness" of human bond and networks (Bauman 2002). All these characteristics are hardly associable with the actual Mafia organizations, not only the Calabrian one. If we take into consideration Bauman's analysis, the presence of a phenomenon as that of the Mafia, it would even be in contradiction on how to explain "liquid modernity." Compared to the latter, as the author observed: "Any dense and tight network of social bond, and particularly a territorial rooted tight network, is an obstacle to be cleared out of the way" (Bauman 2002, p. 14). Mafia networks have precisely these characteristics: They are built by dense social bonds and have always been profoundly settled in the territory. In particular, the 'Ndrangheta—as we will see—is a "solid" reality, constituted by consistent and resistant "material," namely by a stable structure and powerfully close even though geometrically variant.

The prospective adopted in the report of 2008 of the Anti-Mafia Parliament Commission, thus, appears paradoxical that, looking to surpass the reading of the 'Ndrangheta as an archaic phenomenon, proposes an interpretation in terms of a *postmodern* phenomenon, exactly like "liquid Mafia," able to infiltrate everywhere and to "coexist with unexpected efficiency a *tribal dimension* with an attitude modern and global" (Commissione Parlamentare Antimafia (CPA) 2008, p. 23, my italics).

Actually, just like the other types of Mafia, even the Calabrian one can be considered the product of a process of hybridization between modern and traditional elements, which have fostered its great capacity of adaptation and social variations. The supposed "primordial" 'Ndrangheta is difficult to reconcile with its success of the last decades, in particular with the capacity of territorial expansion and entrenchment, besides the integration into vast transnational illegal traffics.[3]

Recently, it was recognized as one of the most powerful criminal organizations. Today, it is repeated with persistence that the 'Ndrangheta has become the *most* dangerous Italian criminal organization, omitting the fact that for a very long time, its force was underestimated and that the contrast action against it was always insufficient. Its dangerousness also derives from this historical lack of attention, above all political and institutional.

---

[3] Regarding the diffusion of the 'Ndrangheta in nontraditional areas, namely where it was historically born, see Commissione Parlamentare Antimafia (CPA) (2008); Sciarrone (2009); Varese (2011); Dalla Chiesa and Panzarasa (2012); Sciarrone and Storti (2014).

In this article, I will focus my attention, in a selective way, on the organizational dimension of the 'Ndrangheta[4] considering in particular the hierarchic structure and reticular configuration, aspects that are often neglected or superficially analyzed in current studies of the phenomenon.

Family and Blood Connections

The *cosca* or *'ndrina* is the basic unit of the organizational structure of the 'Ndrangheta and corresponds to a Mafia family that takes the name of the boss. Within the *cosca*, a strict hierarchy is in force, established according to the reputation and criminal capacity of the single members. A normative and symbolic apparatus that regulate the entrance and the behavior of affiliates: Charters, formula of identification, codes, and initiation rites set a limit between those who belong to the organization and those who do not. The affiliation—defined by the same Mafiosi "baptism" (Ciconte 1992, p. 30)—offers the possibility to enter to an elective world and to have a disposal a formidable channel of social rise.

Speaking of the 'Ndrangheta, the thesis of "amoral familism" (Banfield 1958), endorsing for example that Mafia groups would have created a real "close family model" (Prefettura di Reggio Calabria 2006, p. 4) that will be diffused in Calabrian society. There is no document or publication regarding the 'Ndrangheta that does not reiterate this aspect, assuming, however, as an obvious and self-evident. It is an aspect that is rarely contextualized from an empirical and analytic level: On one hand, it is not understood according to which elements Calabria should be more family-oriented than the other Southern regions; on the other hand, the social mechanisms that put in relations family connection with action and organizational models are not pinpointed. Thus, it is appropriate to pause on this argument, observing it from a wider perspective that takes into consideration the organizational and relational configuration of the Calabrian Mafia.

Undoubtedly, blood connections are very important: A *cosca* created from a family nucleus is developed, then, through arranged marriages that connect and absorb others.[5] This characteristic is not, however, found only in criminal organizations. For example, also the cohesion of the banking community of the City in London

---

[4] For a long time the organizational dimension of the Mafia—and in particular of the 'Ndrangheta—was considered less relevant, according to a perspective mainly "culturalist" shared also by notorious scholars (for example Arlacchi 1986) and by institutions. Among judges, it was supported, for example, that the 'Ndrangheta had "a primitive structure [...] based more on a familiar than organizational aspect" (Pinotti and Tescaroli 2008, pp. 297–298). On the distinction between culturalist and organizational paradigm in the Mafia phenomenon, see Sciarrone (2009, Chap. 1).

[5] In 'Ndrangheta families, the central figure is of the women that, for example, had often a fundamental role in matrimonial strategies finalized to create alliances between *cosche*. More in general, "Mafia women" as wives, cohabitants, sisters, and mothers are a material, symbolic, and affective support indispensable to honored men. See Siebert (1994, 1997); Fiandanca (2007); Ingrascì (2007); Gribaudi and Marmo (2010).

was based on high confidence and loyalty levels, guaranteed by the tendency to maintain in the family businesses, assuming relatives and marrying other bankers' families (Coleman 1990, p. 110).

In our case, it is important to underline that starting from the family network of the *cosche*, Calabrian Mafiosi forge relationships in every social milieu, looking for references especially in the politico-institutional arena. In this way, around the central nucleus of *cosca*, an extensive and pervasive network of collusion and complicity is structured that allows the accumulation and reproduction of social capital, namely the ensemble of relational resources that represent one of the most important strengths of this criminal organization.[6]

The solidity and cohesion of the Calabrian groups do not only depend on family connections. The significance of these last ones are often attributed to the hypothetical archaic and tribal character of the 'Ndrangheta, while it would probably be read as an effect of the modernization process that created profound transformations in its original structure.[7] The presence of family connections does not impede, furthermore, the explosion of violent conflicts: Often the *cosche*, even those extremely cemented by blood ties, "broke" more for internal disagreement than to conflicts with other criminal groups.[8]

In the same way, nonetheless, a largely diffused opinion, pervading family ties are not the only variable to call into question to explain the limited number of collaborator of justice coming from the Calabrian Mafia. Even in this case, the analysis would be complicated: Instead of re-proposing the same images of the supposed impenetrability of the Calabrian Mafia,[9] it is necessary to understand which are the

---

[6] Social capital is understood here with reference to theoretical perspectives that consider it as the kind of resource available to an actor on the basis of its position in networks of social relations (See Bourdieu 1986; Coleman 1990). In this context, Mafiosi can be seen as specialists in social relations, characterized by a high level of social capital that are derived from relationships established with other actors. From this depends their ability to network, namely the ability to act, depending on the circumstances, as mediators, patrons, and/or protectors in relational structures of a different nature. It might be argued that the strength of the Mafia largely depends on this ability to accumulate and use social capital, but also to establish "external relations" and to rely on a wide and varied "reservoir" of relational resources can be used for different purposes. For the social capital of the Mafia, see Sciarrone (2006a, 2009, 2010, 2011).

[7] A hypothesis of this type seems to be advanced by John Dickie (2011), according to which the organizational model of the 'Ndrangheta has emphasized, over time, his familiar character especially to meet the requirements to make it more cohesive and more impenetrable to the repressive action. As was noted: "Future research should explore when and why organization of the 'Ndrangheta came to be based mainly on blood-related family units, as now seems to be the case" (Truzzolillo 2011, p. 372). In the first judicial documents available, the Calabrian organized group does not seem to rest on *'ndrine* based strictly on family, although it is plausible to assume that the family constitutes the most important recruitment channel.

[8] An emblematic case is that relating to the *cosca* of Piromalli-Molè, one of the most powerful of the 'Ndrangheta (Sciarrone 2010), whose cohesion failed despite strong blood connections (Tribunale di Reggio Calabria 2008).

[9] The dominant theory is that in the 'Ndrangheta, there would be a smaller number of collaborators of justice because of the importance of blood ties: *Repentance* would in fact be discouraged because, first of all, they should accuse their families. They forget, however, that this same constraint

mechanisms and the circumstances that might have favored or not the possibility of collaborating with law enforcement.[10] Definitely, family ties are certainly relevant, but it is also necessary to take into account the organizational structure and the relational system that configure relations within the *cosca* as well as between them.

To pursue the matter it could be useful to make a comparison between the Sicilian and Calabrian Mafia.[11] First of all, we must observe that, in both organizations, the Mafia "families" are distinguished from the biological families of their members. In Cosa Nostra, the Mafia family corresponds in a modest amount to the blood family. This, however, does not mean that blood ties are not important; indeed the parental tie between honored men "is certainly one of the most important elements of the organization" (Dino 2002, p. 73).

As in the 'Ndrangheta, in Cosa Nostra, blood ties, likewise, have weight in determining the power position, so that in some Mafia families, the power positions are transmitted from father to son in virtue of a sort of hereditary charisma (Paoli 2002, p. 45). This explains, moreover, how it is possible to find over time the same organogram of Mafia groups in power in areas of traditional settlement (Lupo 2009; Coco 2013). However, it is interesting to observe how Sicilian Mafiosi have tried to institute a rule to limit the relevance of blood ties, in order to make Mafia power less familiar and personalized.

During mid 1970s, the institution of the *Commissione*, namely the top legal entity of the Sicilian Cosa Nostra,[12] in fact also had as an objective to avoid that the power would convey in an excessive manner in blood families. As it is well-known, an association can be formalized precisely to reduce the impact of family

---

is also present in other Mafias. As noted by Pignatone and Prestipino (2012, pp. 135 +), two judges involved in the first line in the most important investigations against the 'Ndrangheta in recent years, also Sicilian collaborators of justice had to accuse their families. On the other hand, it does not seem that the 'Ndrangheta is talking about less than in other Mafias: "The 'ndranghetisti are not so silent: They talk, and how they talk!" (Pignatone and Prestipino 2012, p. 139). The explanation for the lower number of Calabrian collaborators of justice must be sought elsewhere. For example, in the fact that in Calabria has long been a privileged investigative practices that pointed to "confident" (namely on informally information provided to the police and not according to the criteria laid down by the law on collaborators of justice). By doing so, the two judges continued, it has overlooked the fact that "the collaborator must be sought, built, and followed" (Pignatone and Prestipino 2012, p. 139) and, therefore, "it was necessary to create the conditions so potential collaborators of justice could decide to speak with the judicial authorities" (Pignatone and Prestipino, 2012, p. 137).

[10] For a more profound analysis of these aspects—in particular regarding the organizational and relational nature—that impede the exit of the 'Ndrangheta and, thus, the collaboration with judiciary authorities, see Sciarrone (2006b, p. 6).

[11] For a comparative analysis of these two Mafia, see Paoli (2000).

[12] The *Commissione* is a collegiate entity on regional basis (called also Region), comprised by representatives of Cosa Nostra of the different "provincial commissions." Among the latter one, Palermo has always been in predominant positions. The "province" is in turn made up of representatives of the *mandamenti* that refer to more families territorially contiguous. From what we know, this organizational structure was created at the beginning of the 1950s, changing the model adopted by the American Cosa Nostra, but it was temporarily dissolved in 1960. It was later rebuilt in the mid 1970s (See Paoli, 2000; Dino 2002; Lupo 2009).

relationships when they are no longer a limit and a resource for its operation. This seems to be the case for the Cosa Nostra, as demonstrated by the attempt to give the organization a higher level of formality and to develop a regulatory system partially released from the importance of family relationships.

On the other side, in the Calabrian Mafia, it does not seem that blood ties were a commitment for the amplification of the organization, and neither can it be said that their importance is inversely proportional to the introduction of ritual and formal elements.

Inside the 'Ndrangheta, a distinction also exists, at least on a normative level, between the blood and the Mafia family. The organization of an 'Ndrangheta group is not completely overlaid to the structure of the biological family of their counterparts (Paoli 2000, p. 49). As collaborator of justice, Zagari has stated, the affiliation of a new member could be neither promoted nor completed by people connected to the initiated by parental ties (1992, p 36). This rule is not, however, enough to limit the relevance of blood ties, so that, from birth, the sons of Mafia bosses are considered by right *giovani d'onore* (honored youth). As declared by another collaborator of justice: "One can become an 'ndranghetista for family heritance" (Tribunale di Reggio Calabria 1995, p. 233).

Summarizing, even if in both criminal organizations, the equivalence between the blood and Mafia families cannot be deceptive, the fact remains that in the 'Ndrangheta, the command positions are determined in large measure by family relations and often the power tends to be transmitted though heredity, not necessarily from father to son, but to family members that have demonstrated the capacity to inherit.

The pervading of family ties constitute, thus, a controlling cohesive power for the *cosche* of the 'Ndrangheta. However, it would be reductive to think that the force of the latter is summarized in this element. Blood ties create only one aspect of its complex configuration. The organizational system is anything but close and bent on itself: Rather, it shows an adaptability grade, so that it was imitated by other criminal groups,[13] and is characterized by the presence of a wide range of external relations, in particular with exponents of the bureaucratic-institutional apparatus and the entrepreneurial world.[14]

---

[13] Raffaele Cutolo, one of the most important Neapolitan Camorra bosses, had been "baptized" in the 1970s by some prestigious leaders of the 'Ndrangheta and formed the Nuova Camorra Organizzata (New Organized Camorra), taking as a model several characters of the Calabrian Mafia. It also established the role of the 'Ndrangheta in the genesis of the Sacra Corona Unita (United Sacred Crown) in Apulia, a criminal organization developed in the early 1980s, which has imitated and borrowed organizational models and symbolic apparatus right from the Calabrian Mafia (Massari 1998; Sciarrone 2009).

[14] As evident by numerous legal proceedings, in Calabria, there is a strong blend of business committees and Mafia groups at the institutional, political, and business level, especially with reference to the management of public funds (Commissione Parlamentare Antimafia (CPA) 2008). To remember then that large companies operating in the region often tend to agree closely with the Mafia groups, establishing with them a mutually beneficial exchange. In many cases, the same entrepreneurs research and solicit a pact of collusion (Sciarrone 2009, 2010, 2011).

The Organizational Configuration

Attention will be focused on the organizational dimension. In general, we will talk about a horizontal character of the 'Ndrangheta, counterpointing it to the vertical organization of Cosa Nostra. Analyzing the problem from a dichotomy point of view is deceiving. The question does not only involve the 'Ndrangheta, but all Mafia organizations characterized by a peculiar combination of closure toward the internal and maximum opening toward the external. Closure guarantees internal cohesion, making the group less exposed to enemies' pressure and contrastive actions. The opening, on the contrary, is important because it makes extremely flexible and adaptable criminal groups toward the external, allowing the reproduction of their social networks, as well as facilitating extensions and diversification of their fields of activity. We are not dealing with a faction folded back on themselves, nor structures assimilated to the classical bureaucracy model; but a reticular organizational asset that tries to conciliate—in various forms—internal closure and external opening. Historically, all Mafia groups were crossed by opposite trends between centralization and autonomy together with dispersion. In this perspective, we can read some specific dynamics that affect the 'Ndrangheta.

Since relatively recent times, we did not have any information regarding the existence within the 'Ndrangheta of a superordinate body to the various *cosche*, even if in the past, temporary alliances emerged to manage common business matters. In reality, the presence of forms of territorial coordination seems to be a long-lasting characteristic of the 'Ndrangheta (Nicaso 1990; Mannino 1997; Gratteri and Nicaso 2006).[15] Only in the last years, however, important judiciary investigations, held not only in Calabria, but also in other northern regions (in particular Lombardy, Piedmont and Liguria),[16] have shed light on how the main *cosche* of the 'Ndrangheta—especially those that refer to the province of Reggio Calabria—are connected through a governing and regulating entity for internal conflicts, superior to all individual families.

Also in this situation, one must analyze the structure of the 'Ndrangheta, regarding comparison with some aspect of organizational model of Cosa Nostra. The vertical and hierarchic dimension of the latter is functional to guarantee a greater cohesion from an inter-organizational point of view: It is manifested in particular in the regulation of relationships between different Mafiosi groups. Within a single

---

[15] Organic connections between *cosche* are documented in several judicial investigations since the mid nineteenth century and the beginning of the twentieth century (Mannino 1997, pp. 284 +; Truzzolillo 2011, pp. 371–2) in which are described associative structure in some aspects very similar to those emerged in recent investigations.

[16] Tribunale di Reggio Calabria (2010); Tribunale di Milano (2010); Tribunale di Torino (2011); Tribunale di Genova (2011). These judiciary documents, together with others of previous periods (in particular, Tribunale di Reggio Calabria 1995) constitute the empiric base used in the proposed analysis. The more recent judiciary operations have highlighted the "unitary" character of the 'Ndrangheta, proposing a different vision from the past, in which it was supported on the contrary the existence of a "fragmented" or "fractionated" model of the Calabrian organizations (see Direzione Nazionale Antimafia 2012, pp. 91 +; Pignatone and Prestipino 2012).

family, the organizational structure might appear simpler compared to those found in higher levels: There is a command top, but the power positions formalized in specific roles are relatively few.[17] Individual Sicilian families, thus, do not represent an elevated internal difference; in some cases, an honored man might benefit from a more prestigious status compared to the formal role covered, in virtue of his capacities demonstrated in the field, as for example the ability to exercise violence or to do business. By contrast, in Cosa Nostra, a more complex inter-organizational structure might be observed with a different hierarchy position to coordinate and control the organization on the whole.[18] Control positions within the family settled in a given area are, therefore, directed at ensuring the functioning of the supra-territorial hierarchical level, with coordination and control entities with which they try to give a unified strategic direction to all groups recognized in Cosa Nostra.

Very different is the organization of the 'Ndrangheta where it is revealed a horizontal structure from an inter-organizational point of view,[19] from which basically all *cosche* are at the same level (even if, in fact, some are more powerful than others due to the size of their military, economic, and political capacities and resources).

In the 'Ndrangheta is highlighted, however, at the level of a single *cosca*, a more accentuated internal stratification, a more defined and articulated hierarchy. The career of an honored man has different possibilities to achieve diverse ranks that correspond to specific positions in the hierarchy and internal scale of the *cosca*. The rank fulfilled by an individual is formally recognized by all affiliates of the different groups of the 'Ndrangheta, but actually the exercise of power and the influence associated with a determined role find full legitimation only inside the belonging *cosca*. In other words, only the bosses of the *cosche* are able to exercise superior power, whereas the other command roles are important within the group and sign the progression of the career of the affiliates. This organizational structure—more vertical on the inside and more horizontal on the outside—guarantees in the 'Ndrangheta a more intra-organizational cohesion that is reinforced by a rigid compartment between affiliates that fulfill different ranks.[20]

---

[17] Schematizing and resuming the description provided by one of the most important collaborators of justice of Cosa Nostra, Antonio Calderone, at the base, there are honored man, called also *soldiers* structured in organized group led by a *capo decina*, whereas at the top, there is *capo famiglia* also called *rappresentante* that can be supported by a *vice rappresentante* and one or more *consiglieri* (Arlacchi 1993; Paoli 2000).

[18] Think, for example, of *mandamenti* or *commission*. See note 12.

[19] As collaborator of justice Antonio Zagari has explained: "Each *cosca* is independent from another and is controlled by *capi società* who have the faculty and the power to act autonomously from boss of other cosche even if from a superior rank. This is subject to the rule of respecting each other's territorial boundaries and always remaining one to the other for more general interests of the entire organization, which although divided into many cells still refers to a single basic regulation" (Tribunale of Reggio Calabria 1995, p. 374). Ultimately, each group works formally equal with all others, acting independently in their own territory or in areas of origin and in those of the new expansion (Direzione Nazionale Antimafia 2012, p. 93).

[20] Antonio Zagari has pointed out: "It is not always easy to know ranks and special rules of affiliates of the 'Ndrangheta, especially if those occupy positions and high levels of the organization

The Structure of the Locale

When a group of the 'Ndrangheta extends itself beyond the intimate family unit or when on the same territory there are more *cosche*, affiliates tend to coordinate themselves by adopting a specific structure known as a *locale* in the jargon of the honored men. To a *locale*—that takes the name of the municipality or the area where it refers—a limited number of affiliates should formally belong,[21] but actually the composition can vary and might change according to the situation. This results in the *locale* being fundamentally "authorized" and recognized by other already existing *locali*, among which a primary symbolic role is coved by San Luca, also called the "mother" of the 'Ndrangheta.[22]

The organization of a *locale* expects an articulated structure and with inter-independence among the ranks and command positions. On one side, there are ranks or endowments that establish the hierarchy between affiliates; on the other, the ranks are fulfilled within each structure.[23] Even with some variations throughout time or with a difference from one case to the other,[24] the internal stratification has the following ranks: *Giovane d'onore* (honored youth), *picciotto* (young boy), *camorrista*, *sgarrista*, *santista*, *vangelo* (gospel), *quartino*, *trequartino*, *quintino* or *padrino* (godfather), and *associazione* (association) or *società* (society).[25] On the contrary, regarding the highest ranks, there are *capobastone* or *capo locale* (local boss) and eventually *capo società* (boss of the society), following the roles of *contabile* (account), *crimine* (crime), and *mastro di giornata* (master of the day).

The organizational structure is articulated in two levels: One inferior called *società minore*, and the other one superior named *società maggiore*. Young men

---

because the rule wants that people from a high level are not required to disclose their rank to lower levels. Indeed, affiliates of lower levels are strictly prohibited from addressing questions regarding the hierarchy positions of superiors and elders" (Tribunale di Reggio Calabria 1995, p. 375).

[21] Some collaborators of justice have indicated that 49 or 50 is the minimum amount of members necessary to create a *locale*. It is a rough indication because judiciary investigations have shown the existence of *locali* comprised with an inferior number of members.

[22] It is the *locale* that refers to the village of San Luca, a small municipality in the hinterland of Calabria. The honored man's tradition appoint a high symbolic value, considering it like a sort of originating nucleus of the 'Ndrangheta. See Ciconte (1992); Gratteri and Nicaso (2006); Tribunale di Reggio Calabria (2010).

[23] *Doti* (endowments) are appointed with criminal capacities of affiliates and, thus, they represent a value of merit. To have a determined role, a person needs to have gained a certain *dote*, namely have reached a certain rank inside the hierarchical stratification of the organization.

[24] The sources we are referring to are the declarations of several collaborators of justice (Tribunale di Reggio Calabria 1995) and the reconstructions by investigators based on wiretappings and environmental interceptions (Regione Carabinieri "Lombardia" 2008; Tribunale di Reggio Calabria 2010; Tribunale di Milano 2010; Tribunale di Torino 2011).

[25] Each rank can have additional differentiations: For example, *picciotto* (young boy) might be distinguished by the *picciotto liscio* and *picciotto sgarrista* titles achieved after a certain period of Mafia internship; while *camorrista* might have the following rank of *camorista di sgarro* or *sgarrista*, but he could have the additional rank of *sgarrista di fibbia* and *camorrista formato*. Therefore, the creation of new ranks gradually creates a differentiation and an increment of hierarchical levels.

belonging to the subgroup of *società minore* to whose top it is possible to find the roles of *capo giovane* (young boss), *picciotto di giornata* (daily young boy), and *puntaiolo*. In the *società maggiore*, on the contrary, it is possible to find a rank superior to *sgarrista* or *camorrista di sgarro*. In the course of time, the internal organization of the *società maggiore* have introduced new ranks: Thus, to the top positions were added already cited ranks of *santista*, *vangelo* (gospel), *quartino*, *trequartino*, *quintino* or *padrino*, and *associazione* or *società*. This last one "is a special rank reserved to superior bosses" (Tribunale di Reggio Calabria 1995, p. 372). These new ranks are, in fact, given to those who have access to the top structure created in the 1970s and called *Santa*. It is an organizational level that is hidden to inferior level affiliates and to which, originally, only important boss can access. At the beginning, the ranks of *santista* could be given to only 33 people, but later, there was a certain oversaturation in the attribution of this title and, therefore, it was deemed appropriate to establish new higher-level ranks. This decision was dictated by the need, on one hand, to facilitate the relationships between the most powerful bosses in the management of the business, and on the other hand, especially, to foster relations with external parties. Just to increase this type of relationship, the *santisti* were given the opportunity to join the deviated freemasonry (Sergi 1991; Ciconte 1996; Mannino 1997; Guarino 2004). The latter was in fact for the 'Ndrangheta, more than for other Mafia organizations, the place of meeting and connecting with members of the institutions, politics, the bureaucratic apparatus, the business world, and freelance professionals (Commissione Parlamentare Antimafia (CPA) 2000, 2008).[26]

Collaborator of justice Giuseppe Albanese has declared that:

A *santista*, in order to save the organization, could even betray one hundred *camorristi* or *sgarristi*. There were even examples of this revolutionary principle and even became customary tip-offs to the police with real denunciations by *santisti* (Tribunale di Reggio Calabria 1995, p. 6602).

The creation of the *Santa* testifies, among other things, how within the 'Ndrangheta there is periodically a proliferation of ranks and hierarchy levels. This strategy, besides answering the need to affiliate new members, is able to guarantee another important need: Reinforcing the loyalty of associates and cement the cohesion of the group.

The organizational configuration that results, therefore, confirmed as the tendency to structure the relationship between the *cosche* at a horizontal level is compensated by the tendency to strengthen the vertical character of each *locale*, differentiating roles and leadership positions. This, on one hand, reduces the autonomy of individual members, but on the other hand offers the same incentives to abide by the rules of the organization. Loyalty, along with the ability to drive action

---

[26] The relationship with deviated freemasonry was also important for Cosa Nostra. There are, however, some differences between the two Mafia organizations: "While for Cosa Nostra the pact [with the freemasonry] never represented an influence to its power, for the 'Ndrangheta the alliance went beyond a mere utilitarian relationship that represents the essential characteristics through which it has obtained the current supremacy and diffusion" (Commissione Parlamentare Antimafia (CPA) 2000, p. 128).

demonstrated in the field, can be rewarded by the opportunity to advance in the hierarchy. In other words, the high internal differentiation of roles and positions is useful to the career progression of the affiliates; their loyalty and their commitment can be constantly rewarded by the opportunity to achieve a higher rank within the *cosca*. Career opportunities strengthen the ties of belonging and increase the degree of loyalty and cohesion of the affiliates of the organization.

Rules and Symbols

The perspective of the analysis conducted also suggested focusing on the aspect regarding the rules, which are the base of the framework of criminal organizations. More recent investigations have provided a rich picture of information compared to the "constitution"[27] of the 'Ndrangheta from a formal point of view. For this purpose, it is important to ask how these rules are actually binding, and in particular, in what measure their normative cogency is more or less diversified compared to other roles and to the specific people that fulfill that position. As it is notorious, a hypertrophic normative structure—which seems to characterize the 'Ndrangheta—leaves a lot of room for power games. The latter is not held only by those who know more than others to enforce the rules, but especially by those who can control areas of uncertainty that are created between statement of the rules and their practical application (Crozier and Friedberg 1977).

Another important area to analyze pertains to symbolic dimension.[28] Inside the 'Ndrangheta, there is a vast catalogue of symbols and cultural codes, which is the result of a constant process of "invention of the tradition" (Hobsbawn and Ranger 1983). On the other side, Mafiosi are always identified for their capacity to manipulate and instrumentalize traditional values with the objective to obtain consensus and legitimacy.

Rules, symbols, and cultural codes are then strictly tied to practice and behavior, thus to the concrete function of the organization. It is here where the issue of family ties lies. In general, one may argue that the degree of rituals tends to increase when an association extends beyond the family relationship. If an organization is based only on blood ties, it does not need to be formalized on a ritual level. It is a very important aspect of the 'Ndrangheta: In fact, if anything it is due to the family, as has been repeated for some time, it is not understood why it would require specific mechanisms (such as the rites of affiliation) to make "solemn" the bond of membership or organizational structures articulated in so many hierarchical levels.

---

[27] Regarding the relevance and the function of the "constitution" for the criminal organization, see Leeson and Skarbek (2010).

[28] For example, initiation rites that still today represent the entrance into the Mafia organization, more than a tradition heritage, fulfilling important symbolic functions. Like all boundaries, they divide and unify at the same time: They create barriers, but also connections. For 'Ndrangheta's rituals, see Malafarina (1986); Ciconte (1992); Paoli (2000), Gratteri and Nicaso (2006); Tribunale di Reggio Calabria (2010).

It is true that a criminal organization might be formalized even to redistribute the weight of family relations. It is a concern that emerges periodically as part of some 'Ndrangheta groups, against the resistance of others who want to preserve a greater margin of autonomy and action.

Coordination Among Locali

It is now important to bring into focus the operation of the inter-organizational level trying to understand how it was historically configured, how it changed throughout time, and what its peculiarities are.

During the mid 1980s, a bloody fight between *cosche* in the area of Reggio Calabria caused hundreds of deaths. The Mafia war suddenly finished in 1991 and, according to the declarations of some collaborators of justice, that happened thanks to the intervention of some members of Cosa Nostra and 'ndranghetisti located in Canada. From this moment, they began to talk about a new united entity of the *'ndrine*, a sort of Calabrian "commission" similar to the Sicilian model. It seems, however, more of a coordination structure between groups that does not crush the traditional organizational structure, but on the contrary, it proposes to put in relations the networks of the single Mafiosi with those of the *cosche* and the different *locali*.

The existence of a superior entity was revealed with more evidence in recent years via judiciary investigation (Tribunale di Reggio Calabria 2010, 2012; Tribunale di Milano 2010). As a result, the main *cosche* of the province of Reggio Calabria became connected through territorial structures called *mandamenti*[29] that gather the Ionic, Tyrrhenian, and the urban area of Reggio Calabria's *locali* (Direzione Nazionale Antimafia 2012). These three *mandamenti* express an additional superior entity that coordinates, called *Crimine* or *Provincia* that is overseen by an elected member of different representatives of *locali* for a defined period. This role of *capo-crimine*[30] is not assimilated to that of "capo dei capi" (as it has usually been simplified in journalistic reports), but a figure that has mainly symbolic and delegations' roles.[31] The same affiliates represent those who fulfill this position as a depositary and guarantor of rules and tradition of the 'Ndrangheta.

---

[29] As it is evident, the term is taken from that used in the Sicilian Mafia, see note 12.

[30] To which the same affiliates often refer simply using the term *Crimine*, identifying the role with the representative body. As anti-Mafia magistrates explain, this body plays "a decisive role in its organization, primarily through the protection of the basic rules of the organization (a sort of criminal 'Constitution'), those, in short, that characterize the 'Ndrangheta as such and ensure its recognition over time and space, even far away from the motherland of Calabria; thus ensuring the maintenance of general balance, the control of the appointment of the heads of locali and openings of other venues, the authorization for the transfer of charges, the resolution of any disputes, the submission to the judgment of any wrongdoing in place by persons inside the 'Ndrangheta." (Direzione Nazionale Antimafia 2012, p. 96).

[31] It is a role of *primus inter pares*, (Direzione Nazionale Antimafia 2012, p. 94) which in fact collaborators of justice had already addressed. For example, Giacomo Lauro said that in the 1960s, Antonio Macrì of Siderno was the *capo-crimine*: "Represented the crimine, namely he represented

We are, thus, not in the presence of a strictly vertical and pyramidal structure, but to a model that tries to put in contact and to reciprocate identification among different criminal groups active in different territorial areas.[32] The same model is also reproduced by *cosche* that operate outside Calabria: In some regions of the North Italy, as Lombardy, Piedmont, and Liguria is possible to find the same organizational structure in *locali*, internally distinguished into *società maggiore* and *società minore*, and the attempt of inter-organizational coordination. In particular, in Lombardy, it results the creation of a regional entity called indeed "La Lombardia" with the goal of putting in connection the different *locali* active in the territory. There is also news of a "camera di controllo" (control chamber) created in Liguria and the attempt to create a similar entity in Piedmont.[33] It is important, however, to specify that both *locali* and the superior coordination structures need to obtain "recognition" from the top of the most important 'Ndrangheta *locali* settled in Calabria. In this sense, they need to accept to be under the control of the Calabrian *Crimine*.[34]

From the information available, a network configuration seems to be emerging that, from one side, lower the level of conflict and, from the other side, maximize the social capital of the more consolidated criminal organization. It is an organizational innovation, which makes up a flexible coordination structure, which ensures the consultation for the most important decisions, without compromising the compartmentalization and the autonomy of each group.

---

the whole 'Ndrangheta in the province of Reggio Calabria" (Tribunale di Reggio Calabria 1995, p. 288; See also Ciconte 1996, p. 40+; Mannino 1997, pp. 419, 436, note 84). From what we know, the role of *capo-crimine* has long been covered with boss of the clans of the Ionian side of Calabria. The last judicial investigations show that it was awarded to a member of the clans of the Tyrrhenian coast, preferring, however, an elderly, the octogenarian Domenico Oppedisano, that while boasting a long belonging to the 'Ndrangheta not seem to have behind a career criminal with a high thickness (Tribunale di Reggio Calabria 2010, 2012). As noted by investigators, his "appointment was a compromise between multiple instances of power" related to the historical groups of the 'Ndrangheta (Tribunale di Reggio Calabria 2012, p. 178). In other words, the Ionian *cosche* and as well as those from the city of Reggio accept that this charge is attributed to the Tyrrhenian area, but not to a "strong" man, but to one "wise" person because of its seniority, able to represent the above "tradition." This choice seems justified by the fact that he "looks man who groped mediations between aggressive criminal groups and, therefore, to avoid possible conflict" (Tribunale di Reggio Calabria 2012, p. 179; Pignatone and Prestipino 2012, pp. 6–7).

[32] "In reality, this structure has confirmed the dominance of the leading families of the respective areas, formally legitimizing a function that is exercised in practice in benchmarks for agreements, alliances, and pacification" (Regione Carabinieri "Lombardia" 2008, p. 262).

[33] According to investigators, similar structures would be present also in Australia and Canada. In all cases they are bodies that have a function of both internal coordination both of dialogue and interface with the "motherland" (Direzione Nazionale Antimafia 2012, p.94). For an analysis of the different modes of relationships between groups active in nontraditional areas and those rooted in Calabria, see Sciarrone and Storti (2014).

[34] For example, when the representative of Lombardy tries to become independent from the "motherland," claiming more autonomy compared to the Calabrian Crimine, he is killed (Tribunale di Milano 2010).

The 'Ndrangheta seems to have imitated Cosa Nostra to equip itself as a united organ of coordination, but paradoxically, at the same time, the Sicilian Mafiosi—to protect themselves from collaborators of justice and from more efficient repression strategies from the investigation apparatus—have revealed the tendency to reorganize themselves according to a model that is similar to the Calabrian one, segmenting families and groups in order to render the association more impenetrable.

Both Mafia organizations present a reticular configuration, but Cosa Nostra tends to structure itself more like a "organization network," while the 'Ndrangheta continues to maintain a character of a "network of organizations" with more differentiated knots and ties with variable intensity.[35]

A Pact-Based Organizational Model

Having an organizational structure is important for a group of people who wants to act in mutual agreement to reach specific goals. In this regard, it is possible to distinguish between organizations that are limited to only promoting the coordination of members' actions and others that will encourage the cooperation itself. In general terms, the coordination is easy to achieve, while the cooperation requires specific factors to be launched. As we have seen, in the case of the 'Ndrangheta, it has long been possible to recognize different elements that reveal the attempt to configure united coordinated structures, which, in turn, could encourage more concerted plans of action.[36]

The last judiciary investigations (Tribunale di Reggio Calabria 2010; Tribunale di Milano 2010) have shed light on the dynamics through which the 'Ndrangheta has tried to "institutionalize" an inter-organizational model. The formalization of roles and connections has the goal of creating a legitimate exercise of the power, recognized by members of the groups based on trust and loyalty obtained through positive and negative sanctions. It is an apparent attempt to depersonalize some positions of authority, formalizing more precisely some leadership roles to be set up through election. This process of "democratization", although more apparent than real, shows a commitment aimed at making power within the organization independent of specific forces or factions. It is in this way that it also tends to institutionalize the organization, as shared practices and cognitive schemes of reference are created, which serve to strengthen internal cohesion and solidarity.

---

[35] Regarding the distinction between "network of organizations" and "organization network," see Powell (1990); Podolny and Page (1998); Pichierri (2002).

[36] As we have seen, *cosche* of the 'Ndrangheta do not seem, however, to point to a primarily unitarian and centralized organizational structure, but tends to favor a model that, even preferring a certain level of cooperation, is able in particular to preserve and guarantee wise operational autonomy to each group.

This does not mean to eliminate all conflicts, nor does it ratify the claim of tyrannical domination. The recognition and consolidation of an organizational structure does not necessarily imply a situation of peace and a convergence of interests and objectives. In most cases, arenas instead constitute comparing individuals and groups competing—and often also in the fight—between them. The formation of a "dominant coalition," that is an oligarchical power structure, is thus favored.

From the findings in the last judicial investigations, the *Crimine* appears, above all, as an organization that seeks to play a role in ensuring inter-organizational levels, whereas its power seems much reduced to impose binding decisions at the collective level. The constitution of this entity is important anyway because it shows the attempt to structure interests, to coordinate initiatives, to influence alliances, and, above all, to create meanings socially shared. Certainly, decision-making mechanisms (the executive power) are important, but the symbolic functions and those of representation, particularly the guarantee functions, count even more. In any case, it is important that there is a formalized role—the *capocrimine*—which seems to have the task of acting as a guarantor of the unity of the 'Ndrangheta. The presence of elective and temporary positions is meaningful, together with the mechanism of territorial rotation of the top positions. More than in front of a "corporate" model of organized crime, a "corporative" model emerges, we could also say "consociation," which envisages a system of concertation (rather than a unified decision-making system) and especially shows the importance attributed to the functions of guarantee and recognition.

Conclusive Considerations

Like in other organizations, inside Mafia organizations, there is a complex articulation of positions and roles. For example, alongside activities that are managed and coordinated by the organization at different levels, other are conducted in autonomy by single affiliates who have different leeway and can act with a certain amount of independence in both legal and illegal markets. Furthermore, Mafiosi have an asset of external relations that often manage at a personal level, being careful not to share with others their social capital, so that it constitutes an exclusive advantage. Roles formalized inside the organization do not necessarily coincide with power positions effectively held. One may find a Mafioso who, while not occupying an important role in the criminal hierarchy of the association, is able to exert his influence and power by virtue of the relational resources at his disposal, namely the social capital that is derived for example from the fact to perform functions as intermediaries between social networks of different types. In Mafia organizations, it is possible to find a combination of variably "strong" and "weak"[37] connections. Strong con-

---

[37] As it is notorious, the distinction between strong ties and weak ties is due to Granovetter (1973, 1995).

nections are assimilated to family ties, whereas weak connections are more instrumental and less characterized on an effective level. For a Mafia group, as we said, formalizing the association can mean disempowering the strong connections. It is a process that cannot be pushed beyond a certain threshold: In fact, the attempt to de-personalize roles is mitigated by the recourse to a symbolic and ritual apparatus that are used anyway to strengthen connections of belonging. In the 'Ndrangheta, this is extremely evident if we think there is a proliferation of ranks, rules, and command positions. Reading these dynamics in terms of primitive or traditional elements is too reductive and misleading. In reality, the proliferation of positions and the modalities of assigning the same are functional in the delineation of possible "careers" inside the criminal organization. Moreover, this also happens in the legal organization when trying to reward the loyalty through the ability to stimulate and structure the internal career paths, or by distinctions and differences of roles, positions, and command structures.

The organizational structure that we have described additionally proves useful to that peculiar combination of business and power that characterize the Italian Mafia, and that is evident in the case of the 'Ndrangheta (Sciarrone 2010, 2011). It is in fact criminal organizations oriented not only to the accumulation of wealth, but also to the exercise of power. The presence of different organizational levels allows them to have together on one side the entrepreneur dimension through which Mafiosi seek economic objectives, and on the other side the dimension of "secret society" that characterize them as a group of power (that exercise territorial control through functions of protection and mediation in areas that are more or less confined).

This particular combination between business and power is reflected in the associated presence of strong and weak connections of the organizational configuration. As we said, strong connections are important because they are used to provide organizational and social cohesion, but this type of tie is not enough to guarantee the reproduction and extension of the criminal network. Mafiosi need also another type of "enlarged" social capital able to favor external connections. Hence the importance of weak ties, which are not to be understood as about to break, but as "loose" ties, namely elastic and flexible, such as those that underlie the relationship of complicity and collusion, the true strong point of the Mafia, in particular that of Calabria.

Ultimately, the high level of cohesion and compactness of the 'Ndrangheta not only depends on alleged archaic characters of an original cultural matrix, but also cannot be explained by the mere importance of family ties, which in any case are a powerful bond of association. It is rather necessary to keep in mind the multidimensionality of its organizational configuration, reticular type, and variable geometry, able to guarantee a valid combination of centralization and flexibility, together with an effective mix of strong and weak ties, or closing inward and opening outward.

References

Institutional and Judicial Documents

Commissione Parlamentare Antimafia (CPA). (2000). *Relazione sullo stato della lotta alla criminalità organizzata in Calabria, Doc. XXIII, n. 42, XIII legislatura.* Rome.

Commissione Parlamentare Antimafia (CPA). (2008). *Relazione annuale sulla 'Ndrangheta, Doc. XXIII, n. 5, XV legislatura.* Rome.

Direzione Nazionale Antimafia. (2008, Dec). *Relazione annuale sulle attività svolte dal Procuratore nazionale antimafia e dalla Direzione nazionale antimafia, nonché sulle dinamiche e strategie della criminalità organizzata di tipo mafioso nel periodo 1 luglio 2007–30 luglio 2008.* Rome.

Direzione Nazionale Antimafia. (2012, Dec). *Relazione annuale sulle attività svolte dal Procuratore nazionale antimafia e dalla Direzione nazionale antimafia, nonché sulle dinamiche e strategie della criminalità organizzata di tipo mafioso nel periodo 1 luglio 2011–30 giugno 2012.* Rome.

Prefettura di Reggio Calabria. (2006, Dec). *Lo spazio sicurezza, libertà e giustizia nella Regione Calabria, Conferenza Regionale delle Autorità di Polizia di Stato.* Reggio Calabria.

Regione Carabinieri "Lombardia". (2008). *Indagine "Infinito".* Gruppo di Monza, Nucleo Investigativo. Monza.

Tribunale di Genova. (2011). *Ordinanza applicativa di misura cautelare coercitiva nei confronti di Barilaro Fortunato più 18, Sezione dei giudici per le indagini preliminari.* Genoa.

Tribunale di Milano. (2010). *Ordinanza di applicazione di misura coercitiva nei confronti di Agostino Fabio più 159, Ufficio del Giudice per le indagini preliminari.* Milan.

Tribunale di Reggio Calabria. (1995). *Procedimento penale a carico di Condello Pasquale più 562, Procura della Repubblica, Direzione Distrettuale Antimafia.* Reggio Calabria.

Tribunale di Reggio Calabria. (2008). *Fermo di indiziati di delitto e sequestro preventivo in via d'urgenza nei confronti di Alvaro Giuseppe più 23, Procura della Repubblica, Direzione Distrettuale Antimafia.* Reggio Calabria.

Tribunale di Reggio Calabria. (2010). *Decreto di fermo di indiziato di delitto nei confronti di Agostino Anna Maria più 155, Procura della Repubblica, Direzione Distrettuale Antimafia.* Reggio Calabria.

Tribunale di Reggio Calabria. (2012). *Sentenza resa nell'Operazione "Crimine" nei confronti di Agnelli Giovanni più 126, Sezione Gip-Gup.* Reggio Calabria.

Tribunale di Torino. (2011). *Ordinanza di applicazione della misura cautelare della custodia in carcere nei confronti di Agostino Nicodemo più 190, Sezione dei giudici per le indagini preliminari.* Turin.

Books and Articles

Arlacchi, P. (1993). *Men of Dishonor: Inside The Sicilian Mafia: An account of Antonino Calderone.* New York: William Morrow.

Arlacchi, P. (1986). *Mafia business: The Mafia ethic and the spirit of capitalism.* London: Verso.

Banfield, E. (1958). *The moral basis of a backward society.* Glencoe: The Free Press.

Bauman, Z. (2002). *Liquid modernity.* Cambridge: Polity Press.

Becchi, A. (2000). *Criminalità organizzata. Paradigmi e scenari delle organizzazioni mafiose in Italia*. Rome: Donzelli.

Bourdieu, P. (1986). The forms of capital. In J. Richardson (Ed.), *Handbook of theory and research in the sociology of education*. New York: Greenwood Press.

Ciconte, E. (1992). *'Ndrangheta dall'Unità a oggi*. Bari-Rome: Laterza.

Ciconte, E. (1996). *Processo alla 'Ndrangheta*. Bari-Rome: Laterza.

Coco, V. (2013). *La mafia dei giardini. Storia delle cosche della Piana dei Colli*. Bari-Rome: Laterza.

Coleman, J. (1990). *Foundations of social theory*. Cambridge: Harvard University Press.

Crozier, M., & Friedberg, E. (1977). *L'acteur et le système*. Pais: Seuil.

Dalla Chiesa, N., & Panzarasa, M. (2012). *Buccinasco. La 'ndrangheta al Nord*. Turin: Einaudi.

Dickie, J. (2011). *Blood brotherhoods. The rise of the Italian Mafias*. London: Sceptre.

Dino, A. (2002). *Mutazioni. Etnografia del mondo di Cosa Nostra*. Palermo: La Zisa.

Fiandaca, G. (Ed.). (2007). *Women and the Mafia. Females roles in organized crime structures*. New York: Springer.

Granovetter, M. (1973). The strenght of weak ties. *America Journal of Sociology, 78*, 1360–1380.

Granovetter, M. (1995). *Getting a job: A study of contacts and careers*. Chicago: University of Chicago Press.

Gratteri, N., & Nicaso, A. (2006). *Fratelli di sangue. La 'ndrangheta tra arretratezza e modernità: da mafia agropastorale a holding del crimine*. Cosenza: Pellegrini.

Gribaudi, G., & Marmo, M. (Eds.). (2010). Donne di Mafia. *Meridiana, 67*, 9–173.

Guarino, M. (2004). *Poteri segreti e criminalità. L'intreccio inconfessabile tra 'ndrangheta, massoneria e apparati dello Stato*. Bari: Dedalo.

Hobsbawm, E. (1971). *Primitive rebels. Studies in archaic forms of social movements in 19th and 20th centuries*. Manchester: Manchester University Press.

Hobsbawn, E., & Ranger, T. (Eds.). (1983). *The invention of tradition*. Cambidge: Cambridge University Press.

Ingrascì, O. (2007). *Donne d'onore. Storie di mafie al femminile*. Milan: Bruno Mondadori.

Leeson, P., & Skarbek, D. (2010). Criminal constitutions. *Global Crime, 11*(3), 279–297.

Lupo, S. (2009). *History of the Mafia*. New York: Columbia University Press.

Malafarina, L. (1986). *La 'Ndrangheta. Il codice segreto, la storia, i miti, i personaggi*. Rome: Gangemi.

Mannino, S. (1997). Criminalità nuova in una società in trasformazione. Il Novecento e i tempi attuali. In A. Placanica (Ed.), *Storia della Calabria moderna e contemporanea. L'età presente* (pp. 369–439). Rome: Gangemi.

Massari, M. (1998). *La sacra corona unita. Potere e segreto*. Bari-Rome: Laterza.

Nicaso, A. (1990). *Alle origini della 'ndrangheta. La picciotteria*. Soveria Mannelli: Rubbettino.

Paoli, L. (2000). *Fratelli di mafia. Cosa Nostra e 'Ndrangheta*. Bologna: il Mulino.

Pichierri, A. (2002). *La regolazione dei sistemi locali. Attori, strategie, strutture*. Bologna: il Mulino.

Pignatone, G., & Prestipino, M. (2012). *Il contagio. Come la 'ndrangheta ha infettato l'Italia*. (Ed. Gaetano Savatteri). Bari-Rome: Laterza.

Pinotti, F., & Tescaroli, L. (2008). *Colletti sporchi*. Milan: Rizzoli.

Podolny, J., & Page, K. (1998). Network forms of organization. *Annual Reviews of Sociology, 24*(1), 57–76.

Powell, Wa. (1990). Neither market nor hierarchy. Network forms of organizations. In B. Staw & L. Cummings (Eds.), *Research in organizational behaviour*. Greenwich, CT: JAI Press (Vol. 12., pp. 295–336).

Sciarrone, R. (2006a). Mafia e potere: processi di legittimazione e costruzione del consenso. *Stato e mercato, 3*, 369–401.

Sciarrone, R. (2006b). Passaggio di frontiera: la difficile via di uscita dalla mafia calabrese. In A. Dino (Ed.), *Pentiti*. Rome: Donzelli.

Sciarrone, R. (2009). *Mafie vecchie, mafie nuove. Radicamento ed espansione*. Rome: Donzelli.

Sciarrone, R. (2010). Mafia and civil society: Economico-criminal collusion and territorial control in Calabria. In J. L. Briquet & G. Favarel-Garrigues, (Eds.), *Organized crime and states. The hidden face of politics*. New York: Palgrave Macmillan.

Sciarrone, R. (Ed.). (2011). *Alleanze nell'ombra. Mafie ed economie locali in Sicilia e nel Mezzogiorno*. Rome: Donzelli.

Sciarrone, R., & Storti, L. (2014, Aug 11). The territorial expansion of mafia-type organized crime. The case of the Italian mafia in Germany. *Crime, Law and Social Change*, 61. 37–60.

Sergi, P. (1991). *La 'Santa' violenta*. Cosenza: Periferia.

Siebert, R. (1994). *Le donne, la mafia*. Milan: Il Saggiatore.

Siebert, R. (1997). La mafia e le donne. In L. Violante (Ed.), *Mafia e società italiana. Rapporto '97*. Rome-Bari: Laterza.

Truzzolillo, F. (2011). The 'Ndrangheta: The current state of historical research. *Modern Italy, 16*(3), 363–383.

Varese, F. (2011). *Mafias on the move: How organized crime conquers new territories*. Princeton: Princeton University Press.

Violante, L. (1994). *Non è la piovra. Dodici tesi sulle mafie italiane*. Turin: Einaudi.

Zagari, A. (1992). *Ammazzare stanca. Autobiografia di uno 'ndranghetista pentito*. Cosenza: Periferia.

Chapter 7
The Sacra Corona Unita: Origins, Characteristics, and Strategies

Monica Massari

Origins and Evolution

Commonly defined as the "Fourth Mafia" and often considered on par with the other Mafia-type organizations traditionally rooted in the *Mezzogiorno* (Southern Italy)—the 'Ndrangheta, Camorra, and Cosa Nostra—the Sacra Corona Unita (SCU) is composed of a collection of criminal groups that began operating in Apulia between the late 1970s and early 1980s.[1] According to the founding charter of the SCU, discovered by investigators in the cell of the group's founding father, Pino Rogoli, this association was formally created in 1983 inside prison "to regulate and settle various issues arising between prisoners." In fact, the original process of organization was begun precisely in an attempt to contain the excessive power exercised inside the prisons as well as across the broader area of Apulia by certain Mafia-type organizations with more deeply rooted traditions—such as the Campanian *famiglie* (families) identified in the *Nuova Camorra Organizzata* led by Raffaele Cutolo. In the 1970s, prisons in Apulia recorded a growing presence of prisoners aligned with the Cutolo organization because of its ongoing conflict in Campania with the rival criminal organization associated with the *Nuova Famiglia* led by Michele Zaza, the Nuvoletta brothers, and Antonio Bardellino. According to statements from the leader of the Apulia-based association made before the judiciary in the early 1990s regarding the Cutolo organization:

> The whole world knows what they did, they felt, I don't know, like maybe they were strong, they felt they were like God Almighty, and in those prisons where they went [...] they wanted to do things, take advantage of the situation, and we didn't like that (Tribunale di Brindisi 1994, p. 183).

---

[1] The origin and meaning of the name "Sacra Corona Unita" are not clear, but apparently they derive from a ritual formula belonging to the 'Ndrangheta's cultural background. For further analysis of the birth and development of the Sacra Corona Unita, see Massari 1998, 2009.

M. Massari (✉)
Department of Political Sciences, University of Naples "Federico II", Va L. Rodinò, 22, 80138 Naples, Italy
e-mail: monica.massari@unina.it

N. Serenata (ed.), *The 'Ndrangheta and Sacra Corona Unita,* Studies of Organized Crime 12,   101
DOI 10.1007/978-3-319-04930-4_7, © Springer International Publishing Switzerland 2014

Furthermore, a considerable number of detainees were brought there from tradi-tional Mafia regions,[2] more than 200 individuals over a 10-year period (1961–1972) (Commissione Parlamentare Antimafia 1976, p. 289). After an initial period based on reciprocal non interference or at most a profitable exchange of favors, this pres-ence inevitably became more burdensome for the locals who found themselves in a subordinate position compared to the more influential criminal outsiders. At this point a plan was formulated that, in just a few years, would lead to founding an autonomous Mafia association that would extend its supremacy mainly into the provinces of Brindisi, Lecce, and Taranto, three cities in the southern part of Apulia.

The level of intolerance among local criminals against the rough methods used by Cutolo's Camorra to establish control over several areas of criminality in Apulia was, thus, at the origins of forming this association. But the crucial element that actually led to the establishment of this new criminal operation was the existence of close relationships of friendship and collaboration with several *'ndrine* (families) from the Calabrian 'Ndrangheta.[3] In any case, the presence of the 'Ndrangheta in the region had been a well-known fact for some time, since the moment Apulia became an attractive area from many aspects for any criminal association looking to expand its traffic into a context that was, on the whole, still unexplored. This con-text was, in fact, free from any intense law enforcement activities and unobstructed by any firmly established indigenous criminal presence with criteria for division of the territory. In addition, the profit potential was further increased by the special geographical position of Apulia, close to the ports of what was then Yugoslavia, a transit point for most of the traffic between the East and West, and tradition-ally linked to commercial relationships with Albania, Greece, and the Middle East. Therefore, the SCU was able, especially during the mid 1990s, to establish close ties with new partners operating just across the small span of sea separating the two coasts, and became the main Italian intermediary for exploiting the lucrative opportunities opened up by the Balkan conflict (Jamieson and Silj 1998, p. 22; Di-rezione Nazionale Antimafia (DNA) 2008, p. 803). One of the main activities of the SCU during this early phase was tobacco smuggling, subsequently joined by illegal gambling, drug trafficking, extortion, loan sharking, and robbery—all activities that until then had been handled in a disorganized and fragmented manner (Apollonio 2010, p. 75).

It was precisely the 'Ndrangheta that bestowed a sort of formal investiture on the *pugliesi* bosses to independently operate their various illegal activities (especially tobacco smuggling, drug trafficking, and extortion). This investiture was also for-mally recognized in the founding charter of the SCU, which carried the statement "The SCU was founded by G. R. on 1 May 1983 with help from *compari diritti*

---

[2] These individuals were considered linked to Mafia organizations and were therefore ordered to relocate to regions distant from their original areas for the purpose of severing existing ties with their clans. In reality, these preventative measures were soon not only shown to be completely ineffective but, over the course of time, also had numerous adverse effects.

[3] The 'Ndrangheta is divided into basic units called *'ndrine*, composed of one or more groups, deeply rooted on the local territorial level, whether a neighbourhood or a village. Each *'ndrina* largely relies on blood ties between members. The biological family almost always overlaps with the criminal family and represents the cornerstone of the *'ndrina*'s internal structure.

(rightful godfathers)" (Raggruppamento Operativo Speciale Carabinieri 1993, p. 10), specifically to emphasize the role played by certain *capibastone* from the 'Ndrangheta in founding the Apulia-based association.[4] These relationships would continue to remain so constant over time that many outstanding individuals from the SCU were initiated—*battezzati* (baptized) in the language of the 'Ndrangheta—by the Calabrian clans. Given the detention of the leader of the Apulia-based association—in prison since 1981 because of a long sentence for homicide—one of the most important tasks, that is the power of deciding the promotion of members from one level to the next in the internal hierarchical structure, was carried out specifically by the Calabrians.

In this regard, as will be discussed further in the following pages, it is interesting to note right away the many analogies on the symbolic-ritual level between these two organizations. The SCU actually received much of its *cultural* legacy from the 'Ndrangheta, assimilating rules, ceremonies, and the wording of oaths, as well as structural characteristics. Prison represented the context where a cultural legacy from a different origin was learned and absorbed, a legacy that was later reworked by the Apulia-based association with an approach aimed at favoring a sort of cultural syncretism.

Although the existence of the SCU as a Mafia association was only recognized in a courtroom in May 1991, its period of greatest expansion actually occurred during the 1980s and early 1990s. This was the phase when the Apulia-based consortium experienced some ups and downs—with arrests, trials, and defections—which would cause it to implement a strategy of violent conflict against the State and other criminal organizations operating on the local criminal landscape. This phase would culminate in an actual *rifondazione*, or rebirth, of the association currently called the *Nuova* (New) *Sacra Corona Unita*.

Characterized by a ruthless recourse to violence, a low level of internal cohesion, a utilitarian orientation inclined to unrestrained competition, and a tendency toward conspicuous consumption and wealth, rather than a strengthening of the internal power structures of the organization, the SCU has undergone an intense judicial counteroffensive over the past few years. Currently, the still dominant Salento *famiglie* (families) seem to have opted for a strategy of low visibility, and the association has also shown renewed interest in criminal opportunities available on the other side of the Adriatic—in Albania, Montenegro, and other Balkan countries—in trafficking drugs and weapons, as well as more traditional activities such as robbery and extortion.

The Ritual and Symbolic Apparatus

From an *external* point of view, it appears evident that the SCU—like other traditional Mafia organizations—adopted the structural arrangement typical of secret societies as an organizational system of reference. In this, we find a general orga-

---

[4] *Capobastone* is the highest rank a 'Ndrangheta affiliate can achieve after having moved up through the internal hierarchy.

nizational blueprint composed of the existence of a more or less developed ritual-symbolic legacy, formalized mechanisms for selecting and recruiting members, and an internal hierarchy that envisages different levels of power. From a sociological standpoint, the secret society is characterized by the fact that it constitutes a *voluntary* formation—from the moment of its creation when there is a clear constitutional charter—and at the same time a *secondary* formation, considering it is created within a greater society already formed differently.[5] The secret constitutes the visible sign of the boundary, the barrier every secret society attempts to erect toward the outside, a different world from which it wishes to distinguish itself, but of which it must still be a part. "We all felt like we were part of a special elite," recalled Tommaso Buscetta about his years of service in Cosa Nostra (Arlacchi 1994, p. 70), confirming the widespread sensation of separateness and, at the same time, superiority caused by admission into a Mafia brotherhood. This psychological dimension frequently facilitates psychological distance from a broader social context, which becomes at times perceived as blurry and detached, no longer having any significance. Evidence suggesting this sense of *distinction* with respect to the surrounding society can be found to some extent in all traditional Mafia associations (Arlacchi 1992, 1994).

Obviously, a group that decides to conceal one of the inspirational principles for its activities must constantly deal with strategies of dissimulation and the dangers of disclosure. The duty to maintain total secrecy regarding the existence of the association, as well as its activities and members, is absolute. Quite frequently, the survival itself of the association depends precisely on this ability to successfully manage this secrecy, intended as both an instrument of protection against the outside, as well as a means of safeguarding the pursuit of the group's established objectives. The secret always has the danger of betrayal as a counterpart; the temptation to break the barrier erected between men by silence is always present, precisely because it is connected to a psychological dimension of constant tension between those energies that resist and energies that reveal potential temptations for yielding. The historical dimension of the secret society tends to create within itself, through a strict formulation of rules, methods of behavior, and unchanging rituals, inevitably clashes with the broader social context. But the secret society must draw models for its institutions and resources precisely from this context; and this entails an endless process of adaptation, especially in criminal groups (Lau Fong 1981, p. 14).

In the SCU, just as in other traditional Mafia associations, the moment of initiation coincides with a *new* dimension of belonging, but the process of acquiring a strong, stable identity never seems to end. The complex symbolic architecture that underpins this organization emerges clearly from the many ceremonies envisaged inside the organization for passage from one rank to the next. With initiation, the member advances along a particularly elaborate path, which seems to draw its origins—as we have mentioned previously—from the oldest 'Ndrangheta traditions.[6]

---

[5] This refers to principal sources from socioanthropological literature on secret societies: Simmel 1989; Davis 1971; Hutin 1955; Lau Fong 1981; MacKenzie 1968.

[6] Regarding the ways the SCU came into contact with the environment of the 'Ndrangheta, and began borrowing codes, statues, and rituals, see Massari 1998.

The process of assimilation regarding criminal operations arriving from other areas, and the special influence exercised by Calabrian cultural and symbolic legacy appear particularly evident in ceremonies for promoting a member to the highest levels in the organization. Every *dote* (endowment)[7] is characterized by its own symbolic elements, despite the substantial homogeneity in the organization of the various phases of the ritual. All the ranks in the internal hierarchy allude to the ideal founding fathers; fantastic, mythological characters, or, in some cases, historic personages notoriously belonging to Masonic and *Carbonari* secret societies.[8] Tracing the birth and existence itself of the organization back into the obscure night of centuries past obviously helps provide greater power and legitimacy to the bonds of membership.

The member who has received a determined *dote* can be identified through symbols of recognition that frequently consist of tattoos on different parts of the body and small incisions in the skin, each attesting to membership at a certain level within the organization. Every initiate is required to learn special formulas, the so-called *rintagli* (literally "frills" or "embellishments"), which make his membership known at different levels of the hierarchical ladder.

The ceremony calls for the member to swear to different oaths, one for every *movimento*;[9] an explicit reference is always made in these oaths to the rank occupied until then and the rank achieved by the end of the ritual. The specific identity never seems to be acquired once and for all; this is always subject to constant redefining and reoccurring advancements; the *rank* becomes the objective to reach in order to rise constantly higher.

Another peculiar element in the rituals adopted by the SCU is represented by the use, during the ceremony, of special *symbolic* objects that represent, for all practical purposes, *real* ritual tools. In addition to the pin, used to make the incision on the hand or finger and called *armatura* (armor) in the language of the 'Ndrangheta, and the small sacred image, depicting Saint Michael the Archangel in both the SCU and the 'Ndrangheta, these also include: The white silk handkerchief, which represents the purity of the soul of the initiate; the *spartenza* (shared goods), frequently symbolized by several cigarettes, which—as the legacy of the association—must be equally shared among the participants in the ritual; a poison pill as a means for committing suicide in case the principles of loyalty to the organization are ignored; a gun to punish the member in case of betrayal; a lemon, which serves to "heal the wounds of our wise comrades"; and a ball of cotton, which, according to legend, symbolizes Mont Blanc, a place considered holy (Massari 1998).

---

[7] The hierarchical ranks present in the organization are indicated with *dote* or *regalo* ("endowment" or "gift").

[8] The rituals of the Sacra Corona Unita, like those of the 'Ndrangheta, make frequent reference to the three Spanish knights (Osso, Mastrosso, and Carcagnosso) who, according to legend, were part of the secret Spanish society called *Garduña*, formed in Toledo in 1412. Other figures considered the founding fathers of the various levels of membership are: Conte Ugolino, Fiorentin di Russia, Cavalier di Spagna, Giuseppe Garibaldi, Giuseppe Mazzini, Alfonso La Marmora, Peppe Bono, Peppe Giusto, Peppe Ignazio, Carlo Magno, Cavour, and others (Massari 1998).

[9] The *movimento* refers to the ceremony in which an individual becomes a member, or a member is promoted to the various ranks in the organization.

As one gradually advances up the hierarchical ladder of the brotherhood, the ceremonies become more and more complex, and new ritual elements are added along with new methods of recognition; the upper sphere of membership must be kept as secret as possible. Regarding this, one of the most interesting ceremonies is precisely that which includes the promotion to the highest *dote* in the organization: The *diritto al medaglione con catena* or, using a different term for the position, *crimine distaccato*. The investiture ceremony is fairly similar to those for the lowest levels, but a new element enters into this when the oath is recited. As opposed to the other *doti*, where only the initiate swears the loyalty oath, in this ritual all the participants simultaneously swear absolute bonds of loyalty to each other. Beyond this rank, there is nothing more; the course is finished: "I swear to no longer accept any other *dote* from any other body of association, aside from this one, composed of the established Holy Circle of Honor" [Giuro di non accettare altre doti da nessuno altro corpo di società formata, oltre questo, composto dal sacro circolo d'onore costituito] (Raggruppamento Operativo Speciale Carabinieri 1993, p. 23). This collective oath, therefore, seems to be an exceptional tool for making single individuals feel the strength of the bonds that unite them and that must remain as strong as possible, especially in the highest spheres of the internal hierarchy.

The principle of secrecy characteristically marks the *cursus honorum* of the member; initiates belonging to lower ranks never know the identity of those at the top of the hierarchy. In fact, a sort of cognitive barrier blocks knowledge of what there actually is after one's own membership level; "a *picciotto* (rank-and-file member) never knows what there is after the *picciotteria*, a *camorrista* never knows what there is after the *camorra*, but he may have fostered some *picciotti*," stated a former member during a hearing (Tribunale di Brindisi 1994, p. 209). As Luigi Malafarina noted in his study of the 'Ndrangheta, "to have mastery over all Mafia jargon, the initiate must move through all levels of his career within the *onorata società* (honored society)" (Malafarina 1986, p. 141).

These rites of passage from one level to the next reveal the desire to ritually reaffirm the internal solidarity between brothers, thus providing the most unified image possible of the organization. Even in cases where the contents of the ritual seem to be complete nonsense—a typical example of an archaizing rant or a sort of "pseudo-masonic phantasmagoria" (Monnier 1994, p. 36)—it still must be respected, rigorously observed, and fearfully protected by members—totally involved in that collective psychological exercise aimed at continuously safeguarding and reinforcing the identity and secrecy of the brotherhood.

But the constant recourse to ritual formulas and the use of a broadly symbolic language (similar, as has been mentioned, to the so-called Calabrian "*baccaghju*") also extend to other aspects of life in the organization; the ritual codification seems very precise and tends to regulate most internal communication in the group. This symbolic jargon is characterized on the one hand by the conventionality of the coded language, where expressions in rhyme and repetitions in verse reoccur frequently, and on the other hand, the figurative use of terms frequently borrowed from common or dialectical language.

From a psychological standpoint, the power of attraction exercised by initiation rites and the transmission of rules contained in the charters or social codes of the organization are clearly evident. These contain a surprising abundance of religious references and symbolic-esoteric images, along with cryptic words and expressions, loaded with mystery and difficult to comprehend. However, the deep meaning of this cultural legacy clearly should not be sought exclusively in the objective content it carries, but rather in the psychological dimension this is capable of creating. In the case of the SCU, this sense of shared identity assumes a crucial role, facilitating the creation of a sense of togetherness, which involves not only individual members but also the overall organization as a whole. Despite the difficulty in establishing to what extent members take this myth seriously and to what extent this may be accepted as a "component of that collective game of fantasy that contributes to the solidarity of the group" (MacKenzie 1968, p. 16), it still appears evident that this symbolic façade has furnished the association with an opportunity to portray itself, in the eyes of its members, as a strong, powerful organization, widely extended across the territory. This simultaneous need for freedom and connections, revealed by every secret society, is expressed in the SCU through a special intensification of the external characteristics precisely in ritual form. As Simmel emphasizes in his analysis of the secret society, this has allowed it to construct a sort of *body*—which is rather unusual, as we shall see—around the *soul*.

Secret and Secrecy

Despite the presence of a well-defined and ritual-symbolic apparatus in the SCU that, as we have pointed out, has given it a special identity, at least in the eyes of the members, the weakness of mechanisms designed to safeguard the secrecy of its existence and organization has been evident right from the start in concrete behavioral practices. From reading judicial documents, especially statements from collaborators of justice with the law, the incompleteness clearly emerges of the process of socialization into the values of secrecy. For example, many members, both inside and outside prison, never refuse the chance to boast of belonging to the brotherhood, and promise membership even to subjects considered unreliable, such as drug addicts. Many local previous offenders seem to have expressly requested to become part of the association, instead of having been chosen after careful selection, as is customary in other traditional Mafia organizations. This happened with some frequency especially in the initial phase of the emergence of the SCU as an autonomous criminal actor, the phase when the objective of successfully expanding its supremacy to the greatest extent over broad sections of territory brought a general carelessness in dealing with the qualitative aspects of membership. However, this initial error turned out to be quite costly; the low quality of the *human material* available contributed enormously to expanding the ranks of those who decided to collaborate with law enforcement (Massari and Motta 2006).

Furthermore, this tendency toward a poor attitude for secrecy is not only found in the conduct of rank-and-file members, but also in the behavior of leaders and bosses.

"The Sacra Corona Unita? It's dead. In fact, it never existed" [La Sacra Corona Unita? È morta. Anzi non è mai esistita] (Sparviero 1996, p. 1). With these words, in the mid 1990s, the founding father of the *pugliese* brotherhood, Pino Rogoli, answered questions from journalists who, during a pause in one of the many trials where he was a central figure, had approached him to ask questions regarding the facts under discussion in the courtroom. He continued:

> We are the victims of a system. If we really were Mafiosi, the situation would clearly be different […] I am not saying we have not committed any crimes, but here among us, the *Mafia culture* [my italics] of the Sicilians or the Calabrians does not exist, and we don't have their resources either" (Sparviero 1996, p. 7).
>
> [Siamo vittime di un sistema. Se fossimo veramente mafiosi la situazione sarebbe diversa (…) Non dico che non abbiamo mai commesso reati, ma qui da noi non esiste la cultura mafiosa dei siciliani o dei calabresi, né abbiamo i loro mezzi].

With these few words, the boss of the SCU, aside from expressing an evaluation of the special nature of the *pugliese* brotherhood (lacking a pre-existing local Mafia culture to draw on as a historical reference), publicly affirmed its existence and presumed disappearance. This gesture completely broke with that code of silence at the heart of the ideology and activities of traditional Mafia operations. Up to that point, no *Mafioso* had ever gone that far. These words were stated specifically by the man who defined himself as the "absolute leader," the unchallenged boss of the organization, wise "father" of these "children" of his, the "old man," the "grandfather" repository of "peace and wisdom" in whom supreme authority resided (Questura di Lecce 1988, p. 37; Tribunale di Brindisi 1994, pp. 263–265). As could be predicted, these statements were destined to spark bitter debate inside the Apulian criminal organization, even provoking a change in the name of the group itself, which from that time on would be reconstituted, as has been mentioned, under the name *Nuova (New) Sacra Corona Unita*. But, in addition, these statements also represented further confirmation of a trend present right from the beginning of the history of this criminal organization. In other words, a lax attitude toward the use of secrets and the practice of secrecy that, as we have already mentioned, made up one of the principal sources of weakness in the entire criminal project. Traces of this general trend, which could be defined as an *excess of words*, both written and spoken, can be found more or less everywhere. So much so that the discovery of the SCU as a criminal actor, endowed with its own special identity distinct from all other forms of criminality long present in Apulia, occurred precisely with the discovery of certain documents containing the founding charter for this new organizational operation and ritualistic oaths that were painstakingly transcribed to facilitate distribution in the prison context. All this openly contravened one of the most important rules in the Mafia universe, the rule that forbids transcription of any information regarding the association.

But upon further inspection of the stories of the various Mafia associations historically present in the *Mezzogiorno*, there have already been various precedents for this. Although all criminal groups have forever celebrated silence as the core value to which members must necessarily conform their behavior, the frequent discovery—since the mid nineteenth century—of criminal codes and charters regarding the rituals of membership and internal rules for conduct has leaked knowledge of many elements to the *outside* world.[10] All this has de facto irreparably eaten away at the aura of secrecy in which Mafia associations have cloaked themselves. The written objectification of secret wordings and oaths—for example, the rites of membership that mark, more than any other element, the fundamental *alterity*, from a sociological standpoint, of every secret society with respect to other types of social groups—inevitably leads to the negation of any presumed unknowable sphere, giving the organization and its members a visibility that can no longer be denied, and is a clear indication of the limited attention given to safeguarding the secrecy of ties to the association. The meticulous transcription of the procedures connected to the most meaningful moments of life inside the group seems to actually be intimately connected to the need to render more immediate construction of a strong cultural identity among individuals originating from a wide variety of criminal experiences and belonging to profoundly different local situations.

The condition of imprisonment of many bosses, along with the particular complexity of the oaths, did not favor oral transmission of those practices necessary to socialize the largest number of members possible, especially in the initial phases. Strategic needs transcended the present rule within the SCU that, according to statements from several collaborators of justice, called for the destruction of documents containing the oaths of membership and ritual ceremonies after these had been committed to memory. "Keep the secret of the rules of the Sacra Corona deep inside your soul for the rest of your life."[11] But, as has been mentioned, the constant lack of attention toward this regulation seems not to be exclusively linked to any lack of experience. Even in the 'Ndrangheta, for example—one of the associations to which the SCU aspired most as an ideal reference—the duty to keep the contents of these codes imprinted in memory was not especially respected, as seen in the frequent discovery of written documents by investigators. Yet, most of the contents of these documents, in addition to actual membership oaths, are expressly dedicated to a whole series of secret code phrases for recognition—the so-called *social precepts* and *rules*—which should safeguard as much as possible the secrecy of the member's identity. Members belonging to different groups use these to make themselves recognizable in contexts where it is difficult to rely on the presence of a third party capable of guaranteeing their common membership. Prison represents one of the places where these secret code phrases are recited, since the need frequently arises here to reveal one's own rank of membership in the brotherhood to other members (Massari 1998).

---

[10] One of the oldest criminal codes appears to be the charter of the Camorra, the so-called *frieno*; its earliest formulation appears in 1820; the existence has also been verified from written codes regarding the 'Ndrangheta since 1897: See Sales 1993; Ciconte 1992; Paoli 2000.

[11] This instruction is contained in point no. 9 of the *Statuto della Sacra Corona Unita* (Charter of the Sacra Corona Unita).

Verbal communication, the ritual repetition of particularly elaborate secret phrases, and the need to see visible confirmations of one's own authority outside one's
self have all represented crucial elements for the SCU in the process of constructing
a new criminal identity. This occurred through a process of cultural hybridization
of elements drawn from different criminal traditions rooted in the past, as well as
profoundly modern forms of social organizations and practices.

Plural Worlds

When considering sources that paint the portrait of the SCU from its beginnings,
the image emerges of a criminal mega-group that incorporated into itself a criminal
army of individuals with diverse origins. The local criminal environment constituted fertile ground from which to draw varied human material. For many criminals
in Apulia, the birth of this organization symbolized a real chance for advancing
their *status* and acquiring a new criminal identity. Real enthusiasm was clearly reflected in the mass memberships confirmed in the early years of the organization.
Consistent with a strategy that aimed at extending as much as possible the sphere
of influence of the new group, rather elastic recruitment policies were adopted that
did not include meticulous scrutiny of each individual criminal career. All sorts of
criminals, including small-time drug dealers and junkies (usually excluded from
other Mafia associations), were admitted into the various *famiglie* that, in some
areas, reached numbers of more than a hundred members. Never before had the
concept of "criminality" itself, particularly the concept of "Mafia criminality," appeared so completely conventional, from the moment when, "more than a compact,
homogeneous operation, the social dimension recalled by this was a cognitive con-
tainer of *plural worlds*, frequently short-lived and not always visible or definable as
criminal" (Dal Lago and Quadrelli 2003, p. 31). Adapting to an economic system
oriented toward values of flexibility, utilitarianism, and the immediate generation of
profit, individuals in most cases already involved in a number of illegal and criminal
activities entered and became part of the SCU in the early 1980s. Generally, these
were smugglers, fences, thieves, drug dealers, and swindlers. Aside from those already in contact with organized crime environments, the ranks of the SCU also contained representatives from the local underworld—"small operators [...] those who
sell marginal illegal services or procure resources through illegal activities" (Dal
Lago and Quadrelli 2003, p. 32)—street criminals (mostly involving predatory activities), and other petty criminals accustomed to acting more or less independently.
The extreme sociocultural heterogeneity of these individuals, combined with membership in fairly diversified criminal subcultures, contributed notably to raising the
level of conflict and propensity for violent encounters arising inside clans as well as
between opposing clans. From a social perspective, alongside the marginal classes
from an agrarian world in a state of dissolution, there was particular representation
from the ranks of the lower middle class from areas bordering the more properly urban context. This may be the origin of the coexistence of profoundly contradictory

attitudes that seem, on one hand, inspired by typical predatory tendencies specific to criminal groups not structured on a continuous, enduring temporal basis; and, on the other hand, by projects of expansion across vast areas of regional territory where a whole range of activities could be established.

Many young leaders who emerged in these early years possessed some of the characteristics typical of gangsters: A generally low level of education, strong behavioral and emotional instability, a particularly precocious criminal career, a marked propensity for conspicuous consumption, and involvement in high-risk, illegal activities (burglaries, robberies, extortion, or low-level drug dealing). The exceptionally violent impulses of these individuals clearly emerge, for example, in the frequency with which they use homicide as a tool for resolving conflicts. According to notes from investigators:

> Young members of the criminal association are particularly hot-headed and ruthless, and always encourage making sure it is well-known that they are ready and able to kill anywhere and, in any case, take advantage of every chance to settle old scores (Questura di Lecce 1987, p. 15).

In fact, the occasionally spectacular use of violence seemed to inspire this *freewheeling* behavior, frequently aimed only at achieving the greatest immediate profit possible.

Over the course of subsequent years, various attempts have been made to counter the gradual "decline" in available raw, human material. For example, more selective membership criteria were introduced until finally, according to the most recent information, reaching the point that new members were admitted only if they were from the same town or village (Direzione Nazionale Antimafia (DNA) 2011, p. 149), as has been the case inside the Sicilian Cosa Nostra for some time now. Furthermore, attempts were made at strengthening the secrecy of the association by adopting a much stricter code of conduct and sanctions aimed at stigmatizing nonconformist behavior by members. But the progressive involvement in particularly profitable activities (such as drug sales and racketeering) over time encouraged the ascendance to power of the most unscrupulous leaders and a violent, bloody regression that unforgettably changed the course of events, especially during the 1990s.

The Use of Violence

The history of the SCU clearly reveals how the dimension of constant conflict in which the group has found itself operating since its early beginnings—internally as well as against the outside world—has constituted one of the elements of greatest weakness.

Since its beginnings during the 1980s, this group has frequently employed armed violence to exert hegemony over the local underworld. In the area of Salento—the southern part of the region where the SCU is still mostly based—118 Mafia homicides were recorded in 1989. This number increased to 145 just a year later.

Violence and terror became common tools for achieving power and reputation (Dino 2008, p. 293).

The specialized use of violence and terror toward competitors and adversaries, and the availability of capital, as well as the possibility of protecting themselves from oppositional activities by law enforcement, all constitute the characteristic features of the polymorphic entity that is the Mafia organization. Violence in particular represents one of the main resources available to the Mafia group. This consists of:

> The availability of specialized personnel and weapons adequate for the purpose of protecting the physical people, goods and markets belonging to the criminal operation, as well as the aim of eliminating obstacles to conducting everyday business (Arlacchi 1988, p. 20).

However many attempts are made to limit the recourse to violence and establish a set of rules and regulations for those circumstances in which this must be applied, the *pure* power of action—the power to inflict injury free from any restraints—still always represents a possible option.

The high level of personalization of power and difficulties encountered in maintaining a certain continuity for the brotherhood, in part resulting from the absence of recruitment procedures based on biological-parental principles, as is the case with the 'Ndrangheta, have in fact closely linked the history of the SCU to individual destinies and actions. Extremely intense criminal careers have encouraged the advancement of young bosses up the command hierarchy; these individuals, in the majority of cases, are appointed from above in virtue of close relationships existing with the top leaders of the organization, rather than as the result of any personal qualities. This has obviously contributed to weakening the base of legitimacy on which the founding leader and his close collaborators of justice had built the broad consensus met by the SCU during its early period of activity. In fact, it became more and more difficult for them to build effective, stable power relations, as well as relationships founded on loyalty and cooperation, on these foundations. As has been mentioned, this leads to the frequent recourse to violence, murder, and various other types of coercive tools to resolve cases of conflict.

According to statements from collaborator of justice Cosimo Capodieci,[12] in the SCU homicide and the consequent burning of the victim's body, represent a sort of symbolic signal sent to all members. This practice, in fact, makes explicit reference to the top-level membership oaths, which stated "[…] the day when you betray us, you will be burned like this sacred image" (Raggruppamento Operativo Speciale Carabinieri 1993, p. 69). Obviously the method used to carry out the homicide also responded to other needs such as, for example, making identification of the victim difficult and eliminating possible traces left by the perpetrators. The many cases of so-called *morti bianche* (white deaths)—that is, individuals who have disappeared and most likely been killed without leaving any trace—could be traced back precisely to this method of carrying out a homicide.

---

[12] A collaborator of justice from the Brindisi *famiglia* of the Sacra Corona Unita.

The tendency toward pragmatism has frequently imposed use and manipulation of friendships and family ties as tools in committing homicides. All traditional Mafia organizations often use the tactic, for example, of getting close to the victim through a friend or relative. Frequently, the criminal association orders the member closest to the designated victim to carry out the killing himself. This is done in an attempt to prevent the condemned individual from becoming cautious or sensing a suspicious atmosphere. Once again Cosimo Capodieci expresses, in his memoir, this state of oppressive mistrust linked to the fear of being approached by another member, the dread of accepting even one invitation, one ride in a car, or arriving at an appointment. The anxiety of being killed led him to foresee his own death; he was certain that sooner or later he would be brought to a place in the country where his body would be made to disappear: "I understood that in my case, in other words the order to kill me, would have to be a case of *lupara bianca* (white *lupara*)."[13] At times, the awareness of having now been condemned by the organization—the knowledge of a death sentence—is at the basis of many members becoming collaborators of justice. Alceste Semeraro, a former member of the SCU, recounts the events that led him to collaborate; the *famiglia* had ordered him to kill one of his own brothers, but his refusal to carry out the order brought his own death sentence.

However, quite frequently these actions are carried out coldly as a repetitive following of orders. There is no escape from executing these sentences. Paradoxically, the execution of the order—the killing itself—shifts the death to the outside, thus postponing one's own death. The sense of death almost seems to become internalized, the possibility of a violent end accepted as a sort of inevitability. The utility of violent action, even the most brutal—necessary for achieving particular objectives—moves any consideration of its ferocity to the background.

Among the motivations for some of the most recent collaborations, there emerges that state of oppressive mistrust and suspicion that leads to critically considering one's own choices and past. The desire is especially felt in the youngest members to "change lifestyle," return to a "normal life," or "close the door of the past." A sense of exhaustion is felt regarding an existence always lived under the sign of danger, risk, or the impending threat of death. Irreparably compromised emotional and family scenarios are almost always somewhere in the background.

Over the past few years, the SCU, like other traditional Mafia associations, seems to have opted for a lower profile aimed at not attracting the attention of law enforcement with violent activity. One of the most recent major SCU killings occurred in 2003 in the area of Lecce, when a boss was killed in front of many witnesses in a café, with the sole aim of sending a clear message to his affiliates to squash their attempts at establishing control over a number of illegal activities in the

---

[13] Memoirs of the collaborator of justice Cosimo Capodieci, unpublished manuscript. The term "*lupara bianca*" refers to a killing where the body of the victim is deliberately hidden. The victim is usually strangled or suffocated and the body dissolved in acid. Although this practice is still in evidence in Sicily—where four cases were recorded in 2011—and in Calabria, it is mostly used during relatively calm phases, during which homicides can be planned far in advance.

area.[14] As mentioned previously, the SCU is currently implementing a more subtle strategy since:

> Any Mafia that manages to guarantee order in the areas where it operates, without using conspicuous forms of violence, ends up being more easily tolerated and in turn seen as a subject that may offer services alternative to the State (Direzione Nazionale Antimafia (DNA) 2011, p. 149).

From the Model to Practice

Around 30 years from its appearance on the national and international criminal scene—thanks mostly to the opportunities offered by illegal trade with the opposite shore of the Adriatic—the history of the SCU has been characterized by events that seem to confirm the fact that the Mafia still represents a successful organizational model. In the same way as other organizational experiences that matured during the final decades of the twentieth century in various areas of the *Mezzogiorno* (for example the *Stidda* in Sicily and *Basilischi* in Basilicata),[15] the SCU represents an unusual example of how the organizational and strategic methods of traditional Mafia associations still constitute a valid reference model for criminal entities immersed in a social, economic, political, and cultural context profoundly different from those at their origins. Far from wishing to pose the question in terms of a conflict between archaism and modernity, or tradition and innovation, what is most striking in the analysis of the stories, cultures, and identities experienced by the SCU over the past few years is the extreme relevance of a whole series of instruments and resources capable, both yesterday and today, of inspiring and transmitting a powerful sense of belonging. Over the course of that process of acculturation begun both inside and outside prison, through frequent contact with members of other Mafia groups from nearby regions, the SCU has appropriated norms, values, behavioral models, and symbolic references that it has later been able to rework independently. In particular, the most archaic expressions of the ritual-symbolic heritage of secret associations of a criminal nature—which can be traced back to the old codes of the 'Ndrangheta and the Camorra under the Bourbons—were rediscovered and readapted to new criminal realities. Customs, rites, symbols, and oaths that seemed to belong to ancient traditions and no longer fully respected, not even by the historic Mafias, went on to constitute the cultural substrate on which the SCU founded its own identity. Precisely because of the desire to become firmly implanted in the shared imagination of individuals belonging to many different worlds, lacking any homogeneous cultural reference, this identity had to be reintroduced as a special *new* identity that was immediately recognizable. Among other things, it is interesting to recall how in the 1970s, the *Nuova Camorra Organizzata* led by Raffaele Cutolo began a similar process, rediscovering the most evocative and spectacular aspects of traditions from

---

[14] Author's personal communication with the Chief Prosecutor of the DDA in Lecce (2012, July 5).

[15] For further information on the Sicilian criminal organization called Stidda, see Massari 2004.

the Camorra and 'Ndrangheta, so as to expand its membership ranks as much as possible, representing itself as a sort of mass-Camorra (Sales 1993, pp. 88–89). In both cases, it seems evident that this choice functioned as part of a project aimed at marking a profound break with respect to the past, and an opportunity for many young members to get out of marginal situations, thus creating bases for moving from a loose and fluid form of criminal association to a better organized criminal system.

Although it began with an enthusiasm for a real process of socialization into the values, culture, and strategies of traditional Mafia associations, the SCU seems not to have been successful in firmly anchoring its present to that historic memory it had artificially appropriated. Arrests, trials, homicides, collaborations with law enforcement, and new criminal opportunities—as well as legal ones—contributed to profoundly changing the profile of this organization and its capability for action. Over the past 10 years, the SCU has undergone a significant transformation since most of its bosses have been incarcerated and a new generation has emerged, often made up of the sons and relatives of the original leaders. In addition, during the 1990s and first half of the following decade, the area of Apulia was deeply involved in criminal displays particularly linked to illegal immigration and the international trafficking of arms, drugs, and women (destined for prostitution markets and originating mostly from Eastern Europe and the Balkans). These developments brought a change in the strategies adopted by the SCU, which, from an original position of factional alignment, shifted to adopting a more properly commercial logic. This strategy envisaged opportunities for meetings and alliances, in view of individual criminal activities, even among members from groups that in the past were in conflict with one another (Motta 2001). Geographical proximity to the Balkans, particularly Albania and Montenegro, encouraged renewed interest in drug-trafficking activities, as well as involvement in more traditional crimes such as robbery and extortion (Massari 2009, p. 247). However, the new leading elite has given priority to implementing a low profile strategy aimed at consolidating the business aspect of the organization through large, diversified investments in the legal economy. Though the traditional Mafia model represented an essential reference point, in its concrete practices, the SCU has not always managed to consolidate methods of conduct, strategies, and resources capable of giving it stability and continuity. Instead of attracting the attention of law enforcement with sensational acts, over the past few years, the SCU—currently led by the so-called second generation composed of the sons of the first bosses still imprisoned—seems more geared toward earning the social consensus of the local population, supplying resources, and showing their willingness to listen to them and satisfy their needs and demands (Direzione Nazionale Antimafia (DNA) 2011 p. 512).

References

Apollonio, A. (2010). *Sacra corona unita: riciclaggio, contrabbando*. Rome: Carocci.
Arlacchi, P. (1992). *Gli uomini del disonore. La mafia siciliana nella vita di un grande pentito Antonino Calderone*. Milan: Mondadori.

Arlacchi, P. (1994). *Addio Cosa nostra. La vita di Tommaso Buscetta*. Milan: Rizzoli.
Arlacchi, P. (1988). *Droga e grande criminalità in Italia e nel mondo*. Caltanissetta-Rome: Sciascia Editore.
Ciconte, E. (1992). *'Ndrangheta. Dall'Unità ad oggi*. Bari-Rome: Laterza.
Commissione Parlamentare Antimafia. (1976, Feb 4). *Relazione conclusiva (relatore: Carraro)*. (VI Legislatura). Rome: Tipografia del Senato.
Dal Lago, A., & Quadrelli, E. (2003). *La città e le ombre. Crimini, criminali, cittadini*. Milan: Feltrinelli.
Davis, F. (1971). *Le società segrete in Cina. 1840–1911. Forme primitive di lotta rivoluzionaria*. Turin: Einaudi.
Dino, A. (2008). Guerre di mafia. In M. Mareso & L. Pepino (Eds.), *Nuovo dizionario di mafia e antimafia* (pp. 290–300). Turin: Edizioni del Gruppo Abele.
Direzione Nazionale Antimafia (DNA). (2008). *Relazione annuale sulle attività svolte dal Procuratore nazionale antimafia e dalla Direzione nazionale antimafia nonché sulle dinamiche e strategie della criminalità organizzata di tipo mafioso nel periodo 1 luglio 2007–30 giugno 2008*. Rome: DNA.
Direzione Nazionale Antimafia (DNA). (2011). *Relazione annuale sulle attività svolte dal Procuratore nazionale antimafia e dalla Direzione nazionale antimafia nonché sulle dinamiche e strategie della criminalità organizzata di tipo mafioso nel periodo 1 luglio 2010–30 giugno 2011*. Rome: DNA.
Hutin, S. (1955). *Le società segrete*. Milan: Garzanti.
Jamieson, A., & Silj, A. (1998). *Migration and criminality: the case of Albanians in Italy*. Ethnobarometer Programme Working Paper No. 1. Rome: Ethnobarometer.
Lau Fong, M. (1981). *The sociology of secret societies. A study of Chinese secret societies in Singapore and Peninsular Malaysia*. Oxford: Oxford University Press.
MacKenzie, N. (Ed.). (1968). *Le società segrete*. Milan: Rizzoli.
Malafarina, L. (1986). *La 'Ndrangheta. Il codice segreto, la storia, i miti, i riti e i personaggi*. Rome: Gangemi.
Massari, M. (1998). *La Sacra Corona Unita*. Bari-Rome: Laterza.
Massari, M. (2004). L'evoluzione della criminalità organizzata e le dinamiche della violenza. In S. Becucci (Ed.), *La città sospesa. Legalità, sviluppo e società civile a Gela* (pp. 51–82). Turin: Edizioni del Gruppo Abele.
Massari, M. (2009). La Sacra Corona Unita: storie, culture, identità. In G. Gribaudi (Ed.), *Traffici criminali. Camorra, mafie e reti internazionali dell'illegalità* (pp. 241–264). Turin: Bollati Boringhieri.
Massari, M., & Motta, C. (2006). Il fenomeno dei collaboratori di giustizia nella Sacra Corona Unita. In A. Dino (Ed.), *Pentiti. I collaboratori di giustizia, le istituzioni, l'opinione pubblica* (pp. 163–183). Rome: Donzelli.
Monnier, M. (1994). *La Camorra*. Lecce: Argo.
Motta, C. (2001). Sacra Corona Unita & Co. Radiografia di un fenomeno. *Dike 2*.
Paoli, L. (2000). *Fratelli di mafia. Cosa nostra e 'Ndrangheta*. Bologna: il Mulino.
Questura di Lecce. (1987, Jan 10). *Rapporto giudiziario di denunzia a carico di Rogoli Giuseppe + altri*.
Questura di Lecce. (1988, Nov 11). *Rapporto giudiziario di denunzia a carico di Rogoli Giuseppe + 125*.
Raggruppamento Operativo Speciale Carabinieri. (1993, May 12). *Studio sulla criminalità organizzata in Puglia, con particolare riguardo alla Sacra Corona Unita*.
Sales, I. (1993). *La camorra, le camorre*. Rome: Editori Riuniti.
Simmel, G. (1989). Il segreto e la società segreta. *Sociologia*. Milan: Edizioni di Comunità.
Sparviero, V. (1996, Nov 13). I pentiti a Brindisi girano armati. *La Gazzetta del Mezzogiorno* p. 1+.
Tribunale di Brindisi. (1994, Sept 27). *Sentenza contro Buccarella Giovanni + 10*.

Chapter 8
Mafia-Like Culture and Its Function in a Newly Formed Italian Criminal Organization. The Case of Sacra Corona Unita

Mariano Longo

Some Initial Remarks

When studying organized crime, one has to distinguish a plurality of dimensions, all part of a very complex phenomenon. Organization is a relevant aspect, and indeed some of the sociological analyses of organized crime focus on the rational coordination of activities and roles (Cressey 1969; Crisantino and La Fiura 1989). The impact on the everyday life of the involved population is also to be taken into account, and this is probably the reason why organized crime has often been understood starting from criminal actions having a strong capability for intimidation (Reuter 1994). A tight control of places and activities, within a territory that the organization assumes as its own, is another relevant character (Arlacchi 1983). Yet, a general definition, (Ruggero 1992; Albanese 1994; Maltz 1994) useful as it may be, is nonetheless partial, as it does not take into account the national, regional, and local aspects of organized crime.[1]

As we are confronted with a set of different definitions of organized crime, all of them centered on characters, which are not exhaustive of the phenomenon as such, it may be useful to refer to Frank Hagan's attempt to summarize, within a content analysis approach, the many dimensions of organized crime. Hagan (2006) identifies a set of characteristics, which are recognized by current literature as aspects of criminal organizations. Although the definitions show no unanimous consensus about the main traits of the phenomenon, some of these traits are more frequently referred to (that is illegal activities, threats, corruption, and public demand), others are less frequently assumed as relevant. In particular, those linked with what one might call the cultural aspects of organized crime (that is restricted membership, initiation, rules, and the code of secrecy) are rarely mentioned, and that is a probable reason for which Hagan refers to them as secondary characteristics of organized crime.

Indeed, in the selection of the different dimensions of organized crime as proposed by Hagan, reference to culture is relatively unimportant. Yet, the cultural

---

[1] Those aspects are particularly relevant in the Italian case, as I will try to show in this paper.

M. Longo (✉)
Department of History, Society and Human Studies, Università del Salento, 73100 Lecce, Italy
e-mail: mariano.longo@unisalento.it

N. Serenata (ed.), *The 'Ndrangheta and Sacra Corona Unita,* Studies of Organized Crime 12,   117
DOI 10.1007/978-3-319-04930-4_8, © Springer International Publishing Switzerland 2014

aspect does matter, especially when attempting to characterize criminal organizations in Italy. It is useful to refer to the distinction Hagan proposes between Organized Crime (initial letters capitalized) and organized crime, the first referring to criminal groups, the second to their activities. Although it is artful to separate the criminal organization from its activities, when one refers to an organized group as endowed with a specific structure, one may stress a set of differences, which are culturally and geographically determined. The structure of the group, probably more than the criminal activities it performs, may vary as referred to its social and cultural environment. As this essay deals with some structural aspects of an Apulian Mafia-like organization (The Sacra Corona Unita, from now on SCU), my hypothesis is that the cultural elements, weird as they may appear, have relevant functions within the criminal group.

By stressing the relevance of culture, I do not intend to adhere to any culturalist conception of criminal organizations. Indeed, when simplistically adopting a culturalist approach, one tends to emphasize the romantic dimension of Mafias,[2] their being an anthropological aspect of the way people act in the "South." This produces a distorted representation of reality, as Mafia-like groups are supposed to be premodern criminal organizations, endowed with a fascination of their own, deriving from mysterious codes and archaic values. Italian Mafia-like groups are, on the contrary, modern and powerful organisms, which take advantage of the opportunities modernity may offer them (just to mention a few examples: Tenders, money laundering, global drug market, illegal dumping, etc.). Yet, notwithstanding the process of modernization, the cultural dimension is still a relevant aspect of Mafias: Culture, myths, and symbols may be intended as an ideological cover to legitimize illegal and violent activities. They are still part of the way Italian Organized Crime represents itself within the criminal groups and in the public sphere. This essay is an attempt to show the relevance of both the cultural and the structural dimensions of a newly formed criminal organization, SCU, operating in Apulia, whose origins date back in the early 1980s.

Going Beyond the Bureaucracy Model

Organized Crime has a structure, that is a set of rules, roles, expectations as well as legitimate forms of action and communication relevant so as to stabilize the group and its boundaries. Yet, it would be naïve to understand the aforementioned structure by adopting the bureaucratic-model: Indeed, roles are unstable, as they are based on equally unstable power relations within the group. Moreover, rules and expectations are not to be intended as clear-cut orientation for the action. They are better understood as an ex-post justification of what has already taken place. In other words, the stabilization of conduct, which is a typical aspect of formal organization, is possible

---

[2] I use the term Mafias (or Mafia-like organizations) to refer to the four main criminal organizations operating chiefly in Italy: Cosa Nostra, Camorra, 'Ndrangheta and SCU.

in Organized Crime not due to the compliance with a normative set. Stable conducts are a by-product of the control capability of the group-leadership, which is, in turn, unstable due to the potentially ever-changing power-relations within the group and the differentiated capability of its members to exercise violence (Longo 1997).

Due to the specific characteristics of Organized Crime, the concept of organization that will be adopted in this essay is quite neutral: It is to be intended as the complex communication and relation pattern within a social group. This pattern is effective in so far as it is able both to give group members bits of information to be employed when choosing among options of action, and to stabilize their expectations related to the conduct of Alter. Such a broadly defined concept of organization safeguards against from a naïve overlapping of bureaucracy and Organized Crime (Cressey 1969).

Indeed, although certain components of bureaucracy such as hierarchy, rules, enrollment, roles, and labor division are also aspects of a criminal organization, the way they work in their respective social contexts is quite different: (1) Bureaucracies are more stable, due to both a more static normative context and well-defined relations among members; (2) on the contrary, criminal organizations are characterized by fluid relations among members and by latent or patent conflicts which, according to the changing power-relations, may challenge the leadership; (3) although the normative context in a Mafia-like criminal organization may have been formalized in written or oral form as a tradition, and although this normative context may define the mutual relations among members and between members and the organization, norms are weak as they are interpreted and re-interpreted according to convenience and to the actual power relations.

We do not intend to deny, as some sociological literature does (Hess 1993), the relevance of the organizational structure in Mafia-like criminal groups. Our intent is to analyze such structure, and its cultural components, as an essential element to describe, statu nascendi, the process by which a new criminal organization defines itself and legitimizes its activities. The bureaucratic metaphor is less pertinent to our purposes than a comparison with older Mafia-like Italian organizations, so to verify the occurrence of typical patterns of conducts, communication, and interactions and to sketch their function within the organization.

One of the reasons why it is difficult to think of Mafia-like groups as endowed with an organizational structure depends on the fact that one tends to overlap the concept of organization with that of bureaucracy. Social representations of Mafia-like organizations, in their turn, emphasize archaic and weird elements: The structure is supposed to be based on a paramilitary hierarchy, complemented with symbolic tools (that is secrecy, rituals, honor, archaic rules, and primitive values).[3] That appears as being inconsistent with the group's concrete tasks and activities (drug traffic, territorial control, protection, control of public funding, etc.) (Reuter 1994).

---

[3] This simplified representation of criminal organizations affected historical analyses as well. See Caracciolo 1992, whose hypothesis is that Italian Mafias (excluding SCU) should be the evolution of a Spanish secret association, dating back to the XV century, the rituals of which should have been imported to Italy by the three founders of Mafia, 'Ndrangheta and Camorra.

On the one hand, the social scientist is confronted with complex rituals and rules, often expressed with a linguistic combination of uncultivated syntax and antiquated words; on the other, criminal groups unscrupulously pursue their illegal tasks, taking advantage of the opportunities modernity may offer (Arlacchi 1983; Catanzaro 1988a, 1988b, 1992; Ciconte, 1992; Sales 1988, 1992).

Our conception of Mafia-like criminal groups is in-between: Symbolic and cultural elements are adopted as a justification of specific organizational structures, which, unlike bureaucracies, base their unstable balance on violence and ever-changing power relations. By selecting SCU as a case study, one may observe what elements were perceived as relevant by its members in the very process of the organization's set-up, so as to create group strategies, boundaries, and internal identity (Merton 1949). The practical task of the organizational adaptation to a social environment (until then immune from organized crime), was partially solved by assuming as a model the organizational structure of older, and more consolidated, Mafia-like groups ('Ndrangheta in particular), as well as by adopting an external tradition, made up of origin-myths, symbols, rituals, and norms, all elements through which the criminal organization attempted to create a group-identity, thus drawing a distinction between itself and the less structured criminal milieu. The intertwined connection between structural and cultural elements shows, at least in the case of SCU, the partial plausibility of a conception of Mafia-like organizations as both an output of distorted modernization processes, and the survival of archaic cultural forms.

Setting Organizational Strategies: Archaic Symbols and Modern Connivance

An apparently scarcely relevant happening has been described in the written justification of the verdict of the first maxiprocesso[4] against SCU, which took place in 1991. The incident I will soon refer to, although devoid of practical consequences for the development of the criminal organization, is nonetheless pertinent so as to explain the perceived importance of an artificial and constructed cultural tradition within the criminal environment close to the organization. This incident is related to the attempt to set up a criminal group in Taranto (an industrial city on the Ionian sea), that was to be affiliated with the SCU group operating in the territory of Gallipoli (another Ionian city). The whole affair has been reconstructed by the judges, by making reference to the correspondence between Porcelli and Fella, both indicted in the maxiprocesso. The letters shows the close interconnection of two apparently separate aspects of the organization: The pragmatic and the symbolical. Whereas planning illegal activities and establishing relations with political power appears to be a rational strategy of a newly formed group, the correspondence insists also on

---

[4] Maxiprocesso is an Italian term used by the media to describe a trial where a large number of people are involved, generally members of Mafia-like groups.

the relevance of the assimilation of the symbolic elements of SCU, including rules and rituals.

Fella, the boss-to-be of "The Dragon" (the name of the criminal group which was to be set up in Taranto) becomes familiar with the complex rituals of the organization by his correspondent. In order to legitimize his group as a Mafia-like unit, Fella should become the guardian of what Porcelli calls "the religion," that is the complex set of symbols, rules, and practices established within SCU. That is necessary, but not enough. Moreover, he should establish close and stable relations with politicians and judges, so to guarantee institutional cover-up to himself and his group (Tribunale di Lecce 1991, p. 78–80). At the same time, the operative aspect of crime is not to be underestimated: The affiliation of Fella to the SCU group in Gallipoli is to be sealed by finding common interests in the field of illegal activities, the drug market in particular, thus defining tight links, connected to specific criminal activities, between the new group in Taranto and the organization.

The sequestered letters demonstrate a naïve, yet strategical, vision of the way the criminal organization should adapt to its social environment. One may detect three distinct and interrelated levels, all endowed with a function of their own: (1) The cultural and symbolic level has the function of giving the affiliated group inner consistency and compatibility with the overall organization; (2) the level of common interests works as a way to connect the new group to the organization on the base of shared illegal activities; (3) the institutional level, whose function is to make the group more stable, since by establishing relations with local institutions (politics and law), the criminal group may count on political and juridical protection, so as to make control and repression looser. The correspondence between Fella and Porcelli shows in the concrete operating of a Mafia-like group what I have stated before, on a more theoretical basis: The symbolic and operative aspects are strictly interrelated. Mafia-like organizations combine symbols (as a way to construct internal identity and external reputation), illegal activities (the core business of Organized Crime), and institutional relationships (as a way to guarantee the group against state repression). Although from the outside one might perceive inconsistency among these different aspects, they are likely to appear perfectly coherent for a member of the criminal group.

The quoted empirical material shows how the organization represents itself both as a projection toward its interior (note the importance of rituals and structural elements) and a projection toward its exterior (note how relevant the adaptation to a hostile environment is for the organization). In particular, institutional connivance is perceived as a prerequisite for the success of the criminal group-to-be. Regardless of the relevance of the described incident for the history and evolution of SCU, it witnesses the fact that its members perceived themselves as a criminal elite, set apart from common delinquents (think of the set of organizational rules emphatically described as "the religion"); and, closely connected to that, it shows its capability to plan explicit strategies, not only in connection to illegal activities, but also as to its capacity to settle relations with state powers (Maltz 1994).

Leadership

Leadership is one of the aspects Mafia-like groups share with more formal types of organizations. As stated above, in a criminal group, leadership may be unstable, as it depends on an ever variable balance of power. Indeed, although it has been verified that, at least during the 1980s, SCU had an organizational structure (hence a leadership, a hierarchy, a labor division, etc.), this structure was extremely loose, as compared to formal organizations. This structural looseness was somewhat compensated by a stark leadership, at least at the symbolical level. Indeed, SCU as a case study of a newly formed Mafia-like criminal organization shows the relevance of group-leadership as an instrument to define group identity and operative strategies. It shows also the close interconnection between organizational and cultural-symbolic elements.

When compared with the so-called traditional Mafias, SCU makes one of its peculiarities evident: It had, as it were, to construct a structure ex nihilo, which resulted in consequential difficulties both at the level of the effectiveness of illegal activities and at the level of inner organization. Both outer and inner difficulties were made less dramatic by a charismatic figure: Pino Rogoli, leader and acknowledged founder of the criminal organism. Indeed, the leadership of Rogoli compensated for the lack of a shared tradition and identity. Rogoli was converted into a strong identity marker for the organization. For example, an initiation code found by the police in the early 1990s expressly mentions Rogoli as the founder of the organization, the one for whom members have to act:

> I swear upon the tip of this dagger, wet with blood, that I will always be faithful to this body of society, made up of active, free, and positive men belonging to SCU, and that I will always act for its founder, Pino Rogoli.
> [Giuro su questa punta di pugnale bagnata di sangue, di essere fedele sempre a questo corpo di società formata da uomini attivi, liberi e affermativi appartenenti alla S.C.U. e di rappresentarne ovunque il fondatore, Giuseppe Rogoli].[5]

Although 'Ndrangheta and Camorra may also make reference to an origin-myth in their initiation-codes, they collocate their founders (e.g. three Spanish knights, Count Ugolino, etc.) back into an ancient past. SCU, on the contrary, chooses Rogoli as its mythical living founder, so showing the relevance of the charismatic leader both for the members of the organization and its future.

Some of the letters sequestered by the police depict Rogoli with epithets stressing his strength and wisdom. He is in turn the "old man," (Tribunale di Lecce 1991, p. 349) the "man of wisdom," the "righteous," and the "peace keeper" (Tribunale di Brindisi 1993, p. 365). In the verdict of the first maxiprocesso, the reader learns about Rogoli's predominant role:

---

[5] See Vv.Aa. (1994, p. 73). The secrecy code is much stricter in older organizations, such as Mafia or 'Ndrangheta. It was unusual that police were able to find copies of initiation code when arresting SCU members. We know (Gambetta 1996, p. 128) that the initiation rite of Cosa Nostra is much simpler than that of other Mafia-like criminal organizations, which implies a Mafioso may learn it by heart, so avoiding written reproductions.

His role was not just liturgical or ritual, since its meaning and scope were deeper and sharper than that for the actual life of the organization. The affiliated members turned to Rogoli whenever the organization was in an actual or potential critical situation, whenever the strength of the associative commitment was threatened by arising internal conflicts and whenever the organization was jeopardized by people who, from the outside or the inside, tried to endanger its stability.

[Il ruolo di Rogoli non si limitava ad essere esclusivamente liturgico o rituale, ma aveva un significato ed una portata ben più profonda ed incisiva nella vita dell'organizzazione, al Rogoli si rivolgevano gli affiliati nei momenti di crisi effettiva o potenziale dell'associazione, quando la saldezza dei vincoli veniva incrinata dall'insorgere di contrasti interni ovvero quando la struttura veniva messa alla prova dall'azione di chi, dall'esterno o dall'interno, tentava di minarne la compattezza].

What follows is a synthetic reconstruction of the functions Rogoli had during the 1980s within the organization:

• ranking people in the higher positions within the organization, which resulted in a control of strategic organizational positions (Tribunale di Lecce 1991, p. 275);
• appointing the so-called capizona (the group leaders in specific local areas), at least until 1989 (Tribunale di Lecce 1991, p. 375);
• settling controversies among affiliated members or groups, often due to the violation of the territorial rules, according to which each group had a monopoly of illegal activities in its respective area of operation;
• judging those who stepped out of the way and reintegrating those who had been temporarily suspended.

The functions of Rogoli within the organization, as reconstructed in official documents, should not induce to think of SCU either as a stable, bureaucracy-like structure or a monolithic organization centered around the charismatic personality of its leader. Although Rogoli was probably able to keep control of the organization until it remained little differentiated, it is plausible to partially disagree with the aforementioned quoted verdict of the first maxiprocesso. Indeed, Rogoli was not immune from attacks, as the power struggles, which affected the life of the young organization since its early years clearly demonstrates (Longo 1997). Whereas he was described as the peace-keeper, his decisions and actions were often conflicting, as they produced new controversies among members and made the mutual commitment ever looser. Although involved in the conflicting relations of power, he was nonetheless able to maintain, according to the informer Cirfeda, his emblematic character (Tribunale di Brindisi 1993). As the organizational structure became more unstable, Rogoli's function assumed a symbolical rather than an operative function: He guaranteed the construction of a fictitious tradition and the reproduction of a group identity within a newly formed criminal organization.

Indeed, notwithstanding the mitigated descriptions of Rogoli as an old and wise man, his figure does not overlap with the romantic image of the traditional boss, fairly judging members of the organization according to merits and faults. He was an innovator, since he inaugurated a Mafia-like organization able to carry out criminal actions ever more effective in the Southern heel of Italy, and as an innovator, he set the character of the organization, its recklessness and lack of scruples.

Culture and Group Identity

A relevant aspect for both the cultural and organizational components of Mafia-like criminal groups are a set of paramilitary rules and rituals. Both rules and rituals are weird, often written in an incorrect language, combining dialectal forms and archaisms, which is one of the reasons why many scholars (for example Hess 1993) found themselves ill at ease admitting their existence.[6] A plausible sociological question is related to the reason why such apparently "decorative" elements, unusual as they may appear from the outside, are essential even within a newly formed criminal organization, such as SCU. Indeed, the case of the Apulian Mafia makes the idea plausible according to which the cultural component is an essential element of any Mafia-like criminal organization. Otherwise, why should both the enrollment of criminals and their ranking higher in the hierarchy be ritualized? Why should the rituals be so obscure, archaic, confusing, and apparently devoid of any clear sense?

As a newly formed organization, SCU could have solved the question of narratives and rituals simply bypassing it. The organization could have structured itself as not connote Organized Crime, so as to guarantee its practical objective: Pursuing more effective illegal tasks and increasing profits. On the contrary, the history of SCU shows clearly the necessity for a new Mafia-like organization to construct its own tradition, eventually borrowing narratives, rituals, and rules from other criminal organizations, and adapting them to the necessities of its members (Tribunale di Lecce 1991, p. 109). Indeed, the police found a consistent number of manuscripts, even tapes, in which, either in written or recorded form, rituals, rules, initiation-formulas had been stored as an attempt of the affiliated members to keep external narratives in mind, which, in so far as they were part of an exogenous oral tradition, had not yet been memorized.[7]

Rituals are aspects of a dual process of identity construction: (1) The criminal organization may adopt them as the identity-horizon, against which it may differentiate itself from common criminality, thus reinforcing internal mutual commitment; (2) the mystery and secrecy connected to rituals and membership make the capacity for intimidation of the organized group even stronger, since they produce an increased sense of fear and impotence among the population, as the members of secret groups are supposed to support reciprocally, which makes criminal activities even

---

[6] See Gambetta (1996, p. 128), who writes about the difficulty to admit the Mafia mythology, by referring to the case of Cosa Nostra: "Perhaps under the influence of conventional rationalism or Marxist prudery, some authors seam ill at ease when faced with the non rational and simply ignore the mythology, implicitly considering it as irrelevant, a mere drop of superstructural dressing. Substituting disbelief for disregard, other write off the symbolism as pure fantasy or, at the most, exaggerations by outsiders with a vested interest in inflating the phenomenon, notably journalists and policemen."

[7] One of the pieces of evidence used by judges to demonstrate that SCU was a Mafia-like organization was the finding of manuscripts where the affiliation formulas had been transcribed. See Tribunale di Lecce (1991, p. 12), which reports the finding of a notebook where "all the formulas which had been handwritten, had to be followed during the initiation ceremony and in the passages-rituals from the lower to the higher ranks of the organization, according to a rigid and complex ritual made up of questions and answers."

more effective. This second aspect is relevant for the concrete activities of criminal groups. Reputation may guarantee equal relations with similar criminal organizations, so that the new criminal structure may plan joint illegal activities with the older Mafias. Moreover, reputation may result in a tighter grip of the organization over the territory in which it operates: Territorial control (which implies a monopoly of certain illegal activities, tolerance of other activities provided that protection is paid, bribe paid by shop keepers and so on)[8] is possible thanks to the criminal reputation deriving from the belonging to Mafia-like Organized Crime. In short, on the one hand rituals and rules were adopted by SCU as a way of legitimizing its being the youngest among the Mafias, with its own boundaries, its mutually supporting members, and its reputation; on the other, through a sophisticated and balanced information leakage about the organization, the mutual commitment of the initiated members, and the organization's willingness to contrast any opposition, SCU reputation increased and, at the same time, the effectiveness of its illegal activities.[9]

The self-representation of SCU as a criminal elite is strengthened by shared rules and formalized rituals, which are essential to the organization in so far as they make the distinction between membership and common criminality even more unmistakable. A side effect is a peculiar allure propagating from the criminal organization, which makes membership and enrollment desirable for common criminals. Indeed, a complex mythology, a set of symbols, narratives, and rituals are now considered by some sociologists as a conspicuous aspect of Mafia-like organizations, even those with a tradition older than SCU ever had.[10] Diego Gambetta, for example, stressed the relevance of myths and symbols in the oldest and best known Italian criminal organization, the Sicilian Mafia. Antonio Calderone, an important former member of Cosa Nostra who turned into a police informer, described his initiation to the judges. Gambetta reports:

> During [Calderone's] initiations the head of the family said: "Now I am going to tell you how the Cosa Nostra was born. It was born during the Sicilian Vespers [AD. 1282] when people rebelled and also the Beati Paoli were born [...]".

And the sociologist comments:

> Some readers may doubt the representative value of these revelations and deride those who subsist on such fantasies. Still, their function is presumably to transmit a shared language, an esprit de corps, a sense of belonging and differentiation akin, mutatis mutandis, to that transmitted by IBM for example, to its recruits (Gambetta 1996, p. 132).

---

[8] See Gambetta, (1996, p. 115) who writes that the symbolic power of the association, in a way which is not dissimilar from marketing rules, makes the capability of intimidation of associates and groups stronger.

[9] A local newspaper, Quotidiano, 26th October 1994, reports about a group of criminals asking for protection money on behalf of SCU, without being associates. SCU is perceived as a brand, which may make the request for protection money successful since the brand enhances the intimidation power of the bribers. This necessity to promote a 'brand' makes the secrecy code difficult to handle: A Mafia-like organization needs to keep a balance between the secrecy of the organization and the necessity of a dosed leakage of information about its existence and dangerousness.

[10] Gambetta (1996, p. 128) shows that rituals, which are similar to those adopted by Mafia-like organizations are used in more socially accepted contexts (masonry, university, and colleges), and, although there are apparently irrational aspects about them, their existence is not called into question.

The function of the reference to a mythical past is the same for the Apulian criminal organization, with the difference that SCU had no past and had to construct it by fictionally combining elements deriving from other criminal traditions (especially from 'Ndrangheta and Camorra), with which SCU members-to-be (Pino Rogoli in particular) came in contact in Apulian jails. A supplementary function is to be ascribed to SCU's cultural and symbolic tools: By adopting elements deriving from different traditions, and thus mocking more consolidated organizations, SCU aspired at being accepted by other groups as an equal partner and competitor.[11]

Cultural elements produce a sort of shared identity regardless of conflicts and contrasts among territorial groups. Throughout the 1980s and part of the 1990s, different groups continued to recognize themselves as part of a greater organizational structure, even those which, in order to differentiate themselves from the mother-organization, chose to adopt a new denomination.[12] Indeed, the very choice of the name of the criminal structure—Sacra Corona Unita (Fiasco 1992), which according to informers was to stress the mutual commitment of the initiated members—was symbolically connotated so to emphasize the sacredness and strength of the union. It was also the name by which the organization was known by the external social environment, a sort of brand, which tended to stress the reputation and intimidation power of the associated groups.

Becoming a Member as a Status Contract

Initiation rituals mark the entry into the organization and are symbolically connotated, so as to stress the belonging to an elite group.[13] Informers maintain that the future associate has to be proposed to the organization by a member ranking higher than picciotto (the lower grade in the hierarchy), and, at any rate, before being accepted, he has to be put under scrutiny for a certain ammount of time (Vv.Aa. 1994, p. 72). Rituals are complex, their climax being the oath formula, which clarifies the contents of the commitment to the association. An approximate translation of one of the formulas sequestered by the police might be:

---

[11] See Vv.Aa., (1994, p. 69). The original connection with 'Ndrangheta and Camorra has been emphasized also by informers. See Tribunale di Brindisi (1993, p. 232,) where one of the informers, Capodieci, gives a clear-cut description of these relations.

[12] See Tribunale di Brindisi (1994, p. 56) where Cirfeta tells the judges the reason why a group of criminals decided to set up a new organization in Lecce (another important Apulian city) due to conflicts with the mother organization that could not be settled. The new group was denominated Rosa dei Venti (the Wind Rose), and, as Cirfeda stresses, although vindicating more autonomy, it considered itself and was still considered a 'ndrina (that is, an affiliated group) of the overall organization.

[13] The initiation ritual (also called baptism) has the symbolic value of a ritual strengthening of the mutual commitment among members, as well as of the authority of the organization, which may punish any deviance. Musio, one of the informers of the police, by describing the baptism in which he was initiated, says: "Everybody repeatedly reminded me that in case I was led astray, I would pay with my life" Tribunale di Brindisi (1991, p. 271).

I swear, upon the tip of this dagger, wet with blood, that I will disown my mother, father, brothers and sisters up to the seventh generation; I swear that I will share every cent, as long as I have blood in my veins, one foot in the grave, and the other in chains, while hugging friends in jail (Vv.Aa. 1994, p. 73).

[Giuro sulla punta di questo pugnale macchiato di sangue di disconoscere madre, padre, fratelli e sorelle fino alla settima generazione...giuro di dividere centesimo per centesimo, millesimo per millesimo, fino all'ultima goccia di sangue, con un piede nella fossa e l'altro alla catena per dare un forte abbraccio alla galere].

If we assume the initiation ritual as a crucial moment in the organization life, one may better understand the peculiarities of Mafia-like groups. The bureaucracy metaphor is useless for understanding the phenomenon, since the commitment linking an initiated member to the criminal group is completely different from the commitment that would tie an employee to the administrative structure where he works. The sense of belonging may be similar (see Gambetta 1996), the content of everyday activities and the individual existence may not. The oath formula shows that, at least in the self-representation of Mafia-like organizations, when entering the group, the member accepts an absolute, unconditional belonging. By swearing the initiation oath, the member-to-be ceases to play the role of the lay-man: He becomes affiliate.

In order to understand the sociological relevance of affiliation as a biographical landmark, a reference to Max Weber may be useful. Within a different context, aimed at explaining the process by which contractual freedom was introduced in the western economic system, Max Weber proposes a distinction between status contracts and purposive contracts. Purposive contracts are typically modern. They assume the commitment of both contracting parties to a specific purpose (or a set of purposes) and nothing else. Status contracts, on the contrary, are typical of more simple societies and imply a process of transformation of the individual, of his social qualities and roles, as he becomes part of a set of mutual commitments within a new social group. Let me quote Weber directly:

[Status contracts] by which political or other personal association, permanent or temporary, or family relations are created, involve a change in what may be called the total legal situation (the permanent position) and the social status of the person involved. To have this effect this contracts were either straightforward magical acts or at least acts having a magical significance. For a long time, their symbolism retained traces of that character (Weber 1978, p. 672).

And, a few lines below:

[...] the majority of these contracts are fraternization contracts [...]. To "fraternize" with another person did not, however, mean that a certain performance of the contract, contributing to the attainment of some specific object, was reciprocally guaranteed or expected [...]. The contract rather meant that the person would "become" something different in quality (or status) from the quality he possessed before [...] Each party must thus make a new soul enter his body [and that] required the mixing and imbibing of blood or spittle (Weber 1978, p. 672).

Without claiming an absolute compatibility of the Weberian concept of status contract with the initiation rituals, some elements are comparable. The oath formula has the ideological function to create reciprocal obligations, which, at least as an ideological self-representation, should mutually bind, now and forever, the new associate to the organization. The ritual has a quasi-magical power: It changes the qualities of the new members. They are by now new people, and their present characters are a direct effect of their admittance to the criminal group.

It is not my intention to maintain that SCU initiation rituals actually have the strength of an ever-lasting bond or that, once they are performed, they have the power to irreversibly change the social quality of the new member. Nonetheless, when the organization admits a new associate, the symbolic elements of the oath formula tend to stress the passage to a new status (disown parents and relatives being the more meaningful clue). Rituals give a representation of the organization as a separated social nucleus where an unconditional overlapping of group will and member will is supposed to take place.

Since Mafia-like organizations (including SCU) are part of our present and complex society, one can hardly accept the idea according to which, as in the cases described by Max Weber, rituals may function as permanent stabilizers of the actual conduct of the initiated member. They can, at the most, temporarily stabilize reciprocal expectations. Yet, a pretended unconditional belonging to the organization plays a relevant role: Indeed, the associate is an initiated member, not an employee, so that his role may be perceived as a diffuse and not a specific role (Parsons and Shils 1962). This means that the organization may ask him to fulfill a variable number of differentiated, not predetermined tasks. Although some of the roles within the organization may be defined according to individual skills and competences, as well as in coherence with a member ranking in the association hierarchy, initiation as a peculiar form of status contract allows the divisions of tasks and roles to be flexible, according to specific and often unforeseeable organizational necessities.

After the initiated has accepted an unconditional belonging to the organization, according to the oath formula, he has to take on omertà (that is the code of silence) as a guideline for his conduct. At the same time, he has to admit the authority of the organization to punish its members, whenever they stray from the "right" way. Here follows a tentative, nonliterary translation of the formula:

> You [the organization] taught me the beauties of omertà, you, rich in honors were a guarantor for me, and shaped me thanks to your formal rules.
> [Omertà bella che mi insegnasti, ricca d'onore mi garantisti sotto un capo di formalità mi apparecchiasti].

And the officiate urges:

> Young men, beware of not being led astray: Shall you, you'll get 3 plus 5 stabs, three on my behalf and 5 on behalf of this noble, honorable society (Vv.Aa. 1994, p. 73).
> [Giovane badate bene a non sbagliare; se sbaglierete da 3 a 5 colpi di pugnale pagherete, 3 a carico mio e 5 a carico di questa nobile onorata società].

Regardless of the specific aspects of the initiation ritual (complexity and verbosity in particular), which may be assimilated to those performed by other Mafia-like organizations ('Ndrangheta and Camorra in particular),[14] what is pertinent to our discourse is the function it has in the organization's life. The ritual marks a rupture,

---

[14] Camorra rituals are described in Rigagnese and Tricarico (1992); 'Ndrangheta rituals are transcribed in Malafarina (1978, 1986). For Cosa Nostra rituals, see Arlacchi (1992) and Gambetta (1996).

which is symbolically connotated to make the biographical passage mnemonically impressed in the new affiliated member. It also serves as a fictitious narrative of the way the association represents itself. Indeed, this narrative seams in contradiction with reality: Organized Crime is often made up of conflicting relationships, among associated groups and among group members. It is a world of changeable alliances, betrayal, power struggle, and fluctuating power relations, which, all the same, play at representing itself as united, supportive, just.

By underlining the fictitious characteristic of the cultural representation of the association, one has not to conceive rituals as a farce, much less a mythical representation of organizational reality devoid of any organizational meaning. On the contrary, the cultural and the organizational aspects of the criminal group interplay and influence each other. Rituals, narratives and the actual praxis of the organization acts are indeed functional to the maintenance of the overall criminal organization.

Rituals and norms, which found the shared self-representation of the association, are to be intended as an ideological background upon which expectations of members are stabilized. Those expectations are precarious, as they are often disregarded. Yet, since they are at the base of any organizational norms, every norm violation has to be justified, thus forcing the members to reaffirm the validity of the normative component of the association, and the group to re-interpret the broken rule.[15] A wiretapping of a telephone call between De Tommasi, one of the local bosses of the organization, and an associate shows how much the initiation rules are taken into consideration by SCU members. De Tommasi speaks to his addressee: "You know how we have to act if we want to follow the rules, don't you? -You know how we have to act?" [Lo sai come si procede, se vogliamo andare a regola aah?-con il giuramento, no?- Sai come si procede]. Rules are the background of correct conduct, as they fix a set of expectations against the ever incumbent possibility of deviation.

Of course, the flexible use of norms (often determined by the ever-changing relations of power) is not exclusive of SCU, as it shares this feature with other Mafia-like criminal organizations, even those with an older tradition and with a more defined structure. Rules are, in fact, applied from time to time according to an ever precarious power balance, so that the higher the hierarchical status of a member is, the more flexible the norms become for him. The lack of normative scruples, which results in a distorted use of rules, is structurally connected to the fact that, in a Mafia-like organization, the interaction among associates, regardless of the mitigated self-narratives of union and integration, are based on tricks, betrayal, and unstable alliances, with members often going back on previously settled compromises. If the rules, including the golden rule of the monopoly of criminal activities in a given territory, were valid once and for all, it would be difficult to explain the cyclical recurrence of violent conflicts among groups. As a newly formed organization, during the 1980s, SCU suffered from a lack of normative stability, which was stronger

---

[15] Our analysis of codes and norms was clearly influenced by ethnomethodology (Garfinkel 1966). According to this approach, social rules are the product of the everyday effort of common people to make them plausible. In the case of SCU and other Mafia-like organizations, the question of power is relevant for the interpretation and the social construction of the normative apparatus.

than within traditional Mafias, due both to the fact that the Apulian organization had not completely assimilated the set of associative "values," and to lack of internal cohesion (among members and territorial groups), which corresponded to a lack of stable leadership and eventually resulted in an instable and loose organizational structure.

Brief Concluding Remarks

During the 1990s, the great project of Rogoli crumbled: His idea to build up a great criminal organization, able to contrast other Mafias (which tried then to infiltrate into Apulia in order to both control local criminality and monopolize criminal activities) resulted in the creation of what journalists and politicians tend to call the "Fourth Mafia." Yet, when put to the test, the SCU showed all its weaknesses. Conflict among groups became ever more frequent and violent. The planned conspiracy with politicians was only partially successful and in some confined parts of the region. Both the judicial system and the police opposed the criminal phenomenon effectively. But although SCU is now a residual organization still rooted in the northern part of Salento (the sub-region where SCU prospered), its relevance must not be underestimated: Indeed, in a territory, which was immune from Organized Crime, it inaugurated new criminal practices, which are still part of the regional criminal culture. As an organized structure, which tried to protect its members, it was perceived as a positive evolution by common criminality. It increased its influence over the little local criminals, whose prestige increased as they were recognized as members of the organization. Some part of the population became supportive to the criminal groups, although that process may not be generalized. Yet SCU was a violent Mafia-like organization, which did not hesitate to plan massacres and to perpetrate bloody crimes.

A side effect was the increasing awareness in the public sphere, which resulted in the constitution of associations devoted to the civic opposition to Organized Crime. Thus, legality and contrast of crime became part of the public debate, which is particularly relevant when one thinks that in the early 1980s, when Apulian Organized Crime was becoming a theme in the public discussion, the first reaction of politicians, the population, and even judges was to deny the existence of the phenomenon in order to protect a consolidated image of the region as immune from Organized Crime, an exception in the South of Italy.

It is particularly hard to sketch scenarios, which was not the goal of this paper. Its intent was to detect some elements, which may be considered as typical of Mafia-like criminal organizations, starting from the analysis of a novel associative phenomenon. In setting itself up, SCU combined organizational structure, cultural, and ritual elements derived from other Mafias, with a particular emphasis on the cultural dimension in such a way as to construct its image as the youngest among Italian Mafia-like organizations.

References

Albanese, J. S. (1994). Models of organized crime. In R. J. Kelly, K. Chin, & R. Schatzberg (Eds.), *Handbook of organized crime in the United States*. Westport: Greenwood Press, 77–90.

Arlacchi, P. (1983). *La mafia imprenditrice*. Bologna: Il Mulino.

Arlacchi, P. (1992). *Gli uomini del disonore. La mafia siciliana nella vita del grande pentito Antonio Calderone*. Milan: Mondadori.

Caracciolo, F. (1992). *Miseria della mafiologia*. Bologna: Monduzzi Editore.

Catanzaro, R. (1988a). *Il delitto come impresa. Storia sociale della mafia*. Editrice: Liviana.

Catanzaro, R. (1988b). Cosa nostra s.p.a. *Micromega, 4*, 47–57.

Catanzaro, R. (1992). Le relazioni con l'impresa e la politica locale. *Asterischi*, 1(2), 57–64.

Ciconte, E. (1992). *La 'Ndrangheta dall'Unità a oggi*. Bari-Rome: Laterza.

Cressey, D. (1969). *Thefts of the nation. The structure and operations of organized crime*. New York: Harper and Row.

Crisantino, A., & La Fiura, G. (1989). *La mafia come metodo e come sistema*. Cosenza: Luigi Pellegrini Editore.

Fiasco, M. (1992). *Puglia. Il crimine: scenari e strategie*. Rome: Sapere 2000.

Gambetta, D. (1996). *The Sicilian Mafia. The business of private protection*. Harvard: Harvard University Press.

Garfinkell, H. (1996). *Studies in Ethnomethodology*. Englwood Cliffe: Prantice Hall.

Hagan, F. (2006). 'Organized Crime' and 'organized crime.' Indeterminate problems of definition. *Trends in Organized Crime*, 9(4), 127–137.

Hess, H. (1993). *Mafia. Le origini e la struttura*. Rome-Bari: Laterza.

Longo, M. (1997). *Sacra Corona Unita. Storia, struttura, rituali*. Lecce: Pensa Multimedia.

Malafarina, L. (1978). *Il codice della 'ndrangheta*. Reggio Calabria: Edizioni Parallelo 38.

Malafarina, L. (1986). *La 'Ndrangheta*. Rome: Gangemi Editore.

Maltz, M. D. (1994). Defining organized crime. In R. J. Kelly, K. Chin, & R. Schatzberg (Eds.), *Handbook of organized crime in the United States*. Westport: Grenwood Press, 21–38.

Merton, R. K. (1949). *Social theory and social structure*. New York: Free Press.

Parsons, T., & Shils, E. A. (1962). Values, Motives, and Systems of Action. In T. Parsons, & Shils, E. A. (Eds.), *Towards a general theory of action. Theoretical foundations for the social sciences* New York: Transaction Publisher, 47–278.

Reuter, P. (1994). Research on American organized crime. In R. J. Kelly, K. Chin, & R. Schatzberg (Eds.), *Handbook of organized crime in the United States*. Westport: Greenwood Press, 91–120.

Rignanese, M., & Tricarico, V. (1992). *Storia dei tre vecchi antenati. Regole e rituali della Camorra*. Manfredonia: Edizioni del Golfo.

Ruggero, V. (1992). Crimine organizzato: una proposta di aggiornamento delle definizioni. *Dei delitti e delle pene*, II(3), 7–30.

Sales, I. (1998). *La camorra, le camorra*. Rome: Editori Riuniti.

Sales, I. (1992). La criminalità organizzata tra modernizzazione e poteri dello stato. *Asterischi,* 1(2), 11–20.

Tribunale di Brindisi. (16 October 1993). *Sentenza contro B. Ciro + 28*.

Tribunale di Brindisi. (23 May 1994). *Sentenza contro M. D'Amico + 9*.

Tribunale di Lecce. (25 May 1991). *Sentenza contro G. De Tommasi + 104*.

Vv.Aa (1994). *La quarta mafia. Percorsi e strategie della criminalità organizzata pugliese*. Rome: Eurispes.

Weber, M. (1978). *Economy and society*. Berkely and Los Angeles: University of California Press.

Chapter 9
Sacra Corona Unita and 'Ndrangheta: "Structural" Differences of Organized Crime

Andrea Apollonio

Sacra Corona Unita and 'Ndrangheta

The history of Italian criminal organizations has always been marked, in large part, by the events of four Mafia organizations, each of which have a specific geographical location: Cosa Nostra in Sicily, Camorra in Campania, 'Ndrangheta in Calabria, and Sacra Corona Unita (SCU) in Apulia. Of these, the first two have always had a high media emphasis and benefit particular attention from scholars. Indeed, we might say that the history of the Mafia corresponds with the period from the unification of Italy to the beginning of the 1990s, with that of Cosa Nostra and Camorra: The first relevant work of the 'Ndrangheta was, in fact, dated 1990 (Nicaso 1990).

Although it is one of the oldest types of Mafia, only in those years did interest in the 'Ndrangheta grow; more recently attention has turned toward the Apulia region, where, for at least a couple of decades, the SCU has operated. In 1994, the latter region "officially" joined the group of Mafia associations, becoming, thus, the "Fourth Mafia" (Commissione 1994).

The SCU and the 'Ndrangheta have always been considered "twin Mafias." Certainly, for reasons of territorial influences and supremacy that almost border each other; a geographical disposition that made the Ionic Sea a proper *mare nostrum* of the two Mafias, and the whole Ionic coast from Gallipoli to Reggio Calabria, the ideal breeding ground for any sort of maritime illegal activity, often comanaged from both organizations. So much so that the whole southern area of Basilicata could have been considered, until a couple of decades ago, a laboratory of exchanging of criminal techniques, a meeting point, and place for the planning of illicit activities of both organizations (Sergi 2001, p. 73).

Geographical proximity is not the mere reason for this conceptual closeness of the two organizations. The 'Ndrangheta had a primary role in the creation of the SCU, a true "sponsorship" of the organization, (Massari 1998, p. 22) since the

A. Apollonio (✉)
Dipartimento di Giurisprudenza—Diritto e procedura penale, Università di Pavia,
Strada Nuova 65, 27100 Pavia, Italy
e-mail: andrea.apollonio01@universitadipavia.it

N. Serenata (ed.), *The 'Ndrangheta and Sacra Corona Unita,* Studies of Organized Crime 12,   133
DOI 10.1007/978-3-319-04930-4_9, © Springer International Publishing Switzerland 2014

founder of the Apulian group, Pino Rogoli—a man was very close to the 'Ndrangheta boss Giuseppe Bellocco—would be annexed to the 'Ndrangheta with a formal
rite of affiliation. As has been authoritatively affirmed: "In Apulia, ties between the
'Ndrangheta and the SCU were long established. The SCU was founded in 1983 as a
sort of Calabrian *'ndrina*" [in Puglia i legami tra la 'Ndrangheta e la criminalità pugliese sono da tempo consolidati. La "Sacra corona unita" venne costituita nel 1983
come una sorta di 'ndrina calabrese] (Gratteri and Nicaso 2006, p. 200). Therefore,
it is evident that the moment of the constitution of the Apulian organization is strictly connected with the more deep and secret dynamics of the 'Ndrangheta.

In addition, as mentioned before, both groups had the benefit of a persisting and
generalized undervaluation of cause and effect of the Mafia phenomenon. Being
considered minor criminal groups has allowed them an uncontested proliferation of
their dangerousness in their respective regions of origin.

These are only some of the more evident reasons that have allowed these two
Mafia groups a close collaboration in vast transnational drug trafficking—coming
from the West—or the numerous routes of weapons or human smuggling—beginning in the East—both reaching the arrival point in Calabria. This partnership has
also permitted them to "operate as a sort of intellectual collective, able to analyze
in a short amount of time their weak points, and to learn from their mistakes [...] to
progressively impart their own knowledge within the organization" [operare come
una sorta di intellettuale collettivo, in grado di analizzare in breve tempo i propri
punti deboli, di imparare dai propri errori [...] di socializzare progressivamente
all'interno dell'organizzazione il proprio sapere] (Scarpinato 2005). That which the
two Mafias accomplish is a continuous re-elaboration of the criminal model and
method, an overlapping and sharing of experiences that put the two groups in contact on both a conceptual and concrete level.

Nevertheless, there are numerous differences between the SCU and the 'Ndrangheta. These, to some extent, must be considered "structural" as they constitute different species of Mafia criminal organizations, different models of illicit capitalism.
Relevant dissimilarities also demonstrated in terms of offensiveness and obstinacy
compared to the social structures of reference.

A Horizontal Structure with "Fragmented" Behavior, a "Pure" Reticular Structure

The SCU was never successful in becoming a complete Mafia: It lacks a well-
defined structure, bosses who know how to impose themselves within the organization, a decision-making structure, and a well-defined territory. This is an assumption that will often recur in writing as an underground fracture that is there to remind
all that this group and the 'Ndrangheta represent, regardless of their undeniable
similarities, two distinct continents.

The "Fourth Mafia" was born from the reactive impulses of Apulian criminality
to a massive presence of affiliates of the Nuova Camorra Organizzata of Raffaele

Cutolo, who intended to take advantage of the Adriatic coasts to open new maritime routes for cigarette smuggling, (Apollonio 2010, p. 74; Tornesello 2013, p. 60) by adopting "a strategy of proper assimilation of the Apulian men" [una strategia di vera e propria assimiliazione dei pugliesi] (Massari 1998, p. 11). As Cataldo Motta, one of the protagonists of the contrastive phenomenon of those years, wrote:

> In the prison of Bari and in the other penitential institutions of the region, at the beginning of the 1980s, not only a great number of affiliations of Apulian detainees to the *Nuova Camorra Organizzata* occurred, but also an attitude of submission to Neapolitan prisoners belonging to the organization: This was the first sign for those who from the criminal part understood—more promptly from the other side!—the gravity of the phenomenon and the risk of losing control of Apulian criminal activities (p. 54).
> [Nel carcere di Bari e negli altri istituti penitenziari della regione, all'inizio degli anni Ottanta, si verificarono non soltanto un gran numero di affiliazioni di detenuti pugliesi alla Nuova camorra organizzata, ma anche atteggiamenti di loro sottomissione ai detenuti napoletani appartenenti alla stessa organizzazione: questo fu un primo segnale d'allarme per chi da parte criminale, comprese — più tempestivamente dell'altra parte! — la gravità del fenomeno e il rischio della perdita del controllo delle attività criminali pugliesi].

For these reasons, the organization employed, since its beginning, an attitude of "Protest Mafia." In this way, lands that had until then remained untouched, as they were extraneous to Mafia activity, suddenly fell into the hands of a criminal organization—the SCU, in fact—that in the course of a few years replaced the presence of the Neapolitans in the handling of the same illegal trafficking.

Since its establishment, the SCU appeared as something slightly different from the classic phenotype of a Mafia association, but rather as a federation among clans located in the Salento and Bari areas, whose criminal strategies were arranged, at the most, among bosses, and were focused on the management of cigarette smuggling and other illicit maritime trafficking (Tornesello 2009). Not having a socio-family connection (usually present in other organizations), but at the base a vast profit that maritime traffickers assured, the organizational structure is subject to continuous detachments and frequent fragmentations. For instance, in 1987, in the peak of its military potency, the SCU could already be considered as divided into three units, inside which a series of capo-Mafia operated: The Brindisi unit, that of the south of Bari, and finally those in the Salento area (Massari 1998, p. 39).

The organization has never been able to express vertical decision making. The Apulian Mafia could be defined, for this, as a horizontal Mafia with a fragmental behavior, characterized by the absence of top brass and from the maximum autonomy of the single clans that create an innovative criminal *network* (Longo 1997, p. 73). It is, without doubt, capable of managing hundreds of kilometers of coastline and a good part of inland Bari and Lecce, but at the same time proves itself quite weak confronted with judicial offenses. "The Apulian criminal organizations, more than large hegemonic groups, is characterized by heterogeneous reticular delinquent clans, who, from time to time, but not necessarily, interact according to some agreement of reciprocal benefit" [La criminalità organizzata pugliese è connotata, più che da grossi gruppi egemoni, da un reticolo eterogeneo di formazioni delinquenziali, che talora—ma non necessariamente—interagiscono secondo intese di rispetto reciproco] (Mantovano 2001, p. 109). This demonstrates how the interactions and the reciprocal relationships among affiliates, or the concatenate relationships that merge in the center—these phenomena that have always observed within Mafia associations (Hess 1993, p. 190)—are almost absent in the SCU, making it an *unicum* in the Italian situation; more "a project of a Mafia association than a completed model" [un progetto di associazione mafiosa che non un modello compiuto] (Arlacchi 1998, XIII).

Shifting attention toward the 'Ndrangheta, every reflection needs to be looked at on a different scale. It should be sufficient to say that no other organization, in their own territorial declination, can better realize the image of *cosca*: The heart of the artichoke, a fruit closed in on itself, whose leathery leaves do not allow anyone to reach the most internal, edible part.

What strongly characterizes the 'Ndrangheta are the blood ties of its affiliates. So much so that, very often, the "criminal" family tends to coincide with the "natural" family: *La cosca* (or *'ndrina*) is based in large measure on a blood-related family, and that sometimes enlarges and develops itself through weddings that absorb other nuclei. The pervading of family relations determine, thus, the hierarchies of command within the *'ndrina* and the power tends to be transmitted via inheritance (Sciarrone 2008, p. 74).

Moving forward with the analysis of the structure, more *cosche* connected among them give birth to a *locale* that represents the core of the Mafia aggregation in a certain territory. The most important element is without doubt the *'ndrina*, managed in absolute autonomy by the *capobastone*. The *locale*, on the contrary, can be defined a sort of "compensation room" to prepare common strategies and make important decisions.

The dominion of the *capobastone* must not be misleading: We are in the presence of a rigidly top-down Mafia (i.e., vertical structure), since the vertex (absolute) command exists only within the clan. Outside of it, there is a purely horizontal structure, aimed at regulating relations between the *cosche*.

At least, formally, all *cosche* in the 'Ndrangheta are on the same level: This, within a Mafioso context in which (dis)values prevail as vendetta and violence, might determine irremediable internal feuds and often generate bitter and bloody fights among them. Thus, between the 1980s and the 1990s, due to a feud among *cosche* in Reggio Calabria, which led to a degeneration of killings on public roads, 'Ndrangheta heads began to create a "network" "that from one side decreased the fighting level and on the other side allowed to maximize the social share of a more consolidated criminal organization" [che da un lato abbassa il livello di conflittualità e dall'altro consente di massimizzare il capitale sociale delle organizzazioni criminali più consolidate] (Sciarrone 2008, p. 80). An efficient and solid network that put in contact representatives of prominent families by avoiding further margins of hate: Far from the fragmented context of the Apulia organization where bosses of each family could not count on the liability of blood ties.

More specifically, making reference to the 'Ndrangheta as more than a horizontal structure, it would be appropriate to define it as a species: A "pure" reticular structure. Indicating with this latter affirmation, a substantial difference with the other Mafia that in a way or another are complex (i.e. with clans connected among them), but that does not reach the informative and logistic interexchange level present in the Calabrian model.

Institutional Connections

Another reason for which the SCU can be considered an atypical Mafia is that it does not possess the most important requirement that would allow it to construct a wider and more powerful system, which in hindsight presents what makes a Mafia group a well-rooted organization in the territory: Institutional connections.

Historically, Mafia power claims a direct connection with the institutional government of the territory in order to establish a network of protection in higher administration levels. As Pino Arlacchi argues: "The Mafia system is a project of power and conquer" [l'ordinamento mafioso è un progetto di potere e di conquista] (2007, p. 91) as it presumes massive infiltrations in politics and institutional offices. Indeed, the forms of control-coordination in institutions must be considered as mere territorial dominance for the Mafia, a constitutive character of its nature of a political group that exercises its function in a specific area controlling everything that takes place within it (Santino 1994, p. 133).

None of this is part of the experience of the SCU in Apulia, which has failed to become whole, to become a "politico-institutional" Mafia. The numerous episodes of corruption and dishonest behavior in the Public Administration in Apulia in the 1990s—remembering that on a national level it was the period of "Tangentopoli"—cannot be counted with the development of the Mafia organization, which is contrary to what some may hypothesize (Sciarrone 1998, p. 158; Gorgoni 1995, p. 98). The expansion of the Mafia model in Apulia did not "hook" politics: The master proof of this assertion can be found in judicial records, where there are no convictions for Apulian politicians for Mafia collusion, in particular with the SCU.

On the other hand, the 'Ndrangheta could be considered the political "Mafia" of all organizations: This organization has expressed its own "Mafia bourgeoisie" better than any other (Santino 2007, p. 108).

Mafia organizations are not extraneous to society, but are on the contrary an integral part of it. It is within society that they must search for consensus, and specifically in those areas in which it is difficult to reach, it is in the collective fear generated by intimidation that Mafia finds its *raison d'être*. Society is a reference point through which the Mafia places itself diagonally compared to other social circles: In fact, they create their own, wider social circle, which spans from underprivileged families to well-off economical operators that manage their operations of smuggling and reinvestment of capital, passing and flowing through both the business and political world. In a similar social circle on Mafia hegemony, which reaches well beyond the narrow confines of the criminal organization, every boundary between legal and illegal is blurred, and subjects that work within are the heart of the *Mafia bourgeoisie*. This concept, developed in the 1990s by Umberto Santino, takes for granted the intertwining of politics and the Mafia because it places people performing illegal (the boss) and legal (professionals, businessmen, especially politicians) functions in the same social circle, all connected by common interests and sharing the same cultural code.

It is well known that when Santino developed the category of *Mafia bourgeoisie,* he had in mind a complex and contradictory Sicilian society. Still, the best representation of an institutionalized criminality and closeness to the Italian State was not provided by Cosa Nostra, but from the 'Ndrangheta in its *bourgeois* aspect: The Santa.

In the mid 1970s, the 'Ndrangheta, which up until then operated mostly as an agro-pastoral organization and closed into its archaic traditions, felt the need to assign new rules and a new criminal structure that could better infiltrate society. That was the birth of the Santa: "A new structure, elitist, a new management, unrelated to the hierarchical tradition of *locali* that was able to move without hesitation, without the limits of the old Honored Society and its subculture" [una struttura nuova, elitaria, una nuova dirigenza, estranea alle tradizionali gerarchie dei *locali* in grado di muoversi in maniera spregiudicata, senza i limiti della vecchia onorata società e della sua subcultura] (Fierro and Oliva 2007, p. 57). The idea is to penetrate into that gray zone that represents the deviated freemasonry in which they could create a better *bourgeoisie*: Judges, lawyers, businessmen, and politicians. The change is epic since the elite of the 'Ndrangheta—those who were able to reach this secret rank—could have relations, even more lucrative, with members of the freemasonry.

With the *Santa*, the 'Ndrangheta succeeds in entering into a gray zone that had been until that time unapproachable, in the place of privileged contact between Mafiosi and politicians. La *Santa*, in conclusion, represents the "bourgeois" evolution of Mafia organizations. Above all, it embodies the tendency of the 'Ndrangheta to solidify connections at the highest institutional levels, which allowed the organization to be considered a "complete" Mafia because it is "political."

The striking differences articulated so far in this work (regarding the structure and the institutional connections) demonstrate a concrete confirmation on an empirical-criminological level compared to the well-known "pentitismo": That is, from one side, the first cause of the scattering of the organization at the turn of the twenty-first century; on the other side, rendered harmless by the complex and impenetrable structure of the 'Ndrangheta. Undeniably, one of the most evident reasons for the defeat of the SCU is to be found in the spread of *pentitismo* in the 1990s that allowed judiciary organisms to break into families with arrests and convictions.

The absence of institutional protection and of a widespread *affectio societas* meant that once captured, the SCU Mafioso realized to have definitively failed the extremely personal goal of enrichment through illicit activity. Not having—in most cases—blood ties between the various affiliates, and no "common" management of Mafia association, it was possible to begin a collaborative relationship with the judges to diminish the heavy consequences of sanctions: "The fierceness of internal conflict that has characterized the various factions in the Apulian association and the resulting fear to deal directly with the murderous violence of their opponents resulted for many in the urge to cooperate with the authorities" (Massari and Motta 2006, p. 168).

Additional Differences: Expansion Models, Entrepreneurial Strategies, and the Social Milieu

In general, all four Italian criminal organizations can be defined as prototypes of transnational Mafia with a strong centrifugal propulsion compared to the socio-geographic contexts of their regions. The particular geographic collocation of Southern Italy, placed in the center of the Euro-Asian macro-region, has undeniably benefitted from the realization of the peculiar transnational feature of the Italian Mafias. Examples of this are the trafficking of drugs, weapons, tobacco, human, and "new slaves," traffics that have always privileged the (less dangerous) maritime routes and the (often chaotic) harbor passages. Additional examples are the immense cycles of money laundering that represents Northern Italy and even Northern Europe. It is there where Mafia commits a systematic camouflaging of its amounted wealth. It goes without saying, the unstoppable globalization of recent decades has had a considerable impact, and allowed capital to "travel with great speed and simplicity, and this speed and simplicity of movement has proved to be the main source of uncertainty for all the rest. They have become the basis of today's dominion" [viaggiare con grande rapidità e facilità, e tale rapidità e facilità di movimento si sono rivelate la principale fonte di incertezza per tutto il resto. Sono diventate l'odierna base di dominio] (Bauman 2011, p. 137). In this context, exporting the Mafia model beyond the territories of its original roots is a phenomenon observed for a long time by scholars, thus repudiating the assumption that the Mafia is a trademark difficult to export (Gambetta 1992).

That which has been described so far is a general framework with which certain substantial differences among organizations, especially the SCU and the 'Ndrangheta, can be noticed. Looking closer, however, the expansion capacity of the SCU is sure enough unequaled to the other Italian groups. Although tobacco trafficking and smuggling are characterized by an intrinsic transnationality, the SCU was never able—both outside Apulia and Italy—to establish organizational cells. The only exception was Montenegro. Here, as journalistic services had documented (Di Napoli 1995; Sisti 2009), some members of the organization had found not only a secure place to hide, as they were fugitives, but at the same time, necessary collusion within the Montenegro government to make the coastline of that country a comfortable logistic base for the crossing of loads of cigarettes.

Ultimately, the criminal history of the Apulian Mafia has a strong territorial peculiarity and is enclosed in regional boundaries, pressed by the 'Ndrangheta and the Camorra from West, and from East by the powerful Albanian and Eastern Europe Mafia groups (Raufer 2000).

On the contrary, it is interesting to analyze how the 'Ndrangheta was successful at "physically" exporting some operational cells in northern areas of Italy, as well as in Southern France or Germany. In this case, we might talk about a "transplant" or "hard exportation": Two concepts, developed by scholars of criminal organizations, that indicate the possibility for a Mafia group to "decide around a table and with scientific rationality to open a branch in a new area" [decidere a tavolino e con razionalità scientifica di aprire una filiale in una nuova zona] (Varese 2011, p. 11), suggesting, thus, the capacity of the group to operate outside their original territory for a long period, so as to take advantage of the economic resources available in that specific territory (Apollonio 2012a, p. 130).

Extremely interesting is the analysis that Federico Varese does regarding the effort of some clans of the 'Ndrangheta to implant some cells in Northern Italy (49), confirming how far more than other factors, new markets (construction, excavation, etc.) look for a "Mafia request" and to determine, therefore, the establishment of clans somewhere else. Regarding the 'Ndrangheta presence in Germany, Francesco Forgione copiously discusses it, underlying how the opening of new commercial bases defines at the same time the establishment of logistic cells for international drug trafficking (Forgione 2009, p. 130). This same Calabria, nowadays, is described as a nerve center for illicit traffic of every type, and its harbor, especially that of Gioia Tauro, a true sorting center for drugs arriving from South America (Apollonio 2012b, p. 77).

The 'Ndrangheta today is present in almost every continent, and its expansion capacity is the subject to careful reflection. It has also succeeded, as in the example of the plain of Gioia Tauro, to transform its territory into a capital of illegal capitalism, injecting it with apparent wealth and thus altering the dynamics of the local economy. Regarding the drive toward migration and the simultaneous attention to the area of origin of the 'Ndrangheta, Francesco Cinnirella wrote: "The archaism with which this Mafia is cloaked is in contrast to the modernity with which it adapts to new situations and new challenges" [l'arcaicità di cui questa mafia si ammanta fa da contraltare alla modernità con cui si adatta ai nuovi scenari e alle nuove sfide] (Apollonio and Cinnirella 2013, p. 99).

Another substantial difference is found in its different kind of capitalistic behavior, or put differently, in the macroscopic errors of "entrepreneurial strategy" of the Apulian Mafia. The SCU, in fact, during the 1990s was never able to diversify its investments, focusing its criminal strategies on maritime trafficking and contraband, used later for drugs, weapons, and human beings. The capital obtained was then reinvested in the same activities to gain the "multiplier" effect. It is noteworthy how Mafia groups behave, in all respects, like real companies, economic utilities sensitive to supply and demand of markets, legal or illegal: An intuition that had come from 30 years of studies on criminal organizations (Arlacchi 1983), and which is now hardly arguable. The consequences of eliminating that area of the market represented by illicit smuggling are well-known, and it is the members of the SCU that subject the market to tight controls by acting as a "native" organization, and who claim to have an (almost) absolute monopoly.

In fact, in February 2000, following the death of two policemen killed by anarmored off-road vehicle of the organization used to transport some "blondes," the Italian government reacted with an unprecedented repressive action: The territory was militarized, law enforcement bodies were strengthened, the Strait of Otranto was barred with an impressive amount of ships and patrol boats, and sophisticated radar were installed and were able to intercept any suspicious movement in the mirror of the sea in front the coast of the Lecce province. Within a year, all the fugitives were arrested, including those who ran the smuggling routes from abroad.

Operazione Primavera, as the Italian repressive action was called, was one of the most brilliant and effective police and judiciary operations in recent Italian history, and succeeded in totally ending the import of raw and essential material for the Apulian criminal organization: Foreign tobacco. As that trafficking was severely reduced, the entire share capital of the organization was dried up: All faded abruptly with the cessation of smuggling activities, and the "Fourth Mafia" proceeded to be downgraded to criminal associations linked to more traditional "ground" illegal activities: Usury, extortion, drugs, contracts, and other legal activities achieved through Mafioso modality.

Before moving to this work's conclusions, it is important to emphasize another important point: Differences in the social contexts in Apulia and Calabria.

Apulia, until the advent of Campania criminality, was considered an "isola felix" (happy island) since it had not yet experienced the Mafia phenomenon in its territory, as had happened to the other southern Italian regions. The fact that a Mafia was suddenly created, and in such a way as was mentioned above, has determined a sharp contrast with the social fabric of the region, unlikely subjected to Mafia dynamics. This is the reason why the activities that led to the birth of the SCU are "external" to the region, tied to the interest of those territories and coasts of another organization.

The fact that, in the 1990s, the Apulian Mafia had won a "share" of support from the lower social classes of Brindisi cannot remain hidden. In those years, smuggling required manpower (from transport to sale), and it was a labor resource for many people (Tornesello); so that, according to a parliamentary inquiry, smuggling had a turnover that far exceeded 10 % of the wealth of the province of Brindisi (Commissione 2001). It was, regardless, a consensus of those "drugged" by the flow of capital into that region that was not based on a common cultural base of the organization. So much that, once flows were arrested, the consensus generated by the (blinded) support to the local economy also heavily diminished.

On the contrary, the 'Ndrangheta, as it is well-known, has ancient origins, and has been for a long time the expression of a rural and underdeveloped society, still marked by sores of banditry and dissatisfaction of the unification of Italy. In this context, an organization proliferated that was strictly connected with its inhabitants. Then, in a process of reciprocity and exchange with the society it referred to, the 'Ndrangheta gradually shaped it, injecting improper and misleading values, such as the concept of revenge, honor, and private justice. This depended on the fact that, at least in some ways, the 'Ndrangheta values and those of the lower classes corresponded, due to the underdevelopment of Calabria, which continued after the second world war in certain areas. As Enzo Ciconte wrote: "Over time it has become an organization of elite who won, albeit slowly and gradually, its autonomy and has had the ability to draw an ideological construct that merged the values of the dominant culture of the lower classes" [essa nel tempo è diventata un'organizzazione di élite che ha conquistato, seppur lentamente e progressivamente, una sua autonomia e ha avuto la capacità di elaborare una costruzione ideologica in cui sono confluiti valori della cultura dominante e delle classi subalterne] (p. 75). Although with different patterns and trends, the clans of the 'Ndrangheta were able to maintain a close relationship of coexistence and legitimacy with local societies, even after having crossed the threshold of the twenty-first century.

The concept of "ideological construction" is what best suits the 'Ndrangheta, and what completely lacks in the SCU during its 20 years of criminal history: For not having found a fertile ground for Mafia values, a society in Apulia perhaps "healthier," who had not known—before then—the stigma of the Mafia attitude.

The Calabrian Mafia and the Apulian "Mafia" Between Remote Past and Upcoming Present

The "structural" differences previously identified have determined, for the 'Ndrangheta and the SCU, two extremely different destinies. Today, the Calabrian Mafia is seen as the most powerful and able to resist any judiciary operation, so that investigations, even parliamentary, focus on this organization (Commissione 2008). Questions need to focus, on the contrary, on the real nature and essence that the SCU has currently adopted. Can the Apulian Mafia still be considered a Mafia, the fearful "Fourth Mafia"?

On one side, there are those who affirm that the SCU—after judicial investigations of the first years of the twenty-first century aimed at fighting the phenomenon of tobacco smuggling—has reinvested itself, operating underground without any noticeable manifestation of violence, and with more extortion activities (Chiarelli 2012). The management form one decade to another has brought on newer members, often sons or nephews of bosses in prison: A real "second generation" of the SCU (Mastrogiovanni 2013), which is not less-threatening than the first. Recalling the report of the *Procura Antimafia of Lecce*, Maria Luisa Mastrogiovanni argues: "Real international criminal networks are in construction that see the Sacra Corona protagonists of criminal affairs on the side of the Camorra and of Albanian, Montenegrin, Romanian, Russian, Turkish and Greek criminal organizations" [si stanno costruendo vere e proprie reti criminali internazionali che vedono la Sacra corona protagonisti di affari criminali al fianco della camorra e delle mafie albanese, montenegrina, romena, russa, turca e greca] (p. 33).

Not everybody agrees that the SCU is still a Mafia. Authoritatively, it has been denied the Mafia character of the criminal stratum present today in Apulia (Tartaglia Polcini 2010, p. 43). The organization, in fact, with the suspension of the maritime smuggling activities and the spread of *pentitismo* in the group, has been pulverized into a myriad of tiny criminal groups often in opposition to one another that are not able to plan or execute widespread trafficking.

Moreover, as the exceptional reservoir of wealth made from cigarette smuggling was once the real "name" of the SCU, a sort of *raison d'être*, it is now a matter consigned to history. The theorization of Ruggero (unpublished, for those years), according to which a crime must be assessed (also) on the basis of the abundance of opportunities (Ruggero 1992, p. 14), finds its perfect empiric coincidence in the criminal history of the SCU; less opportunities, not infrequently the family patchwork falls apart: Precisely what happened in Apulia. The "Fourth Mafia" has turned into a heterogeneous amalgam with poor criminogenic qualities (Apollonio 2010, p. 76).

Thus, all arguments touch upon the distinction between a "simple" criminal organization and Mafia. The differential nodes are shown in the foregoing reflections: The claim over an "institutional" government in the territory, the tendency to monopolize violence and force, the absolute control of illicit trafficking, and the management of parts of legal local economy (Apollonio 2013, p. 134). Mafia organizations are not limited to committing crimes of various species and nature, aiming to some profit, but they pursue a more "institutional," almost legal, goal: The creation of extra-legal governance structures can provide protection to their native land and settle conflicts between subsidiaries, thus legitimizing their presence and their own enrichment. Each regional Mafia's purpose is to create a shadow-state, which can claim the right of life and death over its inhabitants, establish a system of taxation and effective and timely collection, and incorporate itself into circuits of sovereignty true of any state of law.

The SCU, as shown, was never able to complete itself in becoming a "Mafia." Due to the failure of a politico-institutional liaison, the reduced capacity of expansion, an extremely permeable structure from the outside, a "healthier" social composition, and an altogether failure of its impressive smuggling trade, it can be considered *less* Mafia than yesterday. As said in the 1990s, it "legally fits well, as was the case with repeated judicial decisions, within article number 416-bis of the Penal Code, that is, the crime of Mafia-type associations, but does not fully correspond to the exceptional traditional term 'Mafia,' nor to its sociological profile" [ben si inquadra giuridicamente, com'è avvenuto con ripetute decisioni giudiziarie, nella previsione dell'art. 416 bis del codice penale, del delitto cioè di associazione di tipo mafioso; ma non corrisponde pienamente all'accezione tradizionale del termine "mafia", nè al suo profilo sociologico] (Motta 2008, p. 53).Today in Apulia, and, in particular, in the Salento and Bari area, there is certainly a presence of groups of organized crime that can be also quite stubborn and sometimes well-organized. But these cannot be compared, as a whole, to a Mafia structure such as the 'Ndrangheta, which is true "project power and conquest."

On the other hand, however, the 'Ndrangheta, has from the beginning of the last century managed to create in some areas of Calabria—as we have seen—a "new" legal system as opposed to the state (Ciconte 1992, p. 80).

Conclusively, the violent and bloody history of the SCU is exhausted in a couple of decades, spanning from the 1980s until the beginning of the 2000s. It has been a Mafia, although imperfect: This imperfection, ultimately, generated its defeat at the hands of the state, leaving on the ground pieces of a criminal association that cannot be considered the continuation of an Apulian Mafia history.

This, at least, is what can be found empirically. Although, in this field, scientific researches look a little like exploration voyages of past centuries: They are a mixture of experimental method and rational analysis, an epitome of science and empiricism. For this reason, the current situation can be summarized best by Rosario Tornesello: "Where we are is more or less known; however, you will see the end" [dove siamo arrivati è più o meno noto; e comunque lo si vedrà alla fine] (Tornesello 2013, p. 57).

References

Apollonio, A. (2010). *Sacra corona unita: riciclaggio, contrabbando*. Rome: Carocci.

Apollonio, A. (2012a). Criminalità globalizzata. Il modello delle mafie italiane. *Rivista elettronica di diritto, economia e management*, 1, 125. http://www.clioedu.it/riviste/diritto-economia-management/pdf/rivistaelettronica_2012_1.pdf.

Apollonio, A. (2012b). *Cosa Nuova. Viaggio nei feudi della 'Ndrangheta con lo squadrone cacciatori*. Cosenza: Pellegrini.

Apollonio, A. (2013). *Critica dell'Antimafia. L'avanzare della paura, l'arretramento delle garanzie, l'imperfezione del diritto*. Cosenza: Pellegrini.

Apollonio, A., & Cinnirella, F. (2013). Le mafie che migrano: il caso 'Ndrangheta. In A. Apollonio & F. Lamberti (Eds.), *La mafia e le mafie. Percorsi e geografie del crimine organizzato*. Lecce: Pensa.

Arlacchi, P. (1983). *La mafia imprenditrice. L'etica mafiosa e lo spirito del capitalismo*. Bologna: Il Mulino.

Arlacchi, P. (1998). Prefazione. In M. Massari (Ed.), *La Sacra corona unita. Potere e segreto*. Bari: Laterza.

Arlacchi, P. (2007). *Perchè non c'è la mafia in Sardegna. Le radici di un'anarchia ordinata*. Cagliari: AM & D.

Bauman, Z. (2011). *Modernità liquida*. Bari: Laterza.

Chiarelli, M. (2012). *Sacra corona unita. I camaleonti della criminalità italiana*. Rome: Editori Riuniti.

Ciconte, E. (1992). *'Ndrangheta. Dall'unità a oggi*. Bari: Laterza.

Commissione parlamentare d'inchiesta sul fenomeno della criminalità organizzata mafiosa o similare (XI Legislatura). (1994, January 13). *Relazione sulle risultanze del gruppo di lavoro incaricato di svolgere accertamenti su insediamenti ed infiltrazioni di soggetti ed organizzazioni mafiose in aree non tradizionali*. Relatore Sen. Carlo Smuraglia. Rome.

Commissione parlamentare d'inchiesta sul fenomeno della criminalità organizzata mafiosa o similare (XIII Legislatura). (2001, March 6). *Relazione sul fenomeno del contrabbando di tabacchi lavorati esteri in Italia e in Europa*. Relatore On. Alfredo Mantovano. Rome.

Commissione parlamentare d'inchiesta sul fenomeno della criminalità organizzata mafiosa o similare (XV Legislatura). (2008, February 19). *Relazione conclusiva*. Relatore On. Francesco Forgione. Rome.

Di Napoli, G. (1995, June 20). Al di là del mare nella tana del lupo. *Quotidiano di Puglia*.

Fierro, E., & Ruben O. H. (2007). *La Santa. Viaggio nella 'Ndrangheta sconosciuta*. Milan: Rizzoli.

Forgione, F. (2009). *Mafia export*. Milan: Baldini Castoldi Dalai.

Gambetta, D. (1992). *La mafia siciliana. Un'industria di protezione privata*. Torin: Einaudi.

Gorgoni, R. (1995). *Periferia infinita. Storie d'altra mafia*. Lecce: Argo.

Gratteri, N., & Nicaso, A. (2006). *Fratelli di sangue*. Cosenza: Pellegrini.

Hess, H. (1993). *Mafia.Le origini e la struttura*. Bari: Laterza.

Longo, M. (1997). *Sacra corona unita. Storia, struttura, rituali*. Lecce: Pensa.

Mantovano, A. (2001). *Miliardi in fumo*. Lecce: Manni.

Massari, M. (1998). *La Sacra corona unita. Potere e segreto*. Bari: Laterza.

Massari, M., & Motta, C. (2006). Collaboratori di giustizia nella Sacra corona unita. In A. Dino (Ed.), *Pentiti*. Rome: Donzelli.

Mastrogiovanni, M. L. (2013). La seconda generazione della Scu: la pax mafiosa e la ricerca del consenso. In A. Apollonio & F. Lamberti (Eds.), *La mafia e le mafie. Percorsi e geografie del crimine organizzato*. Lecce: Pensa.

Motta, C. (2008). Sacra corona unita e rapporti con la criminalità dei Paesi dell'Est. *Questione Giustizia*, 3, 52.

Nicaso, A. (1990). *Alle origini della 'Ndrangheta. La picciotteria*. Soveria Mannelli: Rubbettino.

Raufer, X. (2000). Come funziona la mafia albanese. *Gli Stati mafia-Quaderno Speciale di Limes*.

Ruggero, V. (1992). Crimine organizzato: una proposta di aggiornamento delle definizioni. *Dei delitti e delle pene,* 3, 145.

Santino, U. (1994). La mafia come soggetto politico. Ovvero: la produzione mafiosa della politica e la produzione politica della mafia. In G. Fiandaca & S. Costantino (Eds.), *La mafia le mafie. Tra vecchi e nuovi paradigmi.* Bari: Laterza.

Santino, U. (2007). Modello mafioso e globalizzazione. *Mafie e globalizzazione.* Trapani: Di Girolamo.

Scarpinato, R. (2005, April 28–29). La dimensione imprenditoriale della criminalità organizzata e le sue nuove forme di manifestazione: l'analisi sociologica, l'accertamento giudiziario, e l'applicazione della normativa di prevenzione ai nuovi fenomeni criminali. In *Relazione all'incontro di studio sul tema "Le misure di prevenzione patrimoniali."* Rome.

Sciarrone, R. (1998). *Mafie vecchie, mafie nuove. Radicamento ed espansione.* Rome: Donzelli.

Sciarrone, R. (2008). L'organizzazione reticolare della 'Ndrangheta. *Questione Giustizia,* 70, 3.

Sergi, P. (2001). La mafia in Basilicata dal 1981 al 2000 nelle relazioni dei Procuratori Generali. *Rivista storica lucana,* 61, 33–34.

Sisti, L. (2009, June 2). The Montenegro connection. *L'Espresso.* http://espresso.repubblica.it/dettaglio/the-montenegro-connection/2100575. Accessed 2 June 2009.

Tartaglia Polcini, G. (2010). *Mafie, narcotraffico e riciclaggio.* Naples: Edizioni scientifiche italiane.

Tornesello, R. (2009). *Tacco e tabacco.* Lecce: Besa.

Tornesello, R. (2013). Storia criminale: il Salento e il futuro remoto. In A. Apollonio & F. Lamberti (Eds.), *La mafia e le mafie. Percorsi e geografie del crimine organizzato.* Lecce: Pensa.

Varese, F. (2011). *Mafie in movimento. Come il crimine organizzato conquista nuovi territori.* Turin: Einaudi.

Appendices

Appendix I

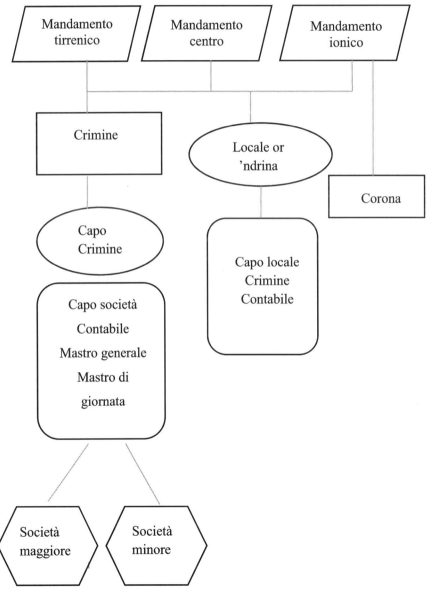

N. Serenata (ed.), *The 'Ndrangheta and Sacra Corona Unita,* Studies of Organized Crime 12,   147
DOI 10.1007/978-3-319-04930-4, © Springer International Publishing Switzerland 2014

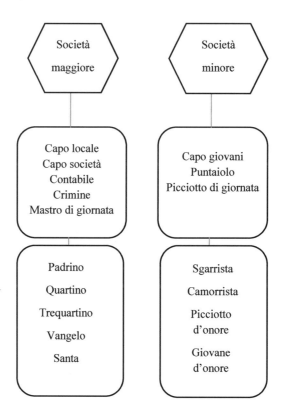

Significance of Structure and Positions (Based on Operazione Crimine 2010, and DIA 2012)

Provincia: It is a regional, national or international authority that helps avoid conflicts and coordinates all the *locali* and *'ndrine*.

Tribunale: It is an authority that judges affiliates whose behavior was doubtful for misdeed or negligence.

Mandamento Tirrenico/Centro/Ionico: It is the territorial division of Calabria. Under each *Mandamento*, there is either an *'ndrina* or/and a *locale*.

Corona: It gathers all *'ndrine* settle in small cities or villages in the *Mandamento Ionico*.

Crimine: It is the superior authority including the representatives of all *locali*.

Capo Crimine: He is the head of the *Crimine*.

Contabile: It is the person who manages all finances and the division of proceeds. Also, he addresses the *baciletta*—the common fund of the organization.

Mastro Generale: It is the spokesperson that reports all the information about the *Società Maggiore* and *Società Minore* to the head of the organization.

Mastro di Giornata: Person who collects all the information that will be later forwarded to the *Mastro Generale*.

'Ndrina: It is a family-based cell and refers directly to the *Provincia*.

Locale: It is created with the union of more *'ndrine* (minimum 49 affiliates). A *locale* usually coincides with a city or a village. The *locale* can have either a *Società Maggiore* and/or a *Società Minore*. The two societies are not in conflicts, indeed they collaborate.

Società Maggiore: It is known also as *Santa* because, to be created, it needs at least seven affiliates with the grade of *Santa*. It is independent in its actions.

Società Minore: It reports all its actions and decisions to *Società Maggiore*.

Structure of Società Maggiore

Capo locale: The head of the *locale*.

  Capo società: The vice of *capolocale*.

  Contabile: Person who manages all finances.

  Crimine: It is the person responsible for planning and executing all criminal activities. It should not be confused with the other *Crimine* (the authority).

> *Capo locale*, *capo crimine* and *contabile* create a triple named *Copiata*; these are three names that an affiliate must know.

Padrino or Quintino: It is the top position of the organization. Few people become Godfathers. These people have specific benefits.

  Quartino: Position created in accordance with the position of *Trequartino* and Godfather.

  Trequartino: Position created in accordance with the position of *Vangelo* (Gospel) and Godfather.

  Vangelo: This person makes his oath with the Gospel, hence the name *Vangelo* (Gospel). This is a very high position that is accomplished for a worthy criminal behavior.

  Santa: First grade of *Società Maggiore*. This person has obtained the *Santa* for criminal merits.

Structure of Società Minore

Capo giovani: This person is the head of the society. He holds the so-called *mezza* (half)—a role that gives him the power to mediate between *Società Maggiore* and *Società Minore*.

  Puntaiolo: The person that oversees how affiliates operate.

  Picciotto di giornata: He has the same function as *Mastro di Giornata* of the *Società Maggiore*.

  Sgarrista: He is a *camorrista* with important functions.

Camorrista: An affiliate with a discrete importance. He does tasks that the *picciotto* cannot do.

Picciotto d'onore: First grade of the organization. He is a person who accomplishes orders.

Giovane d'onore: This person is not yet an affiliate. He will later become a member of the organization because he is the son of an *'ndranghetista*.

Other Positions

Sorella d'omertà: This woman assists fugitives. The highest rank that a woman can have in the organization is *Santa*.

Stella: It is a person who wishes to achieve a specific position within the organization.

Contrasti: People who do not belong to the organization.

Contrasti onorati: People who are not the part of organization, but they are trusted.

Promotions to new positions within the organization are achieved by merits or by seniority. The new appointments are decided on Christmas, Easter and in the month of August.

Appendix II

Clans in Calabria

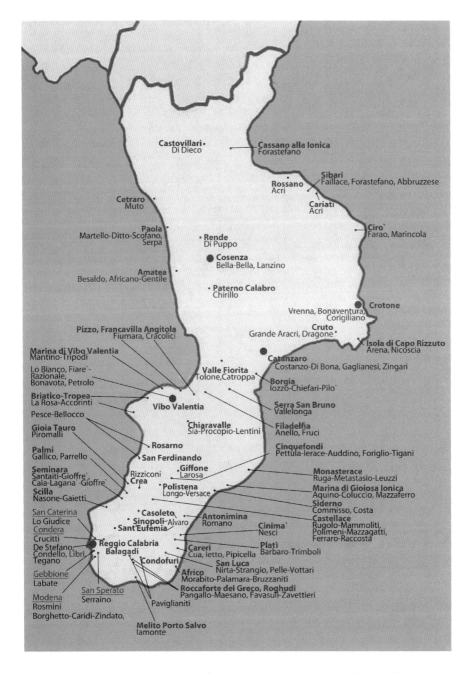

Map 1 Organogram of the Calabrian Mafia based on *Operazione Crimine* 2010, and DIA 2012

Appendix III

Structure of Nuova Camorra Organizzata (1979–1980)

Capo società
Santista
Sgarrista or Capozona
Camorrista
Picciotto

Structure of Sacra Corona Unita-Rogoli (1990)

Capo assoluto
Cupola
Lungotenenti
Cassiere
Capizona
Gruppo di fuoco o della morte
Crimine distaccato
Crimine
Trequartino
Vangelo
Santista
Sgarrista o Dispari
Camorrista
Picciotto

Definition of Positions in the Sacra Corona Unita

Capo assoluto: The absolute head of the organization: Giuseppe Rogoli.
Cupola: An organism formed by the most important lieutenants with the task of taking decisions: kickbacks, punishments and death penalties.
Luogotenenti: Trusted lieutenants of the head with significant responsibilities.
Cassiere: Person who manages the finances.
Capizona: The person who locally represents the organization and its interests, with the help of a congruous number of members.
Gruppo di fuoco o della morte: A team of men defined reliable to accomplish particular tasks, such as punishments or murders of members. Each *capozona* has its own *gruppo di fuoco*.
Crimine: Rank conferred to people who have to commit homicides.
Sgarrista o Dispari: It is the first rank of the organization.
Camorrista: Men with this rank are not yet part of the organization. These men are defined servants of the upper three ranks.
Picciotto: Men with this rank are not yet part of the organization. These men are defined servants of the upper three ranks.

Appendix IV

Clans in Apulia

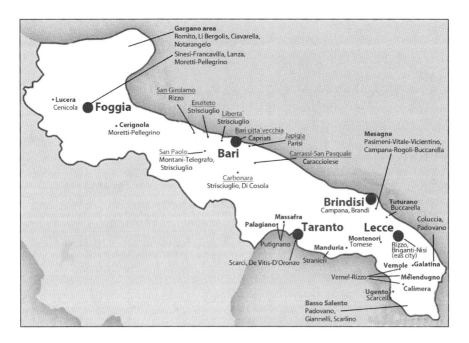

Map 2 Organogram of the Apulian Mafia updated in 2013

Appendix V

'Ndrangheta Oaths

Padrino—Godfather

In nome del Principe Russo, Conte Leonardo e Fiorentino di Spagna, con spada e spadino è formato il Padrino.

In the name of the Prince Russo, Count Leonard and Florentine of Spain, with sword and dress sword the Godfather is formed.

Quartino

In nome del Principe Russo, Conte Leonardo e Fiorentino di Spagna, con spada e spadino è formato il Quartino.

In the name of the Prince Russo, Count Leonard and Florentine of Spain, with sword and dress sword the Quartino is formed.

Trequartino

In nome del Principe Russo, Conte Leonardo e Fiorentino di Spagna, con spada e spadino è formato il Trequartino.

In the name of the Prince Russo, Count Leonard and Florentine of Spain, with sword and dress sword the Trequartino is formed.

Vangelo—Gospel

In nome di Gaspare, Melchiorre e Baldassarre, con una bassata di sole e un'alzata di luna è formata la santa catena. Sotto il nome di Gaspare, Melchiorre e Baldassarre e di nostro signore Gesù Cristo che dalla terra, risuscitò in cielo, noi saggi fratelli formiamo questo sacro Vangelo.

In the name of Caspar, Melchior and Balthazar, with a fall of the sun and a rise of the moon, the holy chain is formed. Under the name of Caspar, Melchior and Balthazar and of our Lord Jesus Christ that from the Earth, resurrected in heaven, we wise brothers form this holy Gospel.

Picciotto d'onore—Honored Young Boy

Come il fuoco brucia questa immagine, così brucerete voi se vi macchiate d'infamità, se prima vi conoscevo come un contrasto onorato da ora vi riconosco come picciotto d'onore.

As the fire burns this image, so will you, if you sully yourself with infamy. If you first were known as an honored contrast, now I know you as honored young boy.

Picciotto—Young Boy

Da questo momento conosco [nome cognome] come picciotto appartenente a questo onorato corpo di società. Giuro con lui di spartire il giusto e l'ingiusto, qui e fuori di qui e in qualsiasi posto. Se macchie d'onore porterà, tragedia e infamità cadranno su di lui e non sulla società.

From this moment, I recognize [name last name] as a young boy of this honored society. I swear to share with him, what is true and what is not, here and out of here, and in every place. If he sullies his honor, tragedy and infamy will fall on him and not on the society.

Camorrista

Come il fuoco brucia questa sacra immagine, così brucerete voi se vi macchiate di infamità. Se prima vi conoscevo come un picciotto da ora vi conosco come un camorrista.

As the fire burns this image, so you will if you sully yourself with infamy. If you first were known as a young boy, now I know you are as a camorrista.

Formula di introduzione—Introduction Formula

This formula introduces to the other honored men the person who will be affiliate during the ceremony.

Quest'uomo onesto e corretto, in una cella nacque e non esce mai un lamento dalla sua bocca. Oggi [...] cosa rappresenta il suo sangue, consiglio al mondo intero che non si tocca. Non è un motivo o un avvertimento, è solamente chiarezza di parola perché lo giuro, non ci sarebbe un momento che non farei cantare la mia pistola. Chi lo [...] dell'umana gente ne dimostri il valore, ogni cosa fece sverginare quello che il giorno nasce dal suo cuore. Se permettete lo voglio presentare, il suo nome è [nome] al di fuori della famiglia [cognome]. Un [cognome] che porti sulle spalle un verde manto. Il colore è quello della speranza, che come si sa è l'ultima a morire, un abbraccio a tutti gli uomini di sostanza augurandogli un radioso avvenire.

This honest and correct man, in a cell was born and never a lament came out of his mouth. Today [...] what his blood represents, I suggest to the whole world not to touch it. This is not a reason or a warning; this is solely for clarification of word, because I swear, there would not be a moment that I would not use my gun. Who [...] will demonstrate the value of human people, everything he deflowered that the day comes from his heart. If you let me introduce him, his name is [name], outside of the family [last name]. A [last name] wearing a green mantle on his shoulders. The color is that of hope, which as we know is the last todie, and a hug to all men of substance wishing them a bright future.

Formula di battesimo del locale—Formula to Consacrate a Place

This oath consacrates the place where a Mafia meeting will occur.

A nome della società organizzata e fidelizzata battezzo questo locale per come lo battezzarono i nostri antenati Osso, Mastrosso e Carcagnosso che lo battezzarono con ferri e catene. Io lo battezzo con la mia fede e lunga favella. Se fino a questo momento lo conoscevo per un locale oscuro, da questo momento lo riconosco per un locale sacro, santo e inviolabile in cui si può formare e sformare questo onorato corpo di società.

In the name of the organized and sacred society, I consecrate this place in the same way our ancestors Osso, Mastrosso and Carcagnosso consecrated it using irons and chains. I consecrate it with my faith and with my lasting speech. If until this time I knew this place as a dark place, from now on, I know it as a sacred, holy and inviolable place where it is possible to form and dismantle this honored society.

Formula per creare una società—Formula to Create a Society

Io formo questo corpo di società a ciampa (ferro) di cavallo e sfera di mezzaluna, con parola mia divina formo e sformo fino a mattina, con parola mia severa formo e sformo come una sfera, con parola da minore sottoposto a maggiore, con parola di omertà è formata la società.

I form the body of this society as a horseshoe and half-moon sphere, with my divine words, I form and dismantle until morning, with my severe word, I form and dismantle as a sphere, with word by a minor subjected to a major, with word of omertà, the society is formed.

Appendix VI

Sacra Corona Unita Oaths

Giuramento iniziale—Initial Oath

These two formulae are the Initial Oath of allegiance that members of the SCU have to pronounce. Words are slightly different since members wrote and modified them according to their memory.

1. Giuro su questa punta di pugnale macchiata di sangue di essere fedele a questo corpo di società, formata da uomini attivi, liberi, franchi e affermativi appartenementi alla SCU. Giuro di dividere la mia vita per la sua e di non trasgredire mai la sua volontà. Sono onorato di entrare a far parte della SCU fondata da lui [Giuseppe Rogoli]. Solo lui può guidicare a bene e a male tutte le trascuranze della nostra SCU. Giuro di dividere centesimo per centesimo con tutti i nostri saggi compagni e di portare onore alla SCU. Saggio compagno, badate bene a non trasgredire questo giuramento altrimenti sarete puniti secondo le regole della nostra SCU.

I swear on the point of this dagger, stained with blood to be faithful to this body of society made up of active, free, frank and forthright men belonging to the SCU. I swear to share my life for his, and to never disobey to his will. I am honored to be part of the SCU created by him [Giuseppe Rogoli]. Only he can judge in the good and bad, the negligence of our SCU. I swear to share cent by cent with all our wise friends and to bring honor to the SCU. Wise friend, be aware to not betray this oath otherwise you will be punished according to the rules of our SCU.

2. Giuro su questa punta di pugnale macchiata di sangue di essere fedele a questo corpo di società, formata da uomini attivi, liberi, franchi e affermativi con tutte le regole e prescrizioni sociali. Giuro di sconoscere padre, madre, fratelli e sorelle, fino alla settima generazione. Giuro di dividere centesimo per centesimo, millesimo per millesimo come fecero i nostri tre vecchi padri fondatori: Conte Ugolino, Fiorentin di Russia e Cavaliere di Spagna che tenevano nella mano destra un pugnale che serviva per intagliare e rintagliare pelle, carne ed ossa; e con un piede nella fossa e l'altro nella catena dò un forte abbraccio alla galera.

I swear on the point of this dagger, stained with blood to be faithful to this body of society made up of active, free, frank and forthright men, and with all the rules and social prescriptions. I swear to abjure father, mother, brothers and sisters up to the seventh generation. I swear to share cent by cent, thousandth by thousandth as our three elder founders did—the Count Ugolino, Herald of Russia and Knight of Spain who held a dagger in the right hand to cut and slashed skin, flesh, and bone up to the last drop of blood; and with a foot in the grave and the other in the chain I embrace the jail.

Battesimo locale—Baptism of a Place

Padrino: saggi compagni siete conformi a santizzare questo locale?

Presenti: conformissimi.

Padrino: conformissimi siete voi, in qualità di santisti, e conforme e conformissimo sono io in qualità di capo società; giusto appunto questa santa sera sotto la la mia responsabilità, vengo a santizzare il locale e lo santizzo come lo santizzarono i nostri tre vecchi fondatori della Santa: Giuseppe Garibaldi, Giuseppe Mazzini e Ferdinando Amato. Loro lo santizzarono sul sacro Monte Bianco, io lo santizzo in questa località. A nome dell'omertà il locale è stato santizzato.

Godfather: wise friends, are you compliant to consecrate this place?

Participants: yes, we are.

Godfather: you are compliant in the quality of consecrators, and I am compliant in the quality of head of this society; right precisely this holy evening under my responsibility, I come to consecrate this place and I consecrate it like our three elder founders of the Santa did—Giuseppe Garibaldi, Giuseppe Mazzini and Ferdinando Amato. They consecrated it on the holy Mont Blanc, I consecrate it in this place. On behalf of the omertà, this place has been consecrated.

Capriata

Una bella mattina di sabato dove spunta e non spunta il sole, un corpo di società dette disposizione a un corpo di cavalieri che mi presero e mi distaccarono per tre giorni e tre notti per prendere conto e sopra conto a carico mio e della settima generazione e a discarico di questa onorata e nobile società fui riconosciuto come un picciotto degno e meritevole e mi fu donato il fiore di camorrista attivo, libero, franco e affermativo con tutte le regole e prescrizioni sociali.

A beautiful Saturday morning where the sun rises and does not, a body of society ordered to a body of knights to take me and transfer me for 3 days and 3 nights in order to know about me and my family up to my seventh generation. At the discharge of this honorable and noble society, I was recognized as a worthy and deserving young boy. I was given the flower of active, free, frank and forthright camorrista with all the rules and social prescriptions.

Sformare il locale—Dismantle the Place

Padrino: saggi compagni siete conformi a sformare il locale?

Presenti: conformissimi.

Padrino: conformissimi siete voi, in qualità di santisti, e conforme e conformissimo sono io in qualità di capo società; giusto appunto questa sera sotto la mia responsabilità, vengo a sformare il locale e lo sformo come lo sformarono i nostri tre vecchi fondatori della Santa: Giuseppe Garibaldi, Giuseppe Mazzini e Ferdinando Amato. Loro lo sformarono sul sacro Monte Bianco, io lo sformo in questa località. Se fino a questo momento lo abbiamo conosciuto come un locale sacro, santo e inviolabile, da questo momento in poi lo riconosceremo come un locale di transito e di passaggio. A nome dell'omertà il locale è stato disantizzato.

Godfather: wise friends, are you compliant to dismantle this room?

Participants: yes, we are.

Godfather: you are compliant in the quality of consecrators, and I am compliant in the quality of head of this society; right precisely this holy evening under my responsibility, I come to dismantle this place and I dismantle it like our three elder founders of the Santa did—Giuseppe Garibaldi, Giuseppe Mazzini and Ferdinando Amato. They dismantled it on the holy Mont Blanc, I dismantle it in this place. If until now, we knew this place as sacred, holy and inviolable, from now on, we recognize it as a place of transit and passage. On behalf of the omertà, this place has been dismantled.

Diritto al medaglione

Giuro di non accettare altre doti da nessun altro corpo di società formata, oltre questo, composto dal sacro circolo d'onore costituito. Giuro di non tradire mai questo sacro circolo d'onore, e soprattutto, giuro di non accettare mai da nessun altro imposizione che non mi sia riconosciuta e rilasciata dal mio capo in testa. Solo con il suo benestare e di tutto il Consiglio Supremo Generale potrà essere il contrario.

I swear not to accept any other ranks from other body of society, aside from this one, composed of the established Holy Circle of Honor. I swear to never betray this Holy Circle of Honor, and above all, I swear to never accept imposition that it is not recognized and issued by my superior. Only with his authorization and of the entire General Supreme Council may be the opposite.

Camorrista

Padrino: Se in questo momento l'abbiamo conosciuto come un camorrista fatto a voce, in un secondo momento come un camorrista fatto e non fidelizzato, ora che è sotto la tirata lo riconosceremo come un camorrista attivo, libero, franco e affermativo, con patti, regole e prescrizioni sociali e con il diritto di spartenza. A nome d'omertà, la terza votazione di camorra è stata rilasciata.

Presenti: ben rilasciata.

Padrino: grazie, bontà vostra.

Godfather: If in this moment, he was known as a orally made camorrista, in a second moment, as a made but not loyal camorrista, now we will recognize him as an active, free, frank and forthright camorrista, with pacts, rules, social prescriptions and with the right of shared goods. On behalf of the omertà, the third vote of Camorra has been released.

Participats: well released.

Godfather: thank you, your goodness.

Pastiglia, armatura, figurina e spartenza—Pill, Shell, Picture Card, and Profit

This long oath is used to consecrate all the tools that a new member of the SCU needs in case of an emergency.

Padrino: Saggi compagni siete conformi?

Presenti: a che?

Padrino: a santizzare pastiglia, armatura, figurina e spartanza?

Presenti: conformissimi.

Padrino: conformissimi siete voi, in qualità di santisti, e conforme e conformissimo sono io in qualità di capo società; giusto appunto questa sera sotto la mia responsabilità, vengo a santizzare armatura, pastiglia, figurina e spartanza e li santizzo come li santizzarono i nostri tre vecchi fondatori della Santa: Giuseppe Garibaldi, Giuseppe Mazzini e Ferdinando Amato. Loro li santizzarono sul sacro Monte Bianco, io li santizzo in questa località. Se in un primo momento l'abbiamo riconosciuta come una pastiglia semplice, da questo momento in poi la riconosciamo come una pastiglia di cianuro. Se in un primo momento l'abbiamo riconosciuta come un'armatura semplice, da questo momento in poi la riconsciamo come un canne mozze. Se in un primo momento l'abbiamo riconosciuta come una figurina semplice, da questo momento in poi la riconosciamo come la figurina del nostro santissimo San Michele Arcangelo. Se in un primo momento l'abbiamo riconosciuta come una spartanza semplice, da questo momento in poi la riconosciamo come una spartanza di Santa. A nome dell'omertà, armatura, figurina, pastiglia e spartenza sono stati santizzati.

Godfather: wise friends are you compliant?

Participants: to what?

Godfather: to consecrate this pill, shell, picture card and profit.

Participants: yes, we are.

Godfather: you are compliant in the quality of consecrators, and I am compliant in the quality of head of this society; right precisely this holy evening under my responsibility, I come to consecrate this pill, shell, picture card and profit like our three elder founders of the Santa did—Giuseppe Garibaldi, Giuseppe Mazzini and Ferdinando Amato. They consecrate them on the holy Mont Blanc, I consecrate them in this place. If until now, we knew this pill as a simple pill, from now on, we know it as a cyanide pill. If until now, we knew this shell as a simple shell, from now on, we know it as rifle. If until now, we knew this picture card as simple picture card, from now on, we know it as the picture of our holy Saint Michael Archangel. If until now, we knew this profit as a simple profit, from now on, we know it as a profit from the Santa. On behalf of the omertà, pill, shell, picture card and profit have been consecrated.

Santista

Padrino: Saggi compagni siete conformi?
Presenti: a che?
Padrino: a rilasciare la prima votazione di Santa a [nome e cognome].
Presenti: conformissimi.
Padrino: conformissimi siete voi, in qualità di santisti, e conforme e conform-issimo sono io in qualità di capo società; giusto appunto questa sera sotto la mia responsabilità, vengo a rilasciare la prima votazione di Santa a [nome e cognome], a carico di [nomi e cognomi dei padrini] come la rilasciarono i nostri tre vecchi fondatori della Santa: Giuseppe Garibaldi, Giuseppe Mazzini e Ferdinando Amato. Se in un primo momento lo abbiamo conosciuto come uno sgarrista fatto a voce da questo momento in poi lo conosciamo come un santista fatto e catechizzato. A nome dell'omertà, la prima votazione della Santa è stata rilasciata.
Presenti: è stata rilasciata.
Padrino: grazie, bontà vostra. Siete conformi?
Presenti: a che?
Padrino: a rilasciare la seconda votazione di Santa a [nome e cognome].
Presenti: conformissimi.
Padrino: conformissimi siete voi, in qualità di santisti, e conforme e conformis-simo sono io in qualità di capo società; giusto appunto questa sera sotto la mia re-sponsabilità, vengo a rilasciare la seconda votazione di Santa a [nome e cognome], a carico di [nomi e cognomi dei padrini] come la rilasciarono i nostri tre vecchi fondatori della Santa: Giuseppe Garibaldi, Giuseppe Mazzini e Ferdinando Amato. Se in un primo momento lo abbiamo conosciuto come un santista fatto a voce da questo momento in poi lo conosciamo come un santista fatto e non partecipante. A nome dell'omertà, la seconda votazione della santa è stata rilasciata.
Presenti: è stata rilasciata.
Padrino: grazie, bontà vostra. Siete conformi?
Presenti: a che?
Padrino: a rilasciare la terza votazione di Santa a [nome e cognome].
Presenti: conformissimi.
Padrino: conformissimi siete voi, in qualità di santisti, e conforme e conform-issimo sono io in qualità di capo società; giusto appunto questa sera sotto la mia responsabilità, vengo a rilasciare la terza votazione di Santa a [nome e cognome], a carico di [nomi e cognomi dei padrini] come la rilasciarono i nostri tre vecchi fondatori della santa: Giuseppe Garibaldi, Giuseppe Mazzini e Ferdinando Amato. Se in un primo momento lo abbiamo conosciuto come un santista fatto a voce, in un secondo momento come santista fatto e non fidelizzato, ora venuto sotto la fidelizzazione, lo riconosciamo come un santista fatto e fidelizzato e con diritto

alla spartanza. A nome dell'omertà, la prima, seconda e terza votazione di santa è stata rilasciata.

Presenti: sono state rilasciate.

Godfather: wise friends are you compliant?

Participants: to what?

Godfather: to issue the first vote of Santa to [name and last name].

Participants: yes, we are.

Godfather: you are compliant in the quality of consecrators, and I am compliant in the quality of head of this society; right precisely this holy evening under my responsibility, I come to issue the first vote of Santa to [name and last name], in the name of [names and last names of Godfathers] like our three elder founders of the Santa did—Giuseppe Garibaldi, Giuseppe Mazzini and Ferdinando Amato. If until now, we knew him as an orally made sgarrista, from now on, we know him as a catechized santista. On behalf of the omertà, the first vote has been issued.

Participants: it has been issued.

Godfather: thank you, your goodness. Are you compliant?

Participants: to what?

Godfather: to issue the second vote of Santa to [name and last name].

Participants: yes, we are.

Godfather: you are compliant in the quality of consecrators, and I am compliant in the quality of head of this society; right precisely this holy evening under my responsibility, I come to issue the second vote of Santa to [name and last name], in the name of [names and last names of Godfathers] like our three elder founders of the Santa did—Giuseppe Garibaldi, Giuseppe Mazzini, and Ferdinando Amato. If until now, we knew him as an orally made sgarrista, from now on, we know him as a santista with no participation. On behalf of the omertà, the second vote has been issued.

Participants: it has been issued.

Godfather: thank you, your goodness. Are you compliant?

Participants: to what?

Godfather: to issue the third vote of Santa to [name and last name].

Participants: yes, we are.

Godfather: you are compliant in the quality of consecrators, and I am compliant in the quality of head of this society; right precisely this holy evening under my responsibility, I come to issue the third vote of Santa to [name and last name], in the name of [names and last names of Godfathers] like our three old founders of the Santa did—Giuseppe Garibaldi, Giuseppe Mazzini, and Ferdinando Amato. If in the first moment, he was known as an orally made santista, in second moment, as made but not loyal santista, now he came for the loyalty. We recognize him as a loyal santista with the right of profit. On behalf of the omertà, the first, second and third vote have been issued.

Participants: they have been issued.

Fazzoletti bianchi—White Handkerchiefs

Padrino: Saggi compagni siete conformi?
  Presenti: a che?
  Padrino: a santizzare i fazzolettini di seta?
  Presenti: conformissimi.
  Padrino: conformissimi siete voi, in qualità di santisti, e conforme e conformissimo sono io in qualità di capo società; giusto appunto questa sera sotto la mia responsabilità, vengo a santizzare questi tre fazzolettini bianchi come li santizzarono i nostri tre vecchi fondatori della Santa: Giuseppe Garibaldi, Giuseppe Mazzini e Ferdinando Amato. Loro li santizzarono sul sacro Monte Bianco, io li santizzo in questa località. Se fino a questo momento li abbiamo riconosciuti come tre fazzolettini di seta semplice, da questo momento in poi li riconosceremo come tre fazzoletti bianchi di seta fine e purissima, che rappresentano la purezza dell'animo. A nome dell'omertà, i tre fazzolettini sono stati santizzati.
  Presenti: i fazzoletti sono santizzati!
  Godfather: wise friends are you compliant?
  Participants: to what?
  Godfather: to consecrate these silk handkerchiefs.
  Participants: yes, we are.
  Godfather: you are compliant in the quality of consecrators, and I am compliant in the quality of head of this society; right precisely this holy evening under my responsibility, I come to consecrate the three silk handkerchiefs like our three elder founders of the Santa did—Giuseppe Garibaldi, Giuseppe Mazzini and Ferdinando Amato. They consecrate them on the holy Mont Blanc, I consecrate them in this place. If until now, we knew them as three simple silk handkerchiefs, from now on, we know them as three white quintessential and refined silk handkerchiefs that represent the purity of the mind. On behalf of the omertà, these handkerchiefs are consecrated.

Appendix VII

Statute of Sacra Corona Unita

These rules were written by the founder of the organization—Giuseppe Rogoli—when he was in prison.

1. L'affraternamento di un fratello solo con la presente formula "madre" può essere iniziata e completata in modo totale di adesione ma con alla presenza di non meno di tre persone: un compare padrone e due uomini d'onore. Avendo poi il compare padrone il dovere di passare subito la "notizia" che poi la "madre" provvederà a passarla per notizia a tutti i figli della Sacra Corona Unita. La base di questo giuramento sarà poi gettata nel più profondo del mare dove che se nemmeno verrà il diluvio universale la si scoprirà e se verrà un giorno uno dei figli la farà conoscere ad altri ne darà gravemente conto se poi la tradisce sarà prima sconosciuto e rinnegato dalla madre dei figli e poi condannato dal supremo consiglio da uno a tre pugnalate alla schiena.
2. Non toccare la moglie degli altri specialmente di chi è carcerato.
3. Di dar poco conto a ricevere conto solo per conto della Sacra Corona Unita.
4. Non litigare mai con il fratello giurato, rivolgersi alla "madre" in caso di disaccordo.
5. Non fare uso di droghe ed essere sempre lucido e responsabile delle proprie azione e dei propri discorsi.
6. Passare tempestivamente tutte le notizie di giornata e quelle che si credono utili ed importanti alla "madre" o al "compare padrone" responsabile del gruppo.
7. Non commettere alcuna azione o spedizione dentro o fuori del carcere senza il consenso della "madre".
8. Vendicare contro chiunque e senza pietà chi offende o ferisce un confratello.
9. Cucirsi sull'anima per tutta la vita il segreto delle regole della Sacra "Corona".
10. Dividere centesimo per centesimo ogni guadagno che non sia personale e lecito e di assistere e sostenere in carcere chi è confratello e di non abbandonarlo mai.
1. A brother can join this society with this formula and he can be initiated and completed with full adhesion at the presence of at least three people: a master and two men of honor. The master has the duty to pass the "news" to the "mother" which will pass it to all the other members of the Sacra Corona Unita. Then, this oath will be thrown into the deepest part of the sea where it will never be discovered even if the Universal Flood arrives; if one day, a member will disclose it to others, he will be taken in charge; if he betrayed the society, he will be denied by the mother and by the members, and then sentenced by the Supreme Council from one to three stabs to the back.

2. Never touch the wife of others, especially of those who are in jail.
3. To give little account and to only receive account on behalf of the Sacra Corona Unita.
4. Never fight with a brother, turn to the "mother" in case of disagreement.
5. Do not use drugs, and be always clear headed and responsible of your own actions and speeches.
6. Promptly pass all daily news and those that you believe being useful and important to the "mother" or the "master" responsible for the group.
7. Do not commit any action inside or outside the jail without the consensus of the "mother".
8. Avenge against everybody, and without any pity, who offended or wounded a brother.
9. Keep the secret of the rules of the SCU deep inside your soul for the rest of your life.
10. Share cent by cent every earning that is not personal and licit and assist and support in jail, a brother and never abandon him.

Appendix VIII

'Ndrangheta Vocabulary (based on Operazione Crimine)

Accoppiata (paired): Five Godfathers who will be the representatives for the new member.

Affiliato spogliato (undressed affiliate): An affiliate expelled from the organization.

Baciletta: Common fund of the groups.

Banco (bench): It is the ensemble of all positions in a *locale*.

Banco nuovo (new bench): It refers to the formation of a new supervisor for a *locale*.

Compenso (reimbursement): Money for those who perform certain crimes.

Completo (complete): A member with a rank.

Copiata: The three names that an affiliate needs to remember. They are—*capo società*, *contabile*, and *crimine*.

Cosca: The *cosca* or *'ndrina* is the basic unit, and corresponds to a Mafia family.

Dote (gift): Ranks within the organization.

Fiore (flower): Synonyms of *dote*.

Formare (to form): Announce a meeting of the society to create new affiliations.

Imbasciate (message): Refer or discover information.

Locale aperto (open locale): A *locale* is considered open when the principal *locale* of San Luca, recognizes it.

Locale chiuso (close locale): A *locale* is considered closed when the principal *locale* of San Luca, does not recognize it.

Locale distaccato (detached locale): When a *cosca* is settled in a different area than the original.

Locale sospeso (suspended locale): When a *locale* is momentarily not operative for contingent causes such as health issues of the *capo locale*.

Mamma (mother): The main *locale*, San Luca, where there is the Sanctuary of Madonna of Polsi.

Mangiata (bust): A meeting.

Mezza (half): Function of connection that the *Capo giovani* has between *Società Maggiore* and *Società Minore*.

Nuove piante (new plants): New members of the organization.

Ritirarsi in buon ordine (retired in good shape): An affiliate that retired to private life, usually old members. However, other affiliates might retire as well, if they are affected by severe health issues.

Spogliato (naked): A member who has lost his "dress," namely his rank.

Stella (star): A person who wishes to receive a very important rank.

Stipendio (salary): Salary for affiliates. The salary depends on the rank.

U ferru (iron): The gun.

Appendix IX

Sacra Corona Unita Vocabulary

Aggio or pensiero (commission or thought): Tax for every case of smuggled cigarettes unloaded in Apulia.

Armatura (shell): Pin used to prick fingers during initiation rites.

Capriata: It is an organ composed of five affiliates who present a person for the baptism as a new member. Members of this committee are: *capo in testa, contabile, maestro di tirata, favorevole* e *sfavorevole*.

Cassiere (treasurer): Person who manages money derived from the different groups.

Collaboratori a cielo scoperto (open air collaborators): Collaborators of the organization who operate outside prison.

Collaboratori a cielo coperto (in jail collaborators): Collaborators of the organization who operate in prison.

Coppa (cup): Symbol of SCU which represents the center of a crown.

Dote (gift): Ranks

Movimento: Ceremony in which an individual becomes a member or receives a promotion.

Authentic Documents

GIURO DI ESSERE FEDELE A QUESTO

CORPO DI SOCIETA FORMATA S.C.U E

DI RAPPRESENTARE OVUNQUE IL SUO FONDATORE

C.R. - GIURO DI DIVIDERE CENTESIMO

PER MILLESIMO SINO ALL'ULTIMA STILLA DI SANGUE

GIURO DI NON TRASGREDIRE IL VOLERE DEL

-NOSTRO SACCIO FONDATORE S.C.U. SOLO LUI PUÒ
GIUDICARE.
BADATE BENE CHE SE TRASGRIDERETE SARETE

GIUDICATI IN PIENE REGOLE DELL'S.C.U.

The Sacra Corona Unita Oath

N. Serenata (ed.), *The 'Ndrangheta and Sacra Corona Unita,* Studies of Organized Crime 12,   169
DOI 10.1007/978-3-319-04930-4, © Springer International Publishing Switzerland 2014

S.C.U. "SACRA CORONA UNITA" CONSISTE IN:

1) OTTO UOMINI INVISIBILI E INSAPUTI:

2) FONDO CASSA

3) SOCIETÀ RISERVATISSIMA

4) COLLETTIVITÀ DEI LAVORI E FINANZIAMENTI

5) IN CASO DI PROBLEMI CONSULTARE IL FONDATORE S.C.U.

6) IN CASO DI DISGRAZIA SARÀ GIUDICATO SEMPRE DA LUI.

The Sacra Corona Unita composition according to the original Statute

```
                    LEGIONE CARABINIERI DI BARI
                         GRUPPO DI BRINDISI
                         NUCLEO OPERATIVO
```

GIURAMENTO   S.C.U.

```
GIURO  SU  QUESTA  PUNTA DI  PUGNALE  BAGNATO  DI
SANGUE  DI  ESSERE  FEDELE  A  QUESTO  CORPO   DI
SOCIETA' FORMATA DA UOMINI ATTIVI,LIBERI, FRANCHI
E  AFFERMATIVI,  APPARTENENTI ALLA S.C.U.    E  DI
RAPPRESENTARE OVUNQUE IL FONDATORE G.R.   GIURO DI
DIVIDERE LA MIA VITA PER LA SUA E NON TRASGREDIRE
MAI LA SUA VOLONTA'.
SONO  ONORATO DI ENTRARE A FAR PARTE DELLA  SACRA
CORONA FONDATA DA LUI.
SOLO  LUI PUO' GIUDICARE IL BENE E IL MALE  TUTTE
LE  TRASCURANZE  DELLA  NOSTRA S.C.U.    GIURO  DI
DIVIDERE  CENTESIMO  PER  CENTESIMO CON  TUTTI   I
NOSTRI  SAGGI  COMPAGNI E DI PORTARE  ONORE  ALLA
S.C.U.
SAGGIO  COMPAGNO  BADATE BENE DI NON  TRASGREDIRE
QUESTO   GIURAMENTO  ALTRIMENTI   SARETE   PUNITO
SECONDO LE REGOLE DELLA NOSTRA SACRA CORONA UNITA

                    --o--

P.S.   LA SACRA CORONA UNITA E' STATA FONDATA   IL
1^ MAGGIO 1983 DA G.R.   E CON L'AIUTO DI COMPARI
DIRITTI.
NELLA S.C.U.  CI SONO LEGGI PRECISE.
CHI  TRASGREDISCE QUESTI REGOLAMENTI SARA' PUNITO
SEVERAMENTE.   IN QUALSIASI CASO SI DOVRA' TENERE
PRESENTE E AL CORRENTE IL SUO FONDATORE G.R.


N.B.   Trattasi  di  appunto   ricevuto  in  data
       26.08.1991 dal R.O.S. di Bari.
```

ge.

Another version of the Initiation Oath used to join the Sacra Corona Unita

ALLEGATO N. 3)

del RAPPORTO GIUDIZIARIO DEL GRUPPO CC   BARI

```
LA SACRA CORONA UNITA E STATA
FONDATAA IL 1Q 5. 1983 DA G.R.
E CON L'AIUTO DI COMPARI DIRITTI.
NELLA S.C.U. CI SONO LEGGI PRECISE.
CHI TRASGREDISCE QUESTI REGOLAMENTI SARA'
PUNITO SEVERAMENTE. IN QUALSIASI COSA
SI DOVRA' TENERE PRESENTE e AL CORRENTE
IL SUO FONDATORE G.R..
```

Per estratto conforme all'originale dell'agenda sequestrata a Giuseppe
ROGOLI.

Bari, 1 24.11.1984

> IL SEGRETARIO GIUDIZIARIO
> Dott. Vito Marino Stricchiola

An extract from Giuseppe Rogoli's agenda in which he states how and when the
Sacra Corona Unita was founded.

LEGIONE CARABINIERI DI BARI
GRUPPO DI BRINDISI
NUCLEO OPERATIVO

FORMULA MADRE DI AFFRATERNAMENTO E REGOLE D'ONORE
DELLA SACRA CORONA.

1. L'AFFRATERNAMENTO DI UN FRATELLO SOLO CON LA PRESENTE FORMULA "MADRE" PUO' ESSERE INIZIATA E COMPLETATA IN MODO TOTALE DI ADESIONE MA CON ALLA PRESENZA DI NON MENO DI TRE PERSONE UN COMPARE PADRONE E DA DUE UOMINI D'ONORE AVENDO POI IL COMPARE PADRONE IL DOVERE DI PASSARE SUBITO LA "NOTIZIA" E IL NOME DEL NUOVO FRATELLO ALLA "MADRE" CHE POI LA "MADRE" PROVVEDERA' A PASSARLA PER NOTIZIA A TUTTI I FIGLI DELLA SACRA CORONA. LA BASE DI QUESTO GIURAMENTO SARA' POI GETTATA NEL PIU' PROFONDO DEL MARE DOVE CHE SE NEMMENO VERRA' IL DILUVIO UNIVERSALE LA SI SCOPRIRA' E SE UN GIORNO UNO DEI FIGLI LA FARA' CONOSCERE AD ALTRI NE DARA' GRAVEMENTE CONTO SE POI LA TRADISCE SARA' PRIMA SCONOSCIUTO E RINNEGATO DALLA MADRE DAI FIGLI E POI CONDANNATO DAL SUPREMO CONSIGLIO DA UNO A <u>TRE PUGNALATE ALLA SCHIENA</u>.

2. NON TOCCARE LA MOGLIE DEGLI ALTRI SPECIALMENTE DI CHI E' CARCERATO.

3. DI DAR CONTO A RICEVERE CONTO SOLO PER CONTO DELLA SACRA CORONA "LA MAMMA".

4. NON LITIGARE MAI CON IL FRATELLO GIURATO, RIVOLGERSI ALLA "MADRE" IN CASO DI DISACCORDO.

5. NON FARE USO DI **DROGHE** ED ESSERE SEMPRE LUCIDO E RESPONSABILE DELLE PROPRIE AZIONI E DEI PROPRI DISCORSI.

6. PASSARE TEMPESTIVAMENTE TUTTE LE NOTIZIE DI GIORNATA E QUELLE CHE SI CREDONO UTILI E IMPORTANTI ALLA"MADRE" O AL "COMPARE PADRONE" RESPONSABILE DEL GRUPPO.

7. NON COMMETTERE ALCUNA AZIONE O SPEDIZIONE DENTRO O FUORI DEL CARCERE SENZA IL CONSENSO DELLA "MADRE".

8. VENDICARE CONTRO CHIUNQUE E SENZA PIETA' CHI OFFENDE O FERISCE UN CONFRATELLO.

formula   madre   di   affraternamento   e   regole
d'onore della Sacra Corona.

—   2   —

9. CUCIRSI SULL'ANIMA PER TUTTA LA VITA IL SEGRETO
    DELLE REGOLE DELLA SACRA "CORONA".

10. DIVIDERE CENTESIMO PER CENTESIMO OGNI GUADAGNO
    CHE NON SIA PERSONALE E LECITO E DI ASSISTERE E
    SOSTENERE IN CARCERE CHI E' CONFRATELLO E DI NON
    ABBANDONARLO MAI.

Trani, 12 maggio 1986

N.B.   Trattasi di un appunto ricevuto dal R.O.S.
        di Bari in data 26.08.1991.

ge.

A copy of the Statute of the Sacra Corona Unita.

Bibliography

Abadinsky, H. (2007). *Organized Crime*. Belmont: Wadsworth.

Apollonio, A. (1998). *Sacra Corona Unita: riciclaggio, contrabbando. Profili penali economici del crimine imprenditoriale*. Rome: Carocci.

Arlecchi, P. (1980). *Mafia, contadini e latifondo nella Calabria tradizionale*. Bologna: Mulino.

Arlecchi, P. (2007). *La mafia imprenditrice*. Milan: Il Saggiatore.

Arlecchi, P. (2010). *La mafia imprenditrice. Dalla Calabria al centro dell'inferno*. Milan: Il Saggiatore.

Barone, L. (1990). L'ascesa della 'ndrangheta negli ultimi due decenni. *Meridiana, 7*(8).

Badolati, A. (2006). *Malandrini*. Cosenza: Klipper Edizioni.

Barbagli, M., & Gatti, U. (2002). *La criminalità in Italia*. Bologna: Il Mulino.

Beccucci, S. (2006). *Criminalità multietnica. I mercati illegali in Italia*. Bari-Rome: Laterza.

Beccucci, S., Ciappi, S., & Massari, M. (1999). *Il crimine organizzato. Strategie di contrasto in tema di narcotraffico e riciclaggio*. Siena: Lalli.

Beccucci, S., & Massari, M. (2001). *Mafie nostre, Mafie loro. La criminalità organizzata italiana e straniera nel centro-nord*. Turin: Edizioni di Comunità.

Boemi, S. (2005). La 'ndrangheta: origini, natura e ramificazioni nell'economia europea del terzo millennio. In S. Morabito (Ed.), *Mafia 'ndrangheta e camorra nelle trame del potere parallelo*. Rome: Gangemi Editore.

Cagnazzo, M. (Ed.). (2007). *Mafia, una guerra senza confini*. Bari: Wip.

Cariati, G. (2000). *Fratelli di Mafia. Cosa Nostra e 'Ndrangheta*. Bologna: Il Mulino.

Casaburi, M. (2010). *Borghesia mafiosa. La 'ndrangheta dalle origini ai giorni nostri*. Bari: Dedalo Edizioni.

Castellaneta, D., et al. (1999). *La mafia che non c'era*. Bari: Palomar.

Cavaliere, C. (2004). *Un vaso di coccio. Dai governi locali ai governi privati. Comuni sciolti per mafia e sistema politico istituzionale in Calabria*. Soveria Mannelli: Rubettino.

Centorrino, M., La Spina, A., & Signorino, G. (1999). *Il nodo gordiano: criminalità mafiosa e sviluppo nel Mezzogiorno*. Bari-Rome: Laterza.

Chiarelli, M. (2012). *Sacra Corona Unita. I camaleonti della criminalità italiana*. Rome: Editori Riuniti.

Chirico, G. (1990). *Una vicenda giudiziaria di associazione per delinquere di tipo mafioso nella provincia di Reggio Calabria (1890–1900)*. (MA Thesis). University of Messina, Messina.

Ciconte, E. (1992). *'Ndrangheta dall'Unità a oggi*. Bari-Rome: Laterza.

Ciconte, E. (1998). *Mafia, Camorra e 'Ndrangheta in Emilia Romagna*. Rimini: Panozzo.

Ciconte, E. (1993). Mafia, 'ndrangheta, camorra: un processo di unificazione? *Studi storici: rivista trimestrale dell'Istituto Gramsci, 34*(4), 829–848.

Ciconte, E. (2011). *'Ndrangheta*. Soveria Mannelli: Rubettino.

Ciconte, E. (2010). *Ndrangheta padana*. Soveria Mannelli: Rubettino.

Ciconte, E. (1996). *Processo alla 'Ndrangheta*. Rome-Bari: Laterza.

Ciconte, E. (2008). *Storia criminale. La resistibile ascesa di mafia, 'ndrangheta e camorra dall'Ottocento ai giorni nostri*. Soveria Mannelli: Rubbettino.

Ciconte, E., Macrì, V., & Forgione, F. (2010). *Osso, Mastrosso, Carcagnosso*. Soveria Mannelli: Rubbettino.

Ciconte, E., & Macrì, V. (2009). *Australian 'Ndrangheta. I codici di affiliazione e la missione di Nicola Calipari*. Soveria Mannelli: Rubbettino.

Ciconte, E., & Romani, P. (2002). *Le nuove schiavitù. Il traffico degli esseri umani nell'Italia del XXI secolo*. Rome: Editori Riuniti.

Carlucci, D., & Caruso, G. (2009). *A Milano comanda la 'ndrangheta*. Milan: Ponte alle Grazie.

Cingari, G. (1988). *Storia della Calabria dall'unità ad oggi*. Bari-Rome: Laterza.

Crinò, P. (Ed.). (2009). *Le subculture mafiose. Tra cavalieri e compagni d'onore*. Naples: Tullio Pironti.

Crupi, P. (1992). *L'anomalia selvaggia. Camorra, mafia, picciotteria e 'ndrangheta nella letteratura calabrese del Novecento*. Palermo: Sellerio.

Dalla Chiesa, S. (1987). *Cultura e politica contro la 'ndrangheta*. Cosenza: Pellegrini.

Delfino, A. (2006). *La nave della 'ndrangheta*. Cosenza: Klipper Edizioni.

De Giorgi, F. (1997). *Cose di casa nostra. Sacra Corona Unita e nuovi assetti criminali nel Salento*. Lecce: Zane.

D'Errico, U. (2009). *Criminalità organizzata e politica in Calabria fra XIX e XX secolo*. (MA Thesis). Sapienza—University of Rome, Rome.

Direzione Investigativa Antimafia (DIA). (2012). *Criminalità organizzata pugliese e lucana. First semester*. http://www.interno.gov.it/dip_ps/dia/semestrali/sem/2012/1sem2012.pdf.

Direzione Investigativa Antimafia (DIA). (2012). *Criminalità organizzata pugliese e lucana. Second semester*. http://www.interno.gov.it/dip_ps/dia/semestrali/sem/2012/2sem2012.pdf.

Di Bella, S. (1989). *La 'Ndrangheta, la setta del disonore*. Cosenza: Pellegrini.

Di Bella, S. (1992). *Alle frontiere della democrazia: La Calabria contemporanea*. Soveria Mannelli: Rubettino.

Dickie, J. (2011). *Blood brotherhoods: The rise of the Italian Mafias*. London: Sceptre.

Di Mauro, G. (2010). *Associazione di tipo mafioso e Sacra Corona Unita. Analisi della Giurisprudenza relativa al fenomeno mafioso nel territorio salentino*. (MA Thesis). Università degli Studi di Milano, Milan.

Dino, A. (Ed.). (2006). *Pentiti. I collaboratori di giustizia, le istituzioni, l'opinione pubblica*. Rome: Donzelli.

Dino, A., & Pepino, L. (Eds.). (2008). *Sistemi criminali e metodo mafioso*. Milan: Franco Angeli.

Direzione Nazionale Antimafia (DNA). (2012). *Sacra Corona Unita e criminalità organizzata pugliese. Second semester 2012* (S. 149–167). http://www.stampoantimafioso.it/wp-content/uploads/2013/01/DNA_Dicembre-20121.pdf.

Emiliano, M. (1993). Rassegna di documenti processuali concernenti le mafie pugliesi. *Quaderni: i diritti di criminalità organizzata, 99*(4).

Errichetti, F. (2012). *La quarta mafia. La criminalità organizzata in Puglia (1980–2010)*. (BA Thesis). University of Milan, Milan. http://www.stampoantimafioso.it/wp-content/uploads/2013/02/LA-QUARTA-MAFIA-LA-CRIMINALITA-ORGANIZZATA-IN-PUGLIA-1980-2010.pdf.

Eurispes. (1994). *Perscorsi e strategie della criminalità organizzata pugliese*. Rome: Eurispes Edition.

Falcone, G. (1983). Strutture organizzative, rituali e "baccagghiu" della 'Ndrangheta. In S. Di Bella (Ed.), *Mafia e Potere. Società civile, organizzazione mafiosa ed esercizio dei poteri nel Mezzogiorno contemporaneo*. Soveria Mannelli: Rubbettino.

Falletti, F. (2007). *Nel mirino della 'ndrangheta*. Rome: Koinè.

Fantò, E. (1992). *Mafia, poteri, democrazia: il caso Calabria*. Rome: Gangemi Editori.

Fantò, E. (1992). *Massomafia: 'Ndrangheta, politica e massoneria dal 1970 ai giorni nostri*. Rome: Koinè.

Fiandaca, G. (Ed). (2007). *Women and the Mafia: Female roles in organized crime structures*. New York: Springer.

Fiasco, M. (Ed.). (1992). *Puglia. Il crimine, scenari e strategie*. Bari: Sapere 2000.

Forgione, F. (2002). La 'ndrangheta. In M. Barbagli & U. Gatti (Eds.), *La criminalità in Italia*. Bologna: Il Mulino.

Forgione, F. (2008). *'Ndrangheta. Boss, luoghi e affari della Mafia più potente al mondo*. Milan: Dalai Editore.

Forgione, F. (2009). *'Ndrangheta. La relazione della Commissione parlamentare antimafia*. Milan: Baldini Castoldi Dalai.

Forgione, F. (2010). Mafia and Civil Society. Economical-Criminal collusion and territorial control in Calabria. In L. Briquet & G. Favarel-Garrigues (Eds.), *Crimes and states*. New York: Palgrave MacMillan.

Forgione, F. (2006). Passaggio di frontiera: la difficile via di uscita dalla mafia calabrese. In A. Dino (Ed.), *Pentiti. I collaboratori di giustizia, le istituzioni, l'opinione pubblica*. Rome: Donzelli.

Forgione, F. (2011). *Porto Franco. Politici, manager e spioni nella Repubblica della 'Ndrangheta*. Milan: Dalai Editore.

Forgione, F., & Mondani, P. (1994). *Oltre la cupola. Massoneria mafia politica*. Milan: Rizzoli.

Fulco, G. (2011). *Da "Armonia" a "Crimine", l'evoluzione della 'Ndrangheta dalla "Santa" a oggi*. (MA Thesis). University of Reggio Calabria, Reggio Calabria. http://www.stopndrangheta. it/file/stopndrangheta_1424.pdf.

Gambino, S. (1971). *La mafia in Calabria*. Chiaravalle Centrale: Edizioni Parallelo 38.

Gambino, S. (1986). *'Ndrangheta dossier*. Chiaravalle Centrale: Frama Sud.

Gorgoni, R. (1995). *Periferia infinita. Storie d'altra mafia*. Lecce: Argo.

Gratteri, N., & Nicaso, A. (2006). *Fratelli di sangue*. Milan: Mondadori.

Gratteri, N., & Nicaso, A. (2010). *La Malapianta*. Milan: Mondadori.

Gratteri, N., Nicasio, A., & Giardina, V. (2009). *Cosenza 'ndrine sangue e coltelli*. Cosenza: Pellegrini.

Gribaudi, G. (2009). *Traffici criminali. Camorra, mafie e reti transnazionali dell'illegalità*. Turin: Bollati Boringhieri.

Guarino, M. (2004). *Poteri, segreti e criminalità. L'intreccio inconfessabile tra 'ndrangheta, massoneria e apparati dello Stato*. Bari: Dedalo Edizioni.

Iadeluca, F. (2007). *Criminalità organizzata e la 'ndrangheta in Calabria*. Rome: Gangemi Editore.

Ingrascì, O. (2007). *Donne d'onore. Storie di mafia al femminile*. Milan: Mondadori.

Ingrascì, O. (2011). "Donne,'ndrangheta, 'ndrine. Gli spazi femminili nelle fonti giudiziarie." *Meridiana* 67.

Ippolito, L. (2006). *Il racket dell'estorsione. Un'analisi contestualizzata*. (MA Thesis). Sapienza—University of Rome, Rome. http://www.liberanet.org/index.php/2011/09/il-racket-dellestorsione-unanalisi-contestualizzata/.

La Camera, C. (2011). *Vincere la 'Ndrangheta*. Rome: Aracne.

Longo, M. (Ed.). (1997). *Sacra Corona Unita: Storia, Struttura, Rituali*. Lecce: Pensa Multimedia.

Longrigg, C. (1997). *L'altra metà della mafia. L'anima femminile di Cosa nostra, 'Ndrangheta e Camorra. Donne che comandano, che subiscono e che combattono. Le loro voci, le loro ragioni*. Milan: Ponte alle Grazie.

Macrì, V. (1993). La 'ndrangheta in Calabria. In F. Occhiogrosso (Ed.), *Ragazzi della Mafia. Storie di criminalità e contesti minorili, voci dal carcere, le reazioni e le proposte*. Milan: Franco Angeli.

Malafarina, L. (1978). *Il codice della 'Ndrangheta*. Reggio Calabria: Edizioni Parallelo 38.

Malafarina, L. (1986). *La 'ndrangheta: il codice segreto, la storia, i miti, i riti e i personaggi*. Rome: Gangemi Editore.

Mantovano, A. (2001). *Miliardi di fumo. Sviluppo, prevenzione e contrasto del contrabbando*. Lecce: Manni.

Marino, G. C. (2007). *Storia della mafia. Dall'"Onorata Società" a Cosa Nostra, la ricostruzione critica di uno dei più inquietanti fenomeni del nostro tempo*. Rome: Newton.

Maritati, A. (1993). La criminalità organizzata in Puglia. In Occhiogrosso, F. (Ed.), *Ragazzi della Mafia. Storie di criminalità e contesti minorili, voci dal carcere, le reazioni e le proposte.* Milan: Franco Angeli.

Maritati, A. (1992). Puglia. Dai tentativi di infiltrazione alla Sacra Corona Unita. *Asterischi. Materiali per una moderna critica del capitalismo* 2.

Martino, P. (1988). Per la storia della 'Ndranghita. *Biblioteca di Ricerche Linguistiche e Filologiche, 25*(1).

Martino, P. (1977). Storia della parola 'Ndrangheta. *Quaderni Calabresi*, 42–43.

Massari, M. (1998). *La Sacra Corona Unita: potere e segreto.* Bari-Rome: Laterza.

Massari, M. (2000). Al di là dei confini. La diffusione della criminalità mafiosa nelle aree non tradizionali: il caso della Puglia e della Basilicata. In R. Siebert (Ed.), *Relazioni pericolose: criminalità e sviluppo nel Mezzogiorno.* Soveria Mannelli: Rubettino.

Massari, M. (1998). Mafia, 'ndrangheta, camorra: un processo di unificazione? *Studi storici: rivista trimestrale dell'Istituto Gramsci,* 38(4), 1031–1050.

Massari, M. (2008). Mafie, culture e identità plurali: il caso della Sacra Corona Unita. *Questione Giustizia* 2.

Massari, M. (2002). Mafie, criminalità transnazionale, globalizzazione: il caso italiano. *Meridiana: rivista di storia e scienze sociali,* 43, 115–133.

Massari, M. (2009). La Sacra Corona Unita: storie, culture, identità. In G. Gribaudi (Ed.), *Camorre, mafie e reti internazionali dell'illegalità.* Turin: Bollati Boringhieri.

Massari, M. (1998). *Sacra Corona Unita: Potere e Mistero.* Bari-Rome: Laterza.

Massari, M. (1997). Potere e segreto nella Sacra Corona Unita. *Studi Storici,* 38(4), 1031–1050.

Massari, M., & Motta, C. (2003). Il ruolo della donna nella Sacra Corona Unita. In *Donne e mafie. Il ruolo delle donne nelle organizzazioni criminali.* Palermo: Università degli Studi di Palermo. Dipartimento di Scienze Penalistiche e Criminologiche, 52–65.

Messina, G. (1992). *L'etimologia della parola "màfia", "camorra" e "'ndràngheta."* Rome: Bonanno.

Minuti, D., & Nicaso, A. (1994). *'Ndranghete. Le filiali della mafia calabrese.* Vibo Valentia: Monteleone.

Minuti, D., & Veltri, F. (1990). *Lettera a San Luca.* Catanzaro: Abramo.

Minuti, D., & Veltri, F. (2008). *Ritorno a San Luca.* Catanzaro: Abramo.

Morabito, S. (Ed.). (2005). *Mafia, 'Ndrangheta, Camorra. Nelle trame del potere parallelo.* Rome: Gangemi Editore.

Motta, C. (2011). Sacra Corona Unita & Co. Radiografia di un fenomeno. *Dike* 2.

Motta, C. (2001). *La Sacra Corona Unita, una mafia diversa dalle altre.* Rome: Giuffrè.

Musolino, E. (1977). *Quarant'anni di lotte in Calabria.* Milan: Teti.

Nicaso, A. (1990). *Alle origini della 'Ndrangheta: la Picciotteria.* Soveria Mannelli: Rubbettino.

Nicaso, A. (2007). *'Ndrangheta. Le radici dell'odio.* Reggio Emilia: Aliberti.

Nicaso, A., & Gratteri, N. (2009). *Fratelli di Sangue. Storie, boss e affari della 'Ndrangheta. La mafia più potente del mondo.* Cosenza: Pellegrini.

Nicaso, A., & Minuti, D. (1992). *'Ndrangheta: le filiali estere della mafia calabrese.* Cosenza: Monteleone.

Nocifera, E. (1982). *Mafia, 'ndrangheta & camorra.* Rome: Edizioni Lavoro.

Paoli, L. (2000). *Fratelli di Mafia. Cosa Nostra e 'Ndrangheta.* Bologna: Il Mulino.

Paoli, L. (2003). *Mafia brotherhood: Organized crime, Italian style.* New York: Oxford University Press.

Paoli, L. (1994). An underestimated criminal phenomenon: The Calabrian 'Ndrangheta. *European Journal of Crime, Criminal Law, and Criminal Justice,* 2(3), 212–238.

Parini, E. G. (2011). 'Ndrangheta. Un prisma di potere. In A. Mammone, N. Nicola Tranfaglia, & G. Veltri (Eds.), *Un paese normale?* Milan: Dalai Editori.

Parini, E. G. (1999). *Mafia, politica e società civile. Due casi in Calabria.* Soveria Mannelli: Rubettino.

Parini, E. G. (2010). The strongest Mafia: 'Ndrangheta made in Calabria. In A. Mammone & G. Veltri (Eds.), *Italy today: The sick man of Europe.* London-New York: Routledge.

Parini, E. G. (1999). Mafia, politica e reazione civile. Due casi in Calabria. *Il Mulino*, 3, 490–498.

Pasculli, A. (2009). Il ruolo della donna nell'organizzazione criminale: il caso barese. *Rivista di criminologia, vittimologia e sicurezza*, 3(2).

Procura della Repubblica Presso il Tribunale di Reggio Calabria, Direzione Distrettuale Antimafia. *Decreto di fermo di indiziato di delitto—art 384 e segg. c.p.p. Agostino Anna Maria + 155*.

Reski, P. (2008). *Mafia. Von Paten, pizzerien und falschen priestern*. Munich: Droemer Verlag.

Parini, E. G. (2013). *The Honored Society. A portrait of Italy's most powerful mafia*. New York: Nation Books.

Ruben, O. H., & Fierro, E. (2007). *La Santa. Viaggio nella 'ndrangheta sconosciuta*. Milan: Rizzoli.

Ruotolo, G. (1994). *La Quarta mafia*. Naples: Tullio Pironti.

Ruotolo, G. (1994). Bionde e profughi sui taxi dell'Adriatico. *Narcomafie*, II(4).

Scarpino, S. (1996). *Storia della 'ndrangheta*. Milan: Fenice 2000.

Sciarrone, R. (2011). All'ombra delle mafie. L'area grigia di Cosa Nostra, 'ndrangheta e camorra. *Il Mulino* 3.

Sciarrone, R. (1993). Il rapporto tra mafia e imprenditorialità in un'area della Calabria. *Quaderni di Sociologia*, 37(5).

Sciarrone, R. (2004). *La Mafia esiste ancora. Mafia e antimafia prima e dopo le stragi del 1992*. Rome: Nuova Iniziativa Editoriale.

Sciarrone, R. (2009). *Mafie vecchie, mafie nuove. Radicamento ed espansione*. Rome: Donzelli.

Sciarrone, R. (2011). Nelle aree grigie di mafia, 'ndrangheta e camorra. *Segno*, 322.

Sciarrone, R. (2008). L'organizzazione reticolare della 'Ndrangheta. In A. Dino & L. Pepino (Eds.), *Sistemi criminali e metodo mafioso*. Milan: Franco Angeli.

Sciarrone, R. (1999). Uno Stato nello Stato. *Narcomafie*, 7(2).

Sciarrone, R., & Mete, V. (2011). Overcoming the 'Ndrangheta: Contrasting methods and continuities of actions. *Modern Italy*, 17(2).

Seccia, D. (2011). *La mafia innominabile*. Bari: Meridiana.

Sergi, P. (1991). *La "Santa" violenta: storie di 'ndrangheta e di ferocia, di faide, di sequestri, di vittime innocenti*. Cosenza: Periferia.

Siebert, R. (Ed.). (2000). *Relazioni pericolose: criminalità e sviluppo nel Mezzogiorno*. Soveria Mannelli: Rubbettino.

Siebert, R. (Ed.). (1997). *Le donne, La mafia*. Milan: Il Saggiatore.

Spezzano, F. (1986). *Il gergo della malavita in Calabria*. Cosenza: Pellegrini.

Svezia, A. F. (2006). *L'infiltrazione mafiosa in Friuli Venezia Giulia. Una terra al confine tra complicità e illusione*. (MA Thesis). University of Pisa, Pisa. http://www.liberanet.org/?p=4656.

Sylos Labini, P. (1986). Puglia regione intermedia. *Delta*, 24.

Vendola, N. (1996). *La mafia levantina. Rapporto sulla criminalià organizzata in Puglia*. Bari: Edipuglia.

Tizian, Giovanni. (2009). *La 'Ndrangheta transnazionale: dalla picciotteria alla Santa. Analisi di un fenomeno criminale globalizzato*. (MA Thesis). University of Bologna, Bologna. http://www.stopndrangheta.it/stopndr/art.aspx?id=15,'Ndrangheta+transnazionale.

Tribunale di Reggio Calabria, sezione GIP-GUP. *Sentenza resa nell'Operazione "Crimine" Agnelli Giovanni + 126. Sentenza n.106/2012*.

Tornesello, R. (Ed.). (2009). *Tacco e Tabacco. Il caso di Brindisi*. Lecce: Besa.

Varano, A. (1996). 'Ndrangheta, neofascismo e massoneria deviata. In L., Violante & A. Bolzoni (Eds.), *Mafia e Antimafia: Rapporto '96*. Bari-Rome: Laterza.

Varese, F. (2006). How Mafias migrates: The case of the 'Ndrangheta in Northern Italy. *Law and Society Review*, 40(2), 411–44.

Veltri, E., & Laudati, A. (2009). *Mafia pulita*. Milan: Longanesi.

Zagari, A. (1992). *Ammazzare stanca, Autobiografia di uno 'ndranghetista pentito*. Cosenza: Periferia.

Zagnoli, N. (1977). A proposito di Onorata società. *Quaderni Calabresi* 42–43.

Zara, V. (1913). *La carboneria in Terra d'Otranto*. Sala Bolognese: Arnaldo Forni.

Filmography

(2010). A che punto è la lotta alla 'Ndrangheta? *Exit*. Rome: La7.

Claudio Bonivento (Director). (2007). *Era mio fratello*. Italy: Rai Fiction Film.

Davide Barletti, & Lorenzo Conte (Directors). (2007). *Fine pena mai: Paradiso Perduto*. Italy: Mikado.

Edoardo Winspeare (Director). (2008). *Galantuomini*. Italy: 01 Distribuzione.

(2005–7). *Gente di mare*. Italy: Raiuno.

Vittorio Sindoni (Director). (2005). *Il Capitano 2*. Italy: Raidue. 1950. Mario Camerini (Director). (1950). *Il brigante Musolino*. Italy: Lux Film.

Gabriele Salvatores (Director). (2003). *Io non ho paura*. Italy: Medusa.

(2011). Il nord e l'assalto delle mafie. *Exit*. Rome: La7.

Ricky Tognazzi (Director). (2013). *L'assalto*. Italy: Raiuno.

(2008). La Mafia al Nord. *Blu notte*. Italy: Raitre.

(2004). La storia della 'Ndrangheta. *Blu notte*. Italy:Raitre.

Ruben H. Oliva, and Enrico Fierro (Directors). (2007). *La Santa. Viaggio nella 'ndrangheta sconosciuta*. Italy.

Lucio Giordano (Director). (1995). *Le bande*. Italy.

Fulvio Wetzl (Director). (2008). *Libera nos a malo*. Italy: Vawe.

(2012). Mafia al nord. *Presa Diretta*. Italy:Raitre.

(2009). Mafia. Le mani sul nord. *Exit*. Rome: La7.

Giorgio Stegani (Director). (1974). *Milano: il clan dei calabresi*. Italy: Overseas Film Company.

(2010). 'Ndranghetisti. *Presa Diretta*. Italy: Raitre.

(2010). 'Ndrangheta del nord. *Anno Zero*. Italy: Raidue.

Index

Printed by Printforce, the Netherlands